Ordnance Survey®

STATLAS UK

A Statistical Atlas of the United Kingdom

First edition 1995.

Published by
Ordnance Survey and HMSO

Romsey Road	St Crispins
SOUTHAMPTON	Duke Street
SO16 4GU	NORWICH
	NR3 1PD

ISBN 0 11 701873 2 (HMSO, softback)
ISBN 0 319 00589 5 (OS, softback)

Designed by Gary Meadows, Design Services, Ordnance Survey.

Edited by David Bradbury, Publishing Services, COI, Hercules Road, LONDON, SE1 7DU.

A catalogue listing for this book is available from the British Library.

Foreword

In no sense is Britain a uniform country. From the geology and climate to every characteristic of the people and culture, our nation's make-up is highly varied and rich in interest. Understanding this is important to the policy-maker and the visitor alike. Moreover, it becomes ever more necessary to compare ourselves with other members of the European Union. *Statlas UK* came about to make all this possible. As a former professor of geography, I well appreciate the value of publications which present data on these subjects in a clear and illuminating visual format. *Statlas UK* is designed to complement the *Britain* handbook (published by Her Majesty's Stationery Office), which is distributed world-wide in large numbers.

Virtually all the information in *Statlas UK* comes from official sources. The statistics derive from a variety of government departments and were arranged by the Central Office of Information. The commentaries were also produced by COI. The boundaries and other mapping came from Ordnance Survey's databases and the Ordnance Survey design team were responsible for the striking portrayal of the data.

Most government information is collected by different departments to underpin the creation of policy or to monitor its progress. The different concerns of separate government departments, differing legal systems in the various parts of the United Kingdom and the variety of administrative arrangements used ensure that some difficulties occur in the way statistics are collected and presented. For example, the boundaries of local government administrative areas do not always coincide with those of health authority areas. Moreover, some statistics are collected with greater frequency than others. Thus the statistics in *Statlas UK* relate to various years; however, we have sought always to use the most up-to-date information available as we went to press. Despite these unavoidable problems, *Statlas UK* illustrates in easy-to-understand form a huge variety of aspects of British life, including the economy, employment, housing, health and the environment.

This publication is intended to inform the public through the use of information collected at the taxpayers' expense. Measuring the value of this is impossible. But all of the partners involved are committed to the dissemination of government information in the spirit of the Citizen's Charter and under the terms of the Government's 1994 regulations on access to government information.

Three-way collaborations are rarely straightforward, especially the first time they are tried. The production of *Statlas UK* has, however, been remarkably trouble-free and I thank Ordnance Survey's partners - the Central Office of Information and Her Majesty's Stationery Office - for their positive approach in producing something which I believe to be of real value.

David Rhind

David Rhind
Director General and Chief Executive of Ordnance Survey

Contents

Industry

Education

Crime

Environment

Travel

Leisure

European Union - Comparisons

Administrative Boundaries 1994

- At present local government is carried out in most of Great Britain on a two-tier basis, the lower tier being districts and the upper tier counties (in England and Wales) and regions (in Scotland).
- Greater London and the 6 metropolitan counties have single tier local government based on London boroughs and metropolitan districts, while in Scotland the 3 islands councils are also single-tier.
- Local government in England is currently being reviewed by the Local Government Commission, which is likely to lead to an increase in the number of 'unitary' local authorities, while Parliament has legislated for new unitary authorities in Scotland and Wales from April 1996 (see page 13).
- Local government in Northern Ireland is carried out through 26 districts, although these have very limited responsibilities compared with local authorities in Great Britain. Some maps in this book present data using the education and library board areas or the health and social services board areas.

The standard regions of England do not form a tier of government. However, many regional statistics are published using these boundaries.

The Isle of Man and the Channel Islands are excluded from most statistics used in compiling this book.

The European Union

- The term 'European Union' (EU) refers collectively to the European Community, the European Coal and Steel Community, Euratom and intergovernmental cooperation on a common foreign and security policy and in the fields of justice and home affairs.
- There are 15 EU member states, of which 3 - Austria, Finland and Sweden - joined in January 1995.
- The United Kingdom joined what is now the EU in January 1973.
- The objectives of the Treaty of Rome include the elimination of customs duties between member states, the free movement of goods, people, services and capital, and the elimination of distortions in competition within the common market.

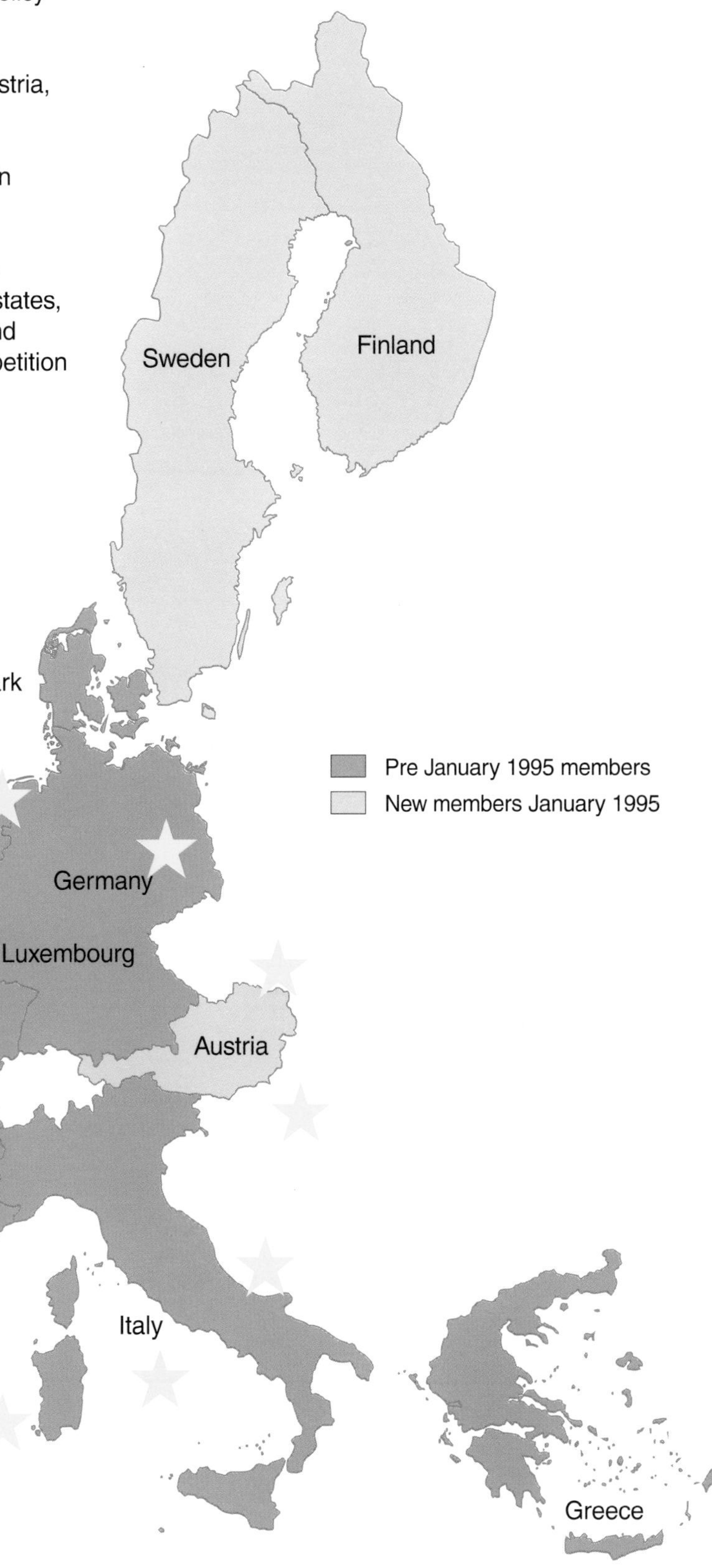

The Commonwealth

- There are 51 members of the Commonwealth, which is a voluntary association of states, nearly all of which were British territories to which independence was granted.
- Her Majesty the Queen is recognised as head of the Commonwealth, and is head of state in the United Kingdom and 15 other member countries.
- Nauru and Tuvalu are special members, entitled to take part in all Commonwealth meetings and activities, with the exception of Heads of Government meetings.
- The newest member of the Commonwealth is South Africa, which left in 1961 and was readmitted in June 1994.

NATO and the WEU

- The North Atlantic Treaty Organisation (NATO) is a 16-member organisation dedicated to collective security.
- NATO's core security functions are to provide a foundation for security in Europe, deter aggression and defend member states against it, and provide a forum for allied transatlantic consultation.
- Britain is also one of the members of the Western European Union, which is the main forum for cooperation and consultation on defence issues for NATO's European members.

NATO and WEU member states

- NATO member
- WEU member
- NATO and WEU member

* Associate members of the WEU
** Observer members of the WEU

Parliamentary Seats

- There are 524 Parliamentary constituencies in England, 38 in Wales, 72 in Scotland, and 17 in Northern Ireland, making a total of 651 in all.
- The General Election took place on April 9th, 1992, with the Conservatives winning 336 seats (giving them a majority of 21), Labour 271, the Liberal Democrats 20 and other parties 24.
- By the end of 1994, 4 seats had changed hands at by-elections, Labour taking Dudley West from the Conservatives and the Liberal Democrats taking Newbury, Christchurch and Eastleigh, also from the Conservatives.

Parliamentary seats, representation by political party, April 1992

Source: Dod's Guide to the Election 1992

European Parliament Seats

- The first direct elections to the European Parliament took place in 1979; subsequent elections have taken place at 5 year intervals.
- From the June 1994 elections, the number of seats allocated to the United Kingdom was increased to 87, 71 of which are English constituencies, 8 Scottish and 5 Welsh.
- The remaining 3 seats are filled by a system of proportional representation using the single transferable vote system with Northern Ireland making 1 constituency.

Party control of Euro-seats, June 1994

- Conservative
- Labour
- Liberal Democrat
- Scottish National Party
- Democratic Unionist Party
- Social Democratic and Labour Party
- Ulster Unionist Party

European elections in Northern Ireland are conducted under a system of proportional representation using the single transferable vote system in a 3-member constituency.

Source: Dod's Guide to the Parliamentary and European Elections 1994

Local Government Control

- County council elections in England and Wales take place once every 4 years (most recently in 1993); some non-metropolitan districts have elections in the 3 other years of the cycle; a third of the seats coming up each time.
- Other non-metropolitan districts, and all metropolitan districts and London boroughs, elect all their councils at one time, again once every 4 years.
- In Scotland local elections are held every 2 years, alternately for districts and regions.
- A large number of councils are not controlled by any one party; moreover, there are still a significant number where many or even most councillors are independent of political parties.

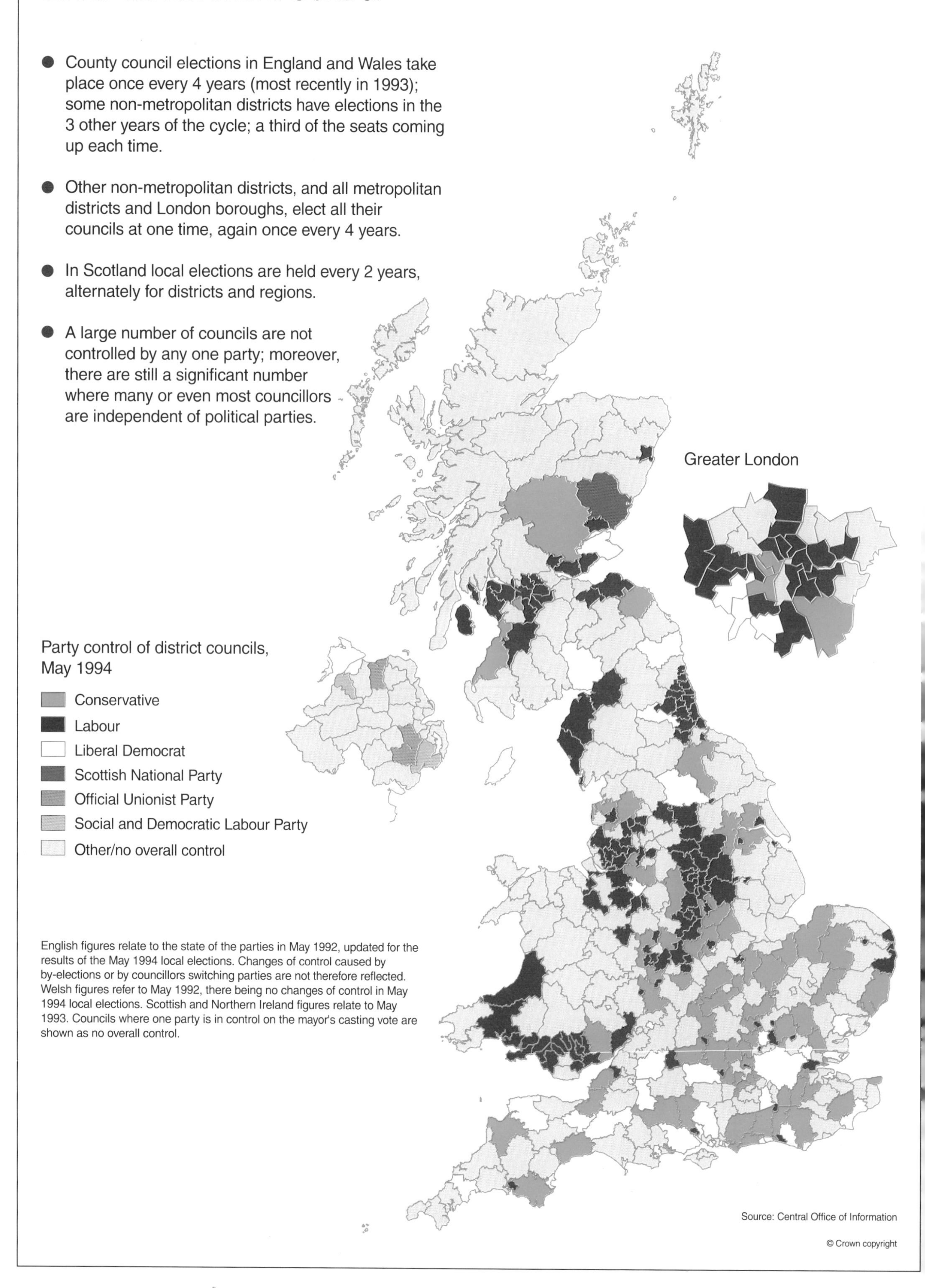

English figures relate to the state of the parties in May 1992, updated for the results of the May 1994 local elections. Changes of control caused by by-elections or by councillors switching parties are not therefore reflected. Welsh figures refer to May 1992, there being no changes of control in May 1994 local elections. Scottish and Northern Ireland figures relate to May 1993. Councils where one party is in control on the mayor's casting vote are shown as no overall control.

Source: Central Office of Information

New Unitary Councils in Scotland and Wales

- New council boundaries are to be introduced in Scotland and Wales under the terms of the Local Government etc (Scotland) Act 1994 and the Local Government (Wales) Act 1994.
- The new arrangements apply from April 1996.
- The new authorities will be unitary - that is, local government functions will be combined in a single tier rather than split between districts and either counties or regions.
- Local government boundaries in England are also being reformed in a rolling programme. As this book went to press, the Local Government Commission for England was recommending the retention of two-tier local government in many areas.

Wales

1 Aberconwy & Colwyn
2 Anglesey
3 Blaenau Gwent
4 Bridgend
5 Caerphilly
6 Caernarfonshire & Merionethshire
7 Cardiganshire
8 Cardiff
9 Carmarthenshire
10 Denbighshire
11 Flintshire
12 Merthyr Tydfil
13 Monmouthshire
14 Neath & Port Talbot
15 Newport
16 Pembrokeshire
17 Powys
18 Rhondda Cynon Taff
19 Swansea
20 Torfaen
21 Vale of Glamorgan
22 Wrexham

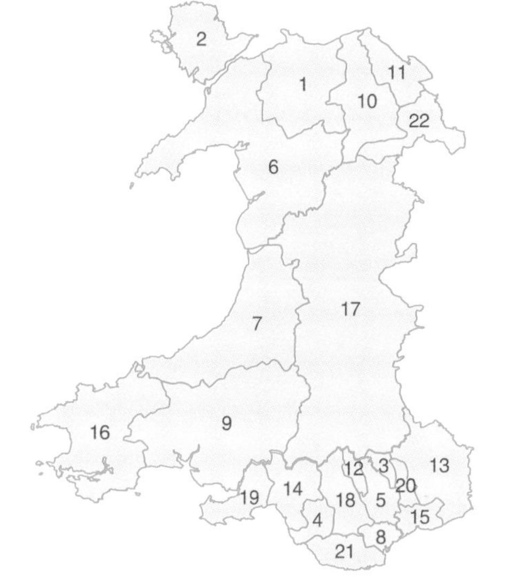

Sources: Welsh Office; The Scottish Office

Size of Electorates

- The average Parliamentary electorate in England in 1994 was about 70 000; it was about 58 000 in Wales, 55 000 in Scotland and 68 000 in Northern Ireland.
- The biggest constituency was Isle of Wight, with 101 000 voters.
- The smallest - by a considerable margin - was the Western Isles, with 23 000 electors.
- A periodic review of Parliamentary constituency boundaries is being carried out at the time of writing.

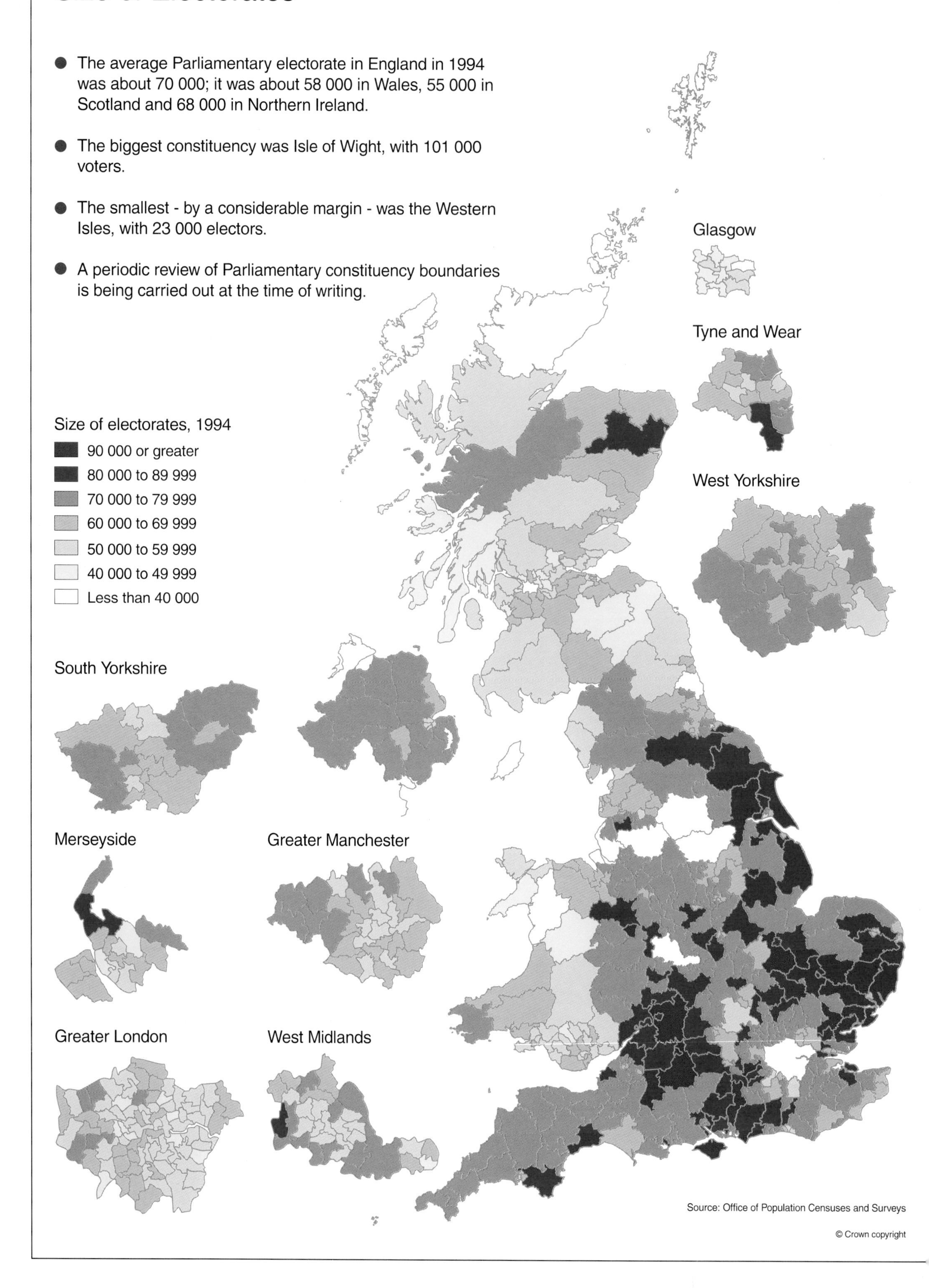

Source: Office of Population Censuses and Surveys

Major Urban Areas

There is no easy statistical definition of a city in Britain. Various approaches have been used in the past, including the extent of built-up area, population density, the status of local authories and the pattern of commuting. All give somewhat different results. The information on this map is taken from population figures for local authorities. Places marked are those districts where the population is 200 000 or more *and* the population density is 1 000 persons or more per square kilometre. Where metropolitan counties meet these criteria, the county is included as one large population centre.

- Towns and cities may be defined by local government area, as here, or in other ways, for example on a local labour market area basis.
- Using either concept London is by far the largest city in Britain.
- With some 6.9 million people, it accounts for about 14 per cent of the population of England.
- The metropolitan counties of West Midlands, Greater Manchester and West Yorkshire all have more than 2 million inhabitants.
- Using the local labour market area concept, four cities have over 1 million people: London, Birmingham, Glasgow and Manchester.

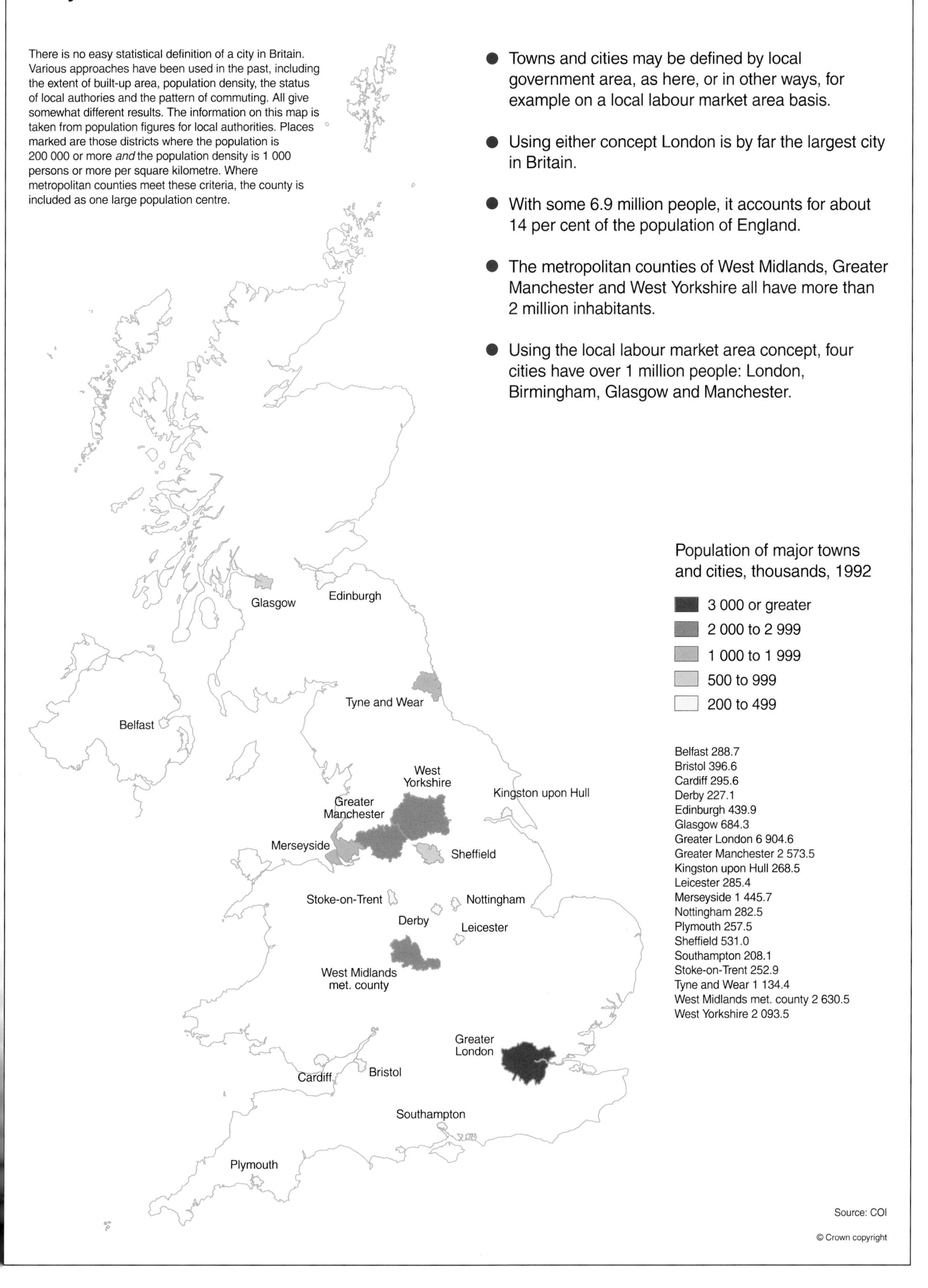

Population of major towns and cities, thousands, 1992

- 3 000 or greater
- 2 000 to 2 999
- 1 000 to 1 999
- 500 to 999
- 200 to 499

Belfast 288.7
Bristol 396.6
Cardiff 295.6
Derby 227.1
Edinburgh 439.9
Glasgow 684.3
Greater London 6 904.6
Greater Manchester 2 573.5
Kingston upon Hull 268.5
Leicester 285.4
Merseyside 1 445.7
Nottingham 282.5
Plymouth 257.5
Sheffield 531.0
Southampton 208.1
Stoke-on-Trent 252.9
Tyne and Wear 1 134.4
West Midlands met. county 2 630.5
West Yorkshire 2 093.5

Source: COI

Population Density

- The population density in Great Britain is about 241 people per square kilometre.
- England is much the most densely populated of the four countries, while Scotland, Wales and Northern Ireland all have population densities below the United Kingdom average.
- Greater London is the most densely populated area in England, with nearly 4 400 people per square kilometre.
- By contrast, there are only 167 people per square kilometre in East Anglia.

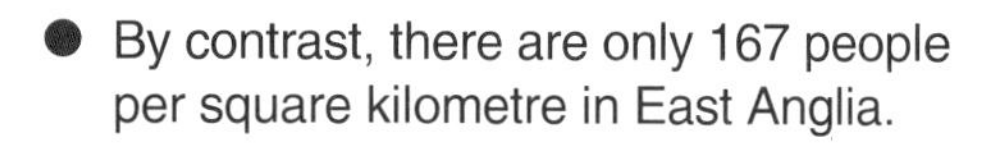

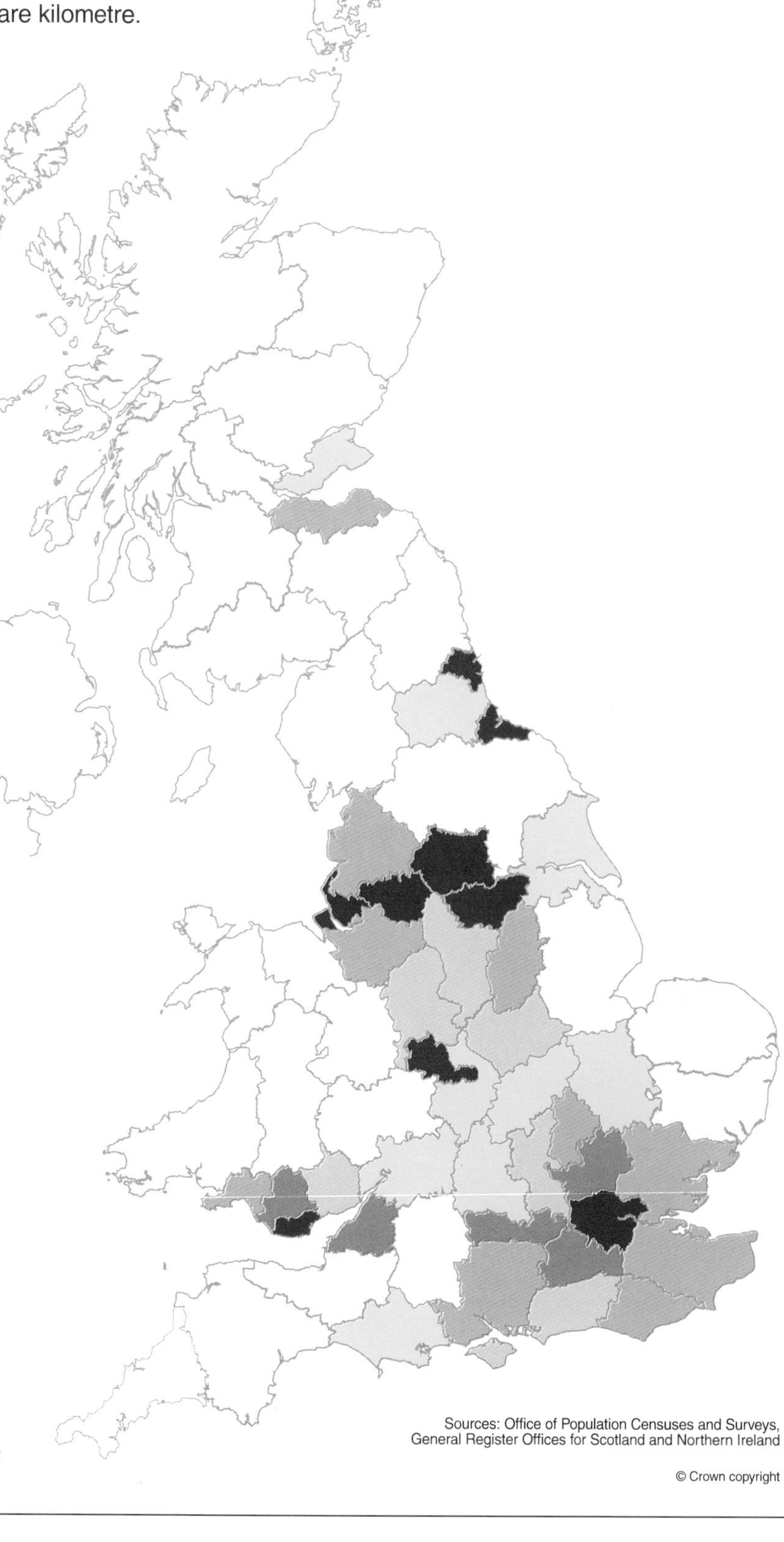

People per square kilometre, 1993

- 1 000 or greater
- 750 to 999
- 500 to 749
- 400 to 499
- 300 to 399
- 200 to 299
- 100 to 199
- Less than 100

Sources: Office of Population Censuses and Surveys, General Register Offices for Scotland and Northern Ireland

Change in Population 1981 - 1992

- East Anglia was the fastest growing region between 1981 and 1992, with an increase in population of over 10 per cent.
- The county of Cambridgeshire experienced the greatest population increase, with a rise of 15 per cent.
- 5 other counties - Buckinghamshire, Cornwall, Dorset, Northamptonshire and Wiltshire - had rises of more than 10 per cent.
- Many of the cities and metropolitan counties had fewer inhabitants in 1992 than in 1981.
- Merseyside and Strathclyde experienced some of the largest falls, of around 5 per cent.
- Although the population of Northern Ireland rose by 4.7 per cent, that of Belfast declined by 8 per cent.
- The population of Shetland fell by 14 per cent, mainly reflecting the loss of oil terminal construction workers who had been temporarily resident in 1981.

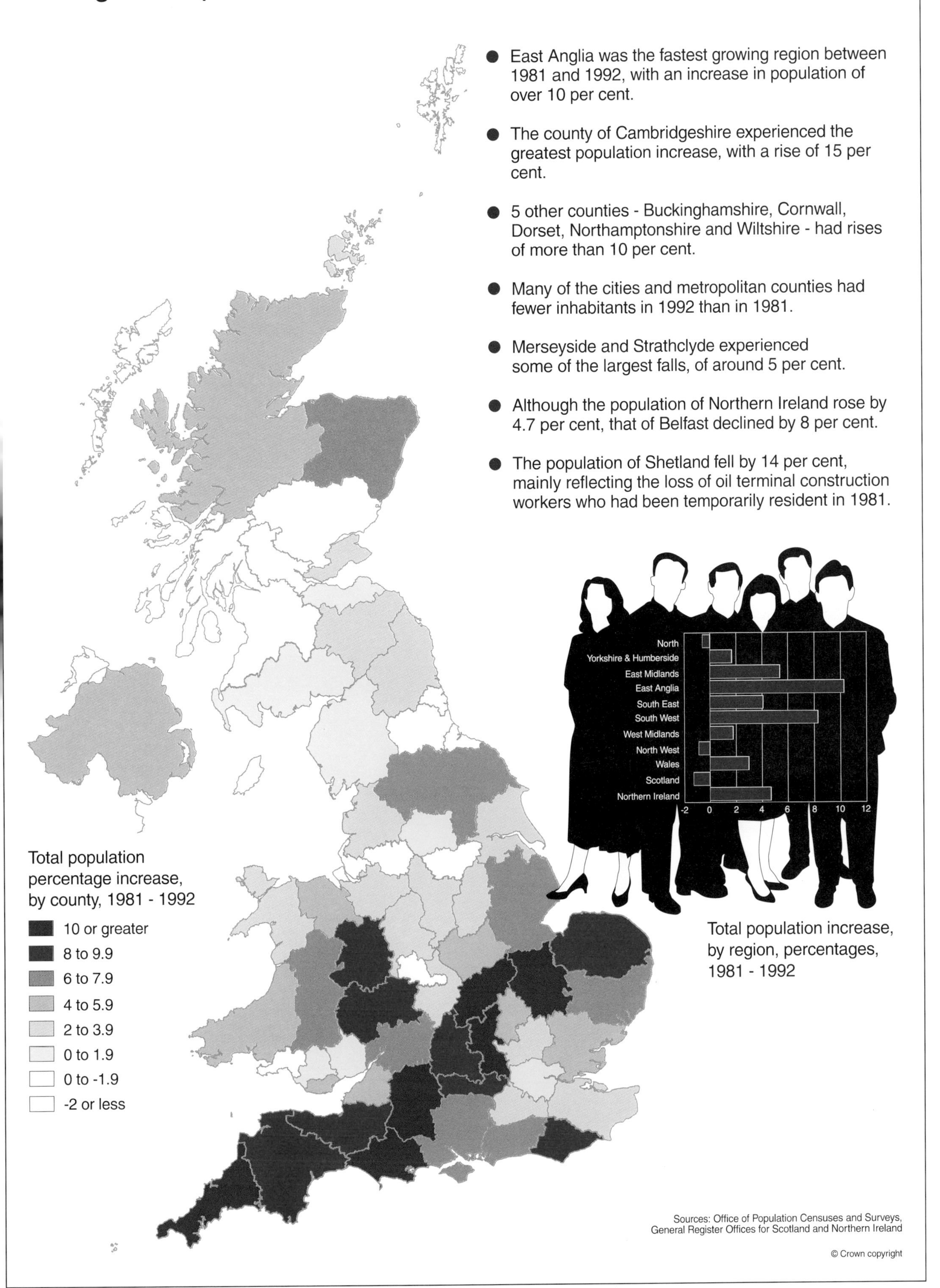

Total population percentage increase, by county, 1981 - 1992

Total population increase, by region, percentages, 1981 - 1992

Sources: Office of Population Censuses and Surveys, General Register Offices for Scotland and Northern Ireland

Birth Rates

- Birth rates are the highest in Northern Ireland: 15.9 live births per 1 000 population in 1992.
- The Isle of Wight has the lowest birth rate (10.5).
- Other southern coastal counties also tend to have relatively low birth rates.
- All regions have experienced an increase in the level of births outside marriage, which now account for over 30 per cent of all live births.
- Merseyside had the highest proportion of births outside of marriage in 1992: 42 per cent.

Live births per 1 000 population, 1992

- 16.0 or greater
- 15.0 to 15.9
- 14.0 to 14.9
- 13.0 to 13.9
- 12.0 to 12.9
- 11.0 to 11.9
- Less than 11.0

Births outside marriage
as a percentage of all births, United Kingdom

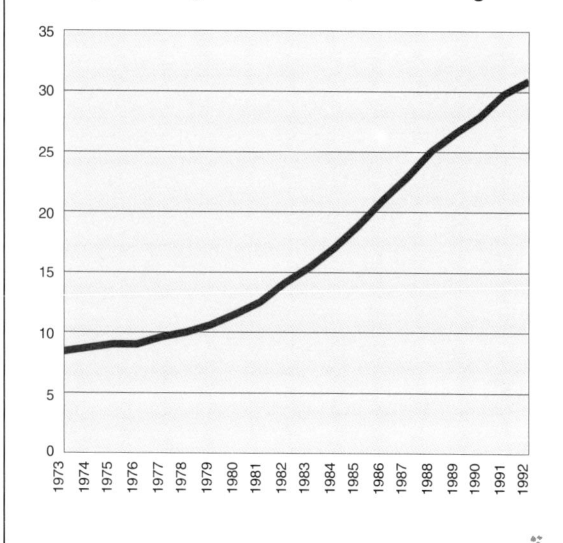

Sources: Office of Population Censuses and Surveys, General Register Offices for Scotland and Northern Ireland

Young People

- Northern Ireland has the highest proportion of young people in Great Britain: over one-quarter of its population is under 16, and it has the highest proportion of under 5s (8 per cent) and of those aged 5-15 (nearly 18 per cent).
- Greater London has a relatively high proportion of under 5s, but a relatively low proportion of the 5-15 age group.
- Dorset has the lowest proportion of under 16s: 17.7 per cent.
- The Isle of Wight has the lowest proportion of under 5s: 5.5 per cent.

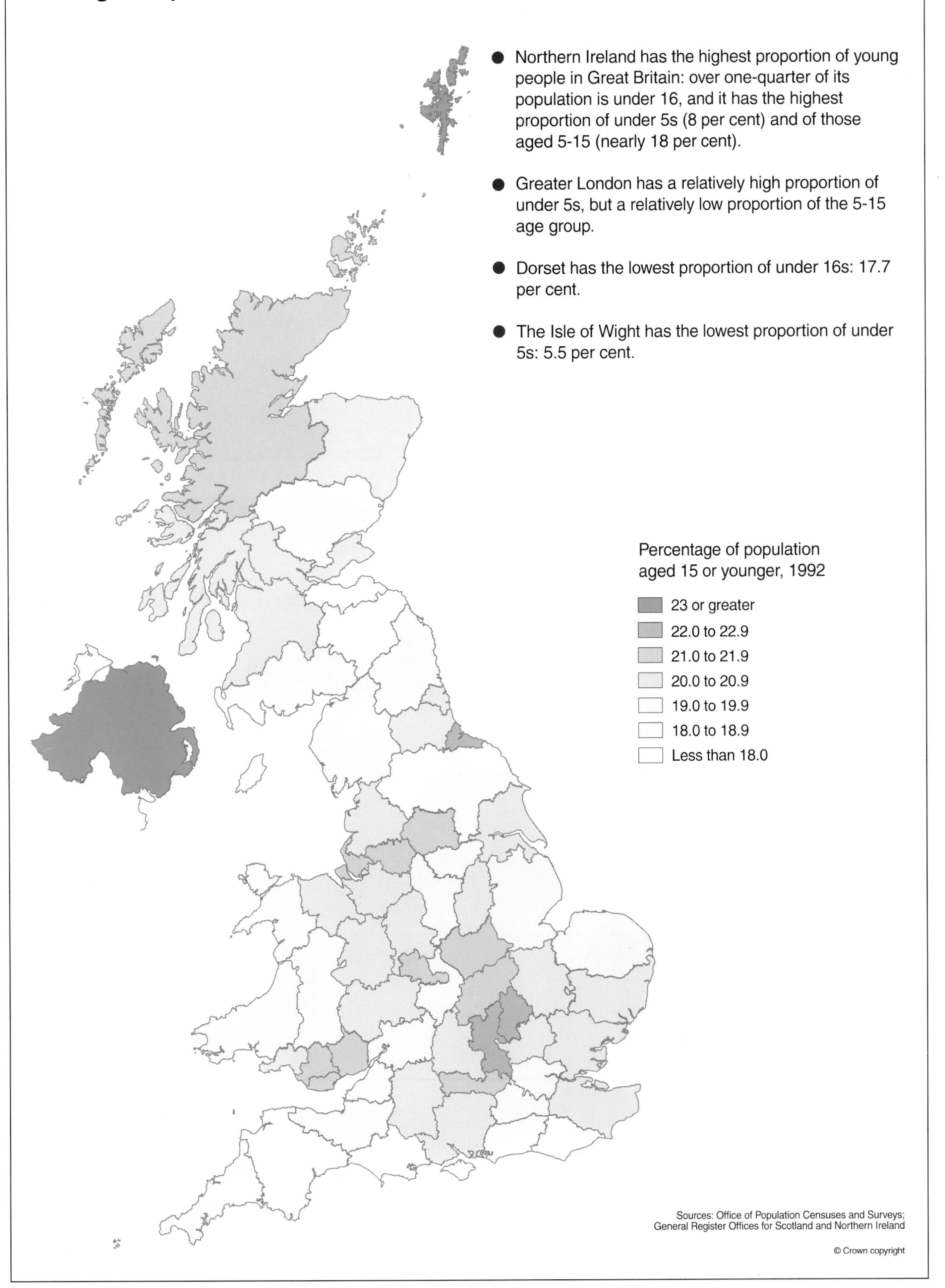

Sources: Office of Population Censuses and Surveys; General Register Offices for Scotland and Northern Ireland

Death Rates

- Death rates reflect the proportion of elderly people in the population.
- Areas such as East Sussex and the Isle of Wight had the highest death rates in 1992.
- Death rates were lowest in parts of the South East and Northern Ireland.
- Age-specific death rates take the age structure of the population into account; on this basis, deaths in the south tend to be below the national average and those in the north above it.

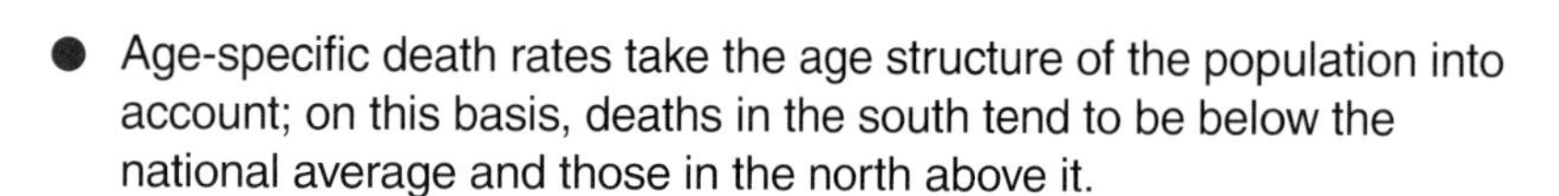

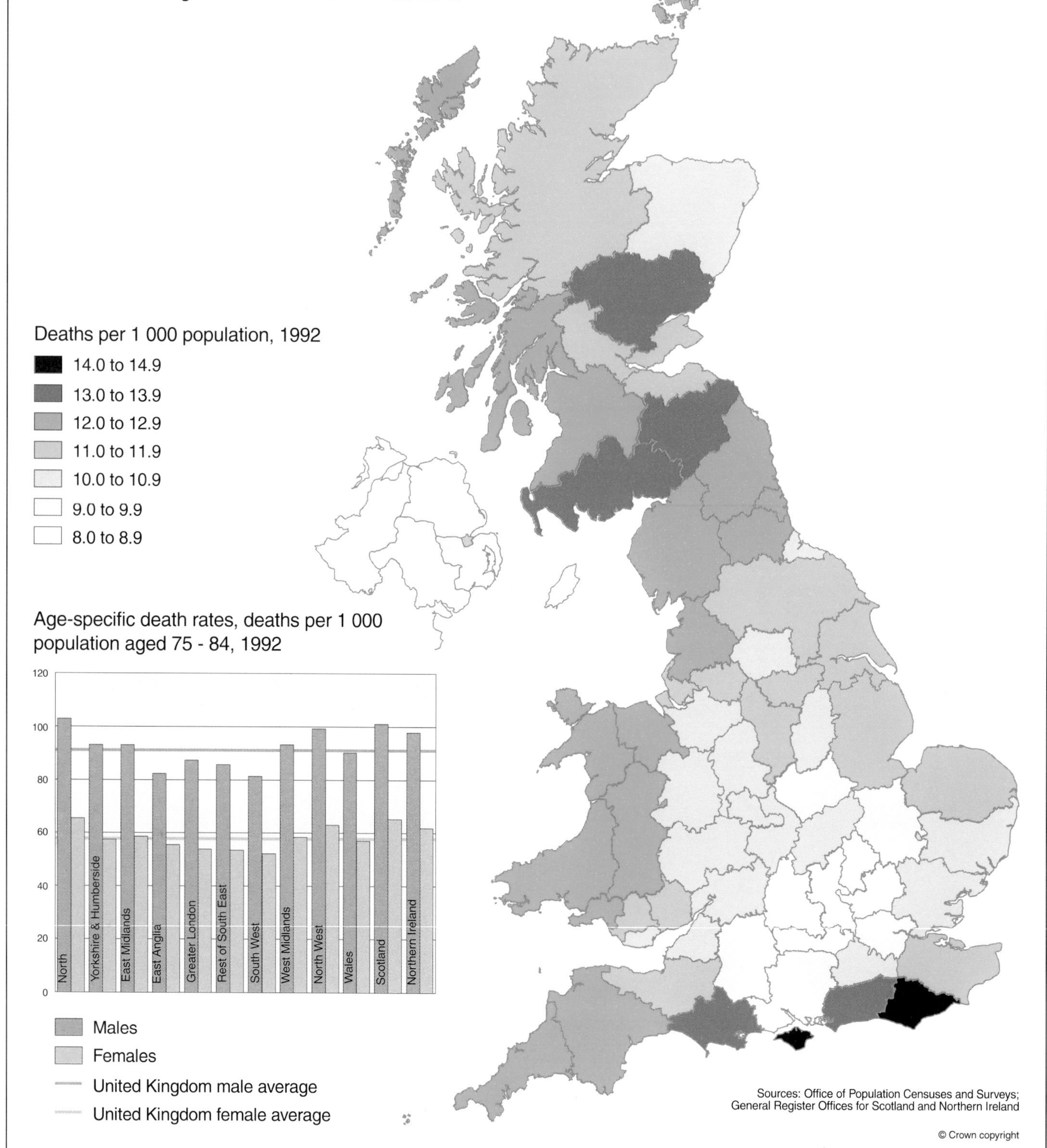

Sources: Office of Population Censuses and Surveys; General Register Offices for Scotland and Northern Ireland

Mortality Rates by Cause

- Generally speaking, cancer is a bigger killer than heart disease in the southern and eastern parts of the United Kingdom, whereas in the north the opposite tends to be the case.
- Scotland has the highest age-adjusted mortality rates for both men and women, and also has the highest mortality rate for heart disease for both men and women.
- However, for cancer the highest rates are for men in the Northern Regional Health Authority Area and for women in the Mersey Regional Health Authority Area.

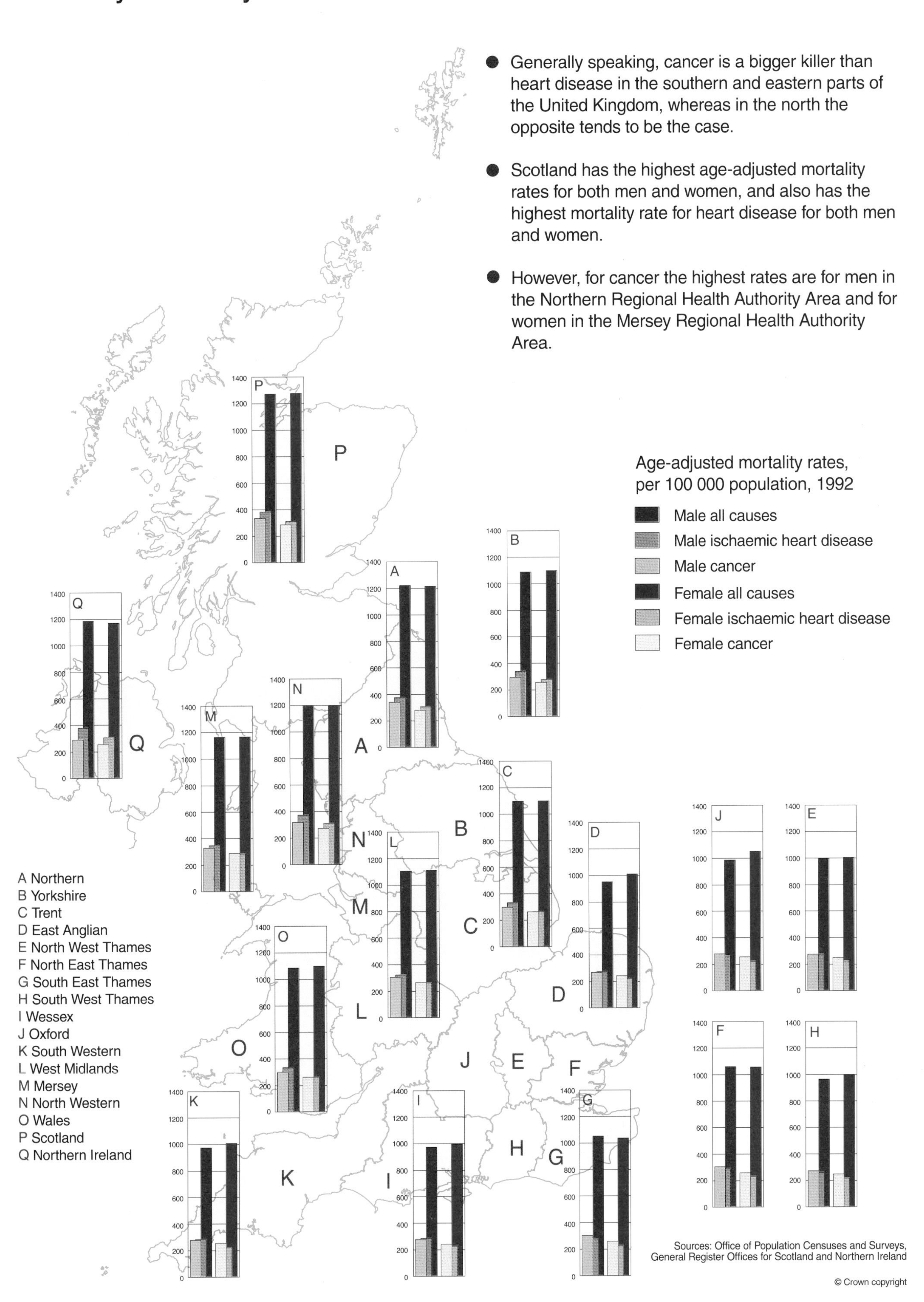

Retired People

- The southern coastal counties tend to have some of the highest levels of retired people.
- By county the Isle of Wight has the highest proportion of its population over pension age: 26.5 per cent in 1992.
- The district with the highest proportion over pension age was Christchurch in Dorset, with over 34 per cent.
- New towns such as Milton Keynes have some of the lowest levels of people of pensionable age.
- Northern Ireland also has a relatively low level of retired people.

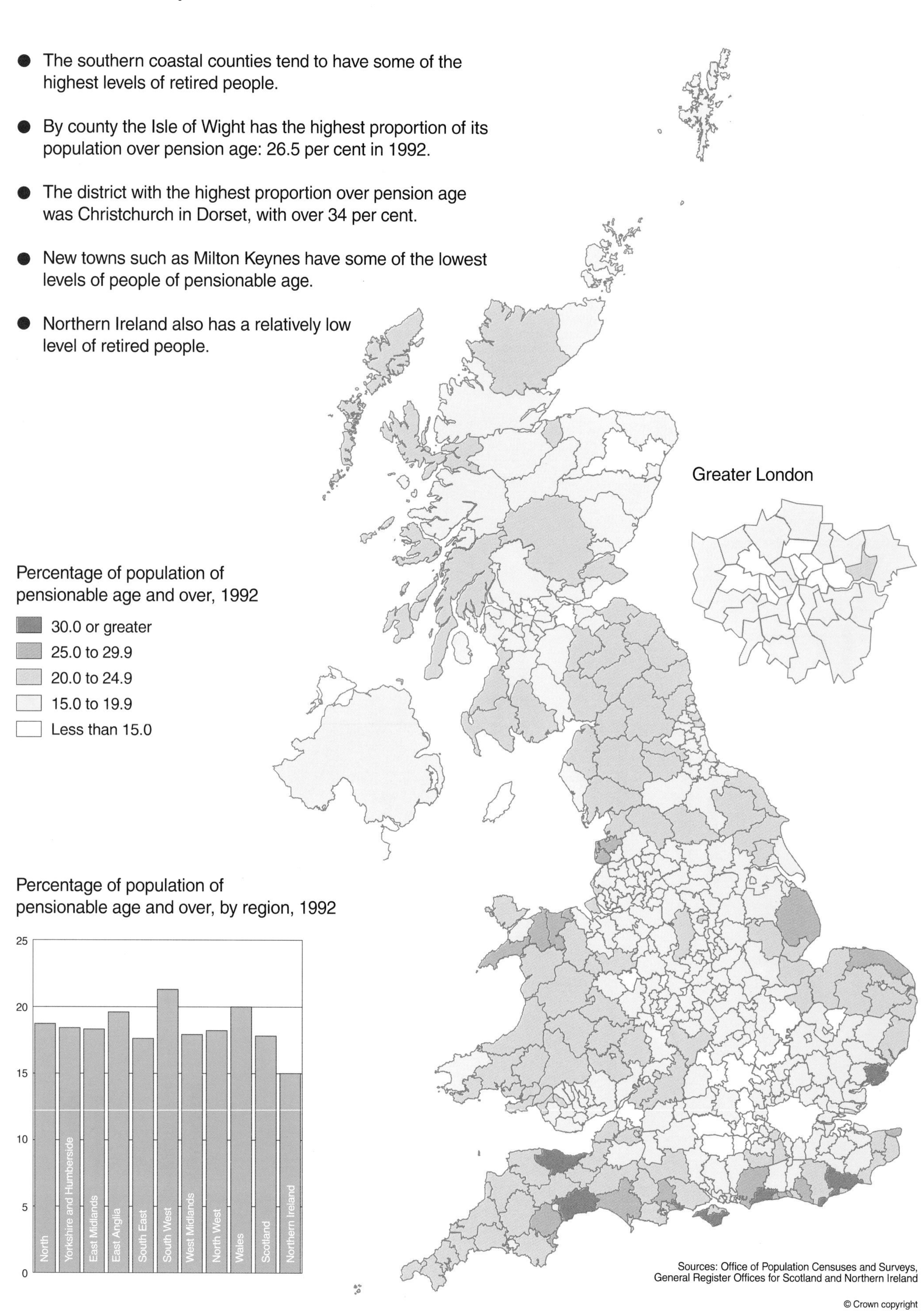

Sources: Office of Population Censuses and Surveys, General Register Offices for Scotland and Northern Ireland

Ethnic Minorities

- According to the 1991 Census, just over 3 million people described themselves as belonging to an ethnic minority group - 5.5 per cent of the population of Great Britain.
- Over two-thirds of the ethnic minority population live in four conurbations: London, the West Midlands, West Yorkshire and Greater Manchester.
- Around 10 per cent of the population of the South East belongs to an ethnic minority group.
- In many rural areas ethnic minority groups form less than 1 per cent of the population.
- Of the main ethnic minority groups, the Chinese are the least likely to live in metropolitan areas.

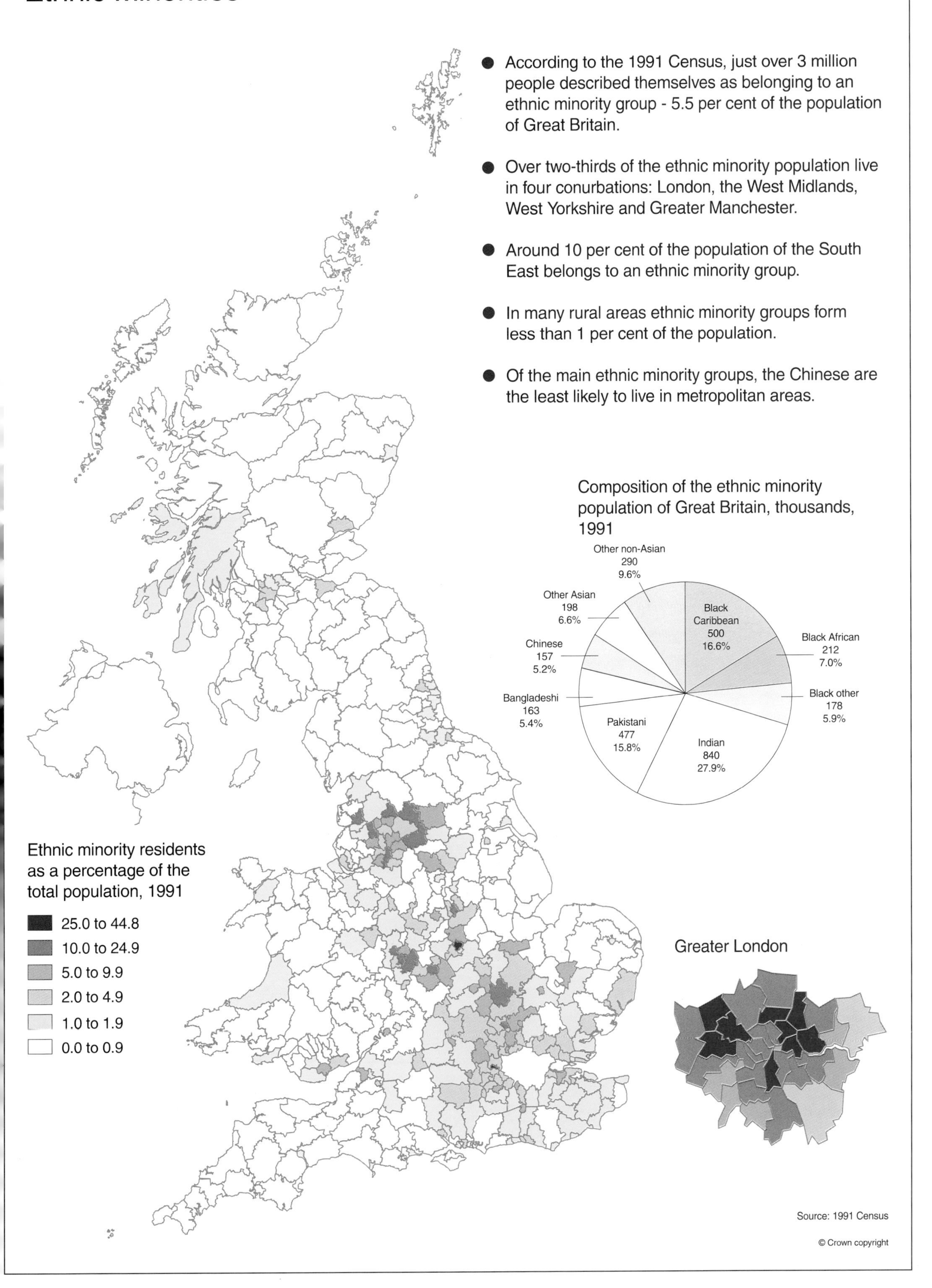

General Practitioners

- In recent years the number of general practitioners (GPs) has been rising and average patient size list has been falling.
- The average number of people on a GP's list in Britain is 1 870.
- This figure is higher in most regional health authority areas in England.
- In the North East Thames and North West Thames areas the average is above 2 000.
- Scotland has the smallest average size of lists, with 1 555 patients on the average GP list.

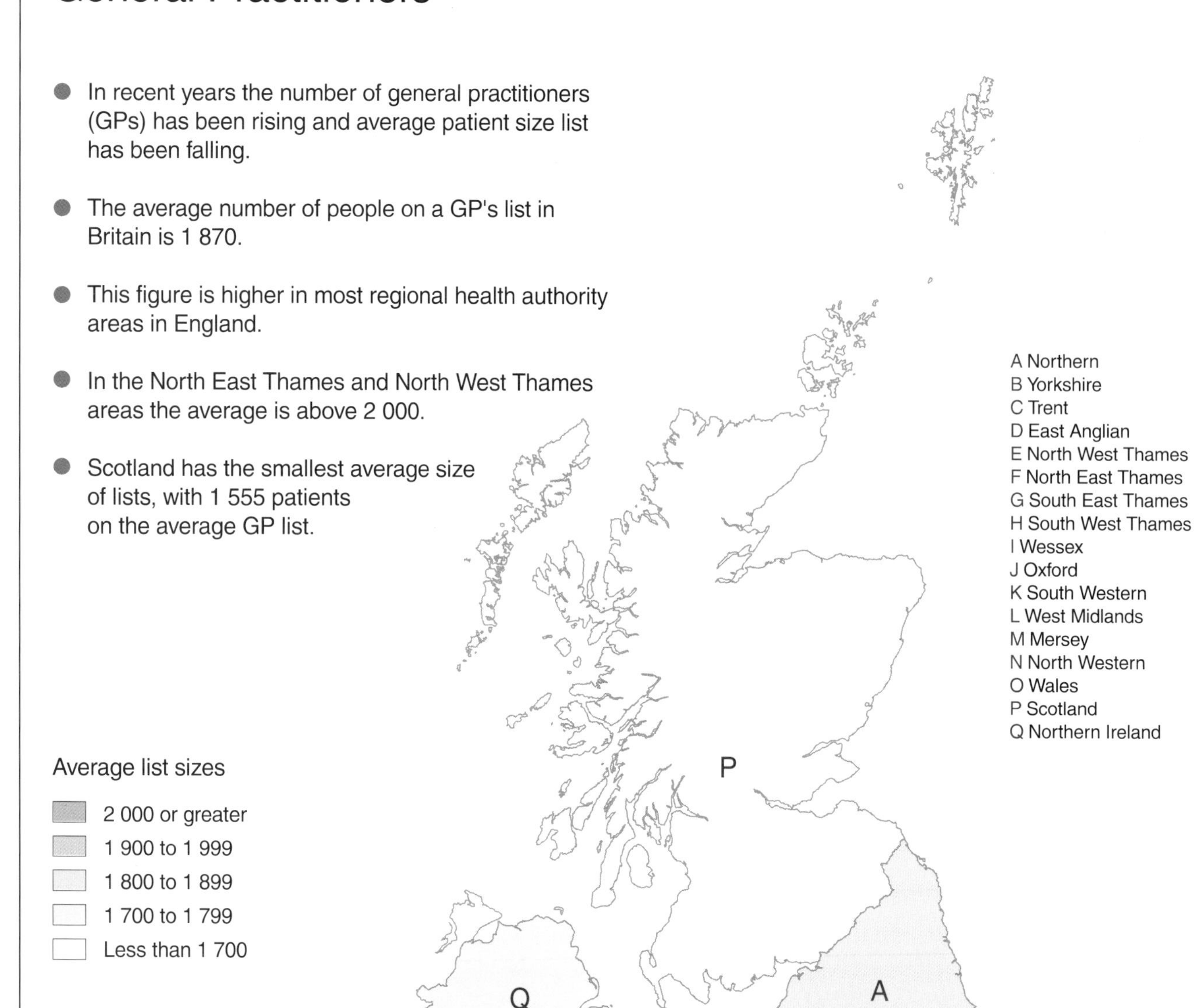

Number of general practitioners

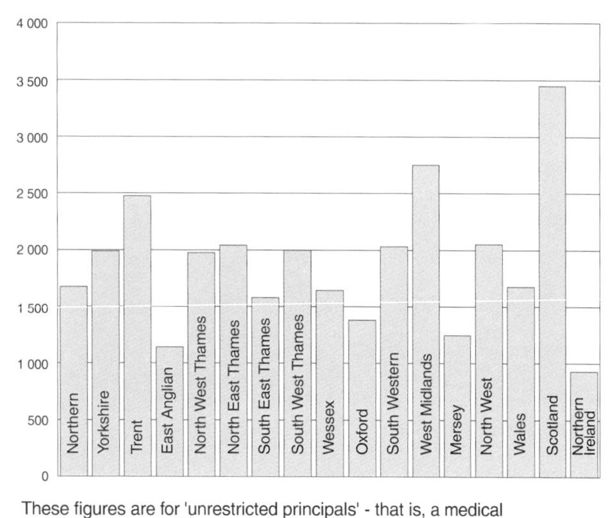

These figures are for 'unrestricted principals' - that is, a medical practitioner who provides the full range of general medical services and whose list is not limited to any particular group or persons.

Sources: Department of Health; Welsh Office; The Scottish Office; Department of Health and Social Services, Northern Ireland

Dentists

- The average number of people on the list of a general dental practitioner in Britain is 1 829.
- The highest figures are in the Trent and West Midlands health authority areas (over 2 200).
- The lowest figures are in the North West Thames and South West Thames health authority areas.
- As with GPs, Scotland has a below average size list for dentists.

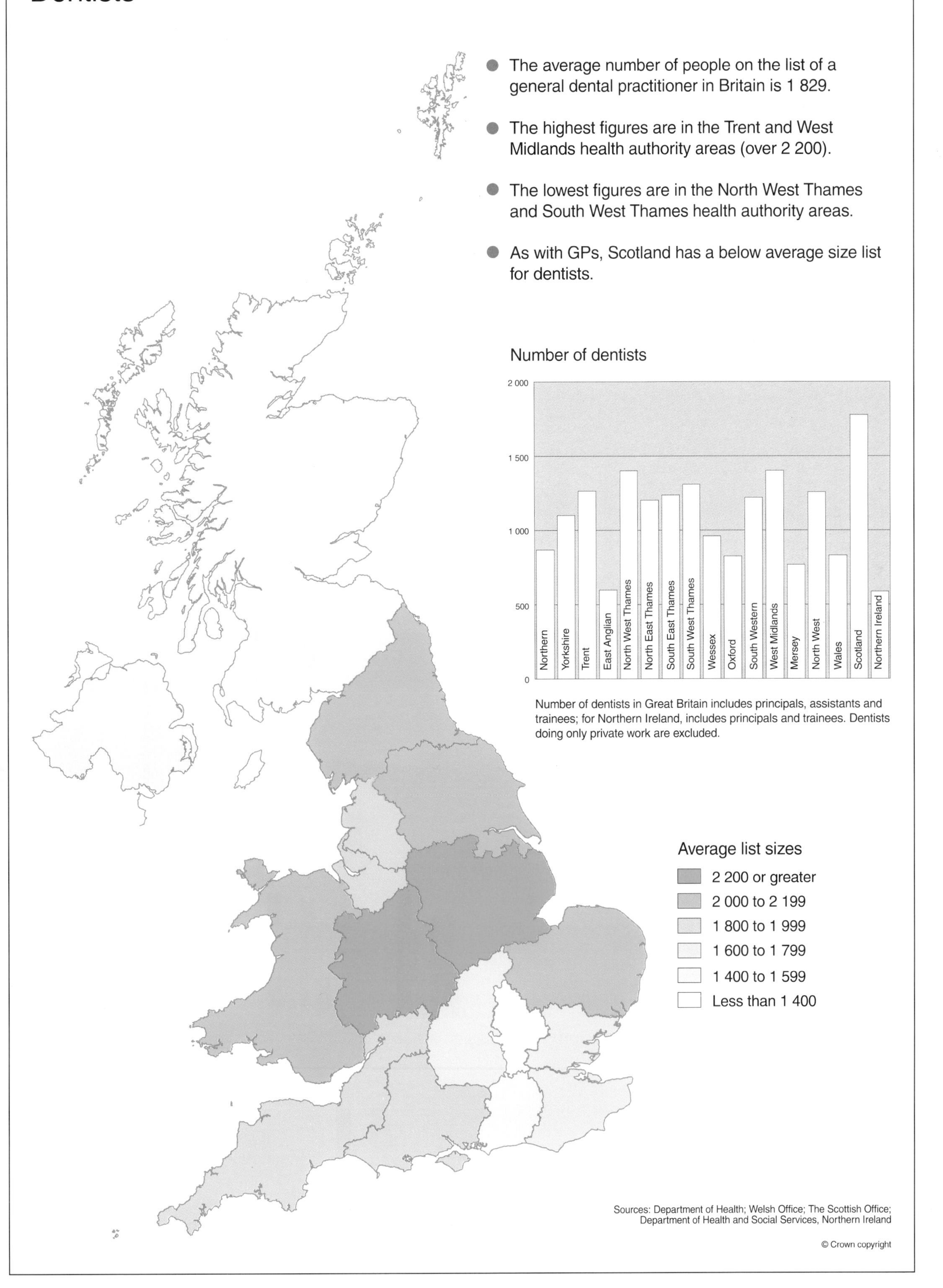

Number of dentists in Great Britain includes principals, assistants and trainees; for Northern Ireland, includes principals and trainees. Dentists doing only private work are excluded.

Sources: Department of Health; Welsh Office; The Scottish Office; Department of Health and Social Services, Northern Ireland

Long Standing Illnesses

- Just under one-fifth of the population reports having a limiting long-standing illness, disability or infirmity.
- The proportion is slightly higher among women than among men in all regions except the North West, where the rates are the same for both sexes.
- Wales and the North have the highest proportions, and the South East the lowest proportion.
- Over half of very elderly women and nearly half of very elderly men (those aged 75 and over) reported such an illness, disability or infirmity.
- Among the very elderly the highest rates for women were in Wales and in men in the East Midlands.

Percentage of persons reporting limiting long-standing illnesses by age and sex, 1991 - 1992

- Males all ages
- Males 65 - 74
- Males 75+
- Females all ages
- Females 65 - 74
- Females 75+

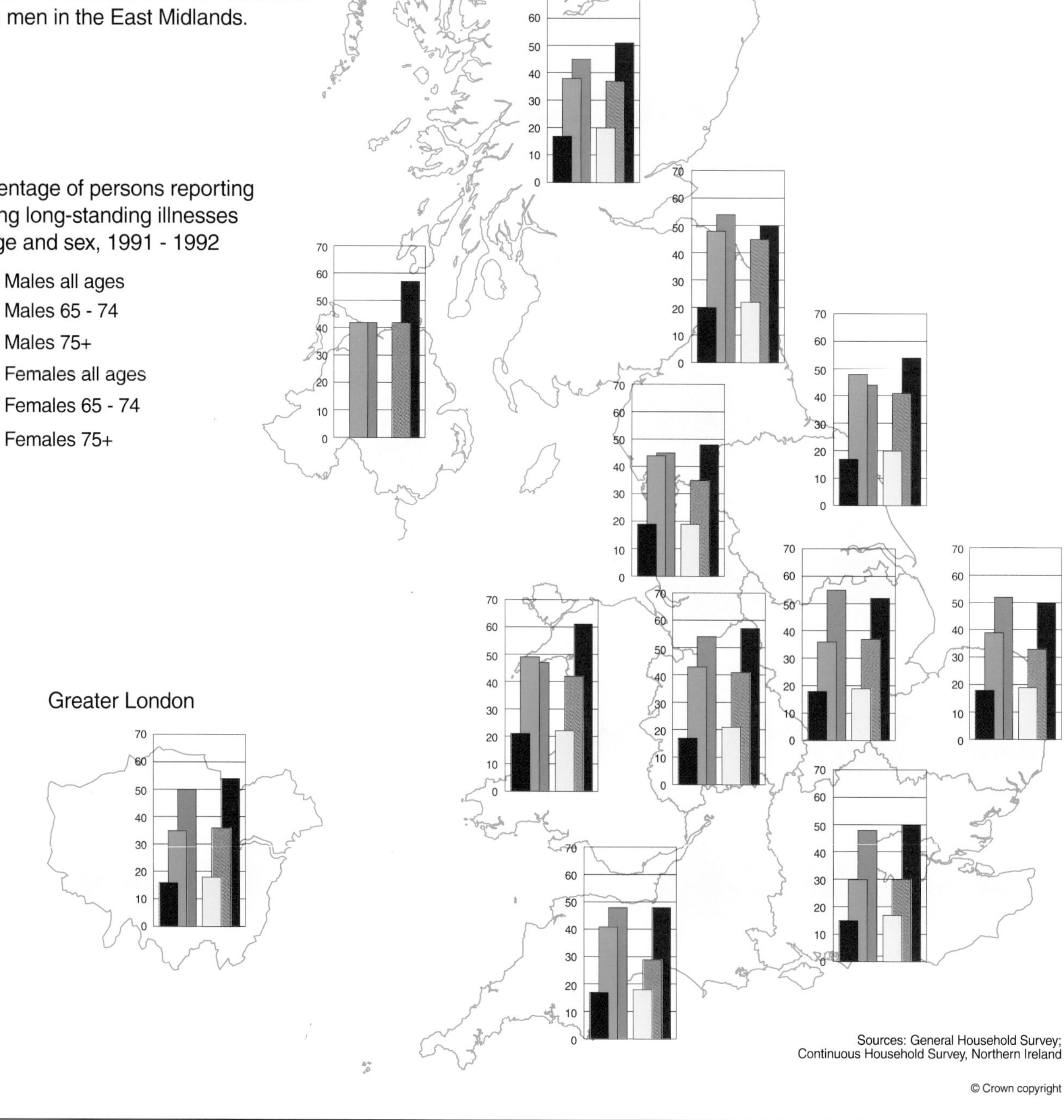

Sources: General Household Survey; Continuous Household Survey, Northern Ireland

Diet

- There has been a significant change in eating patterns, reflecting greater emphasis on health, frozen and convenience foods.
- Consumption of meat and meat products (except poultry) and of vegetables and vegetable products is lower than in 1980 - 1981, but consumption of fresh and other fruit is higher.
- The highest levels of consumption of both meat and meat products and vegetables and vegetable products are in the North region.
- The highest level of fruit consumption is in East Anglia and the South East.
- Consumption of fresh and other fruit was significantly higher in virtually all regions in Great Britain in 1991 - 1992 than in 1980 - 1981; only in the West Midlands was it slightly lower.

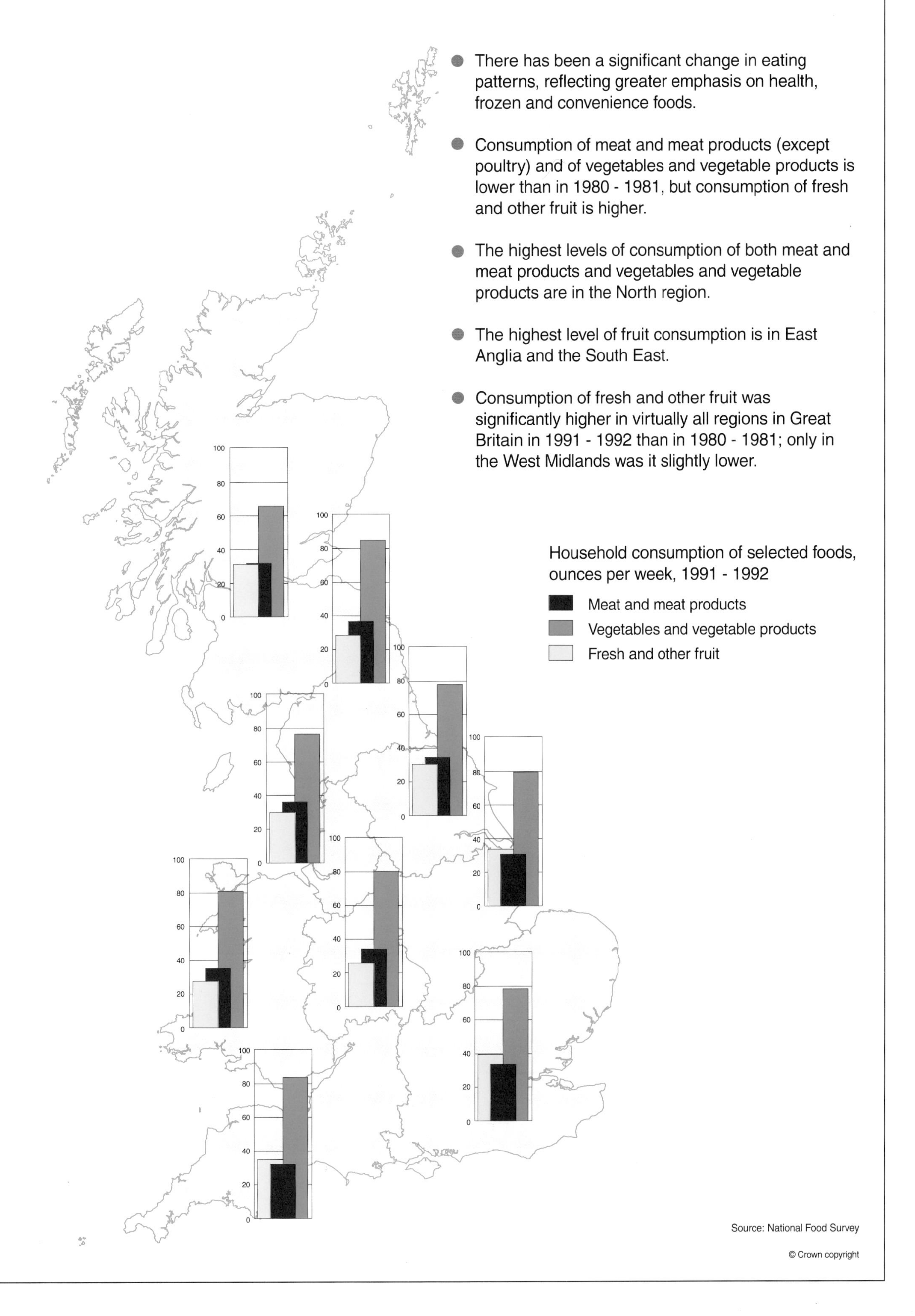

Household consumption of selected foods, ounces per week, 1991 - 1992

Source: National Food Survey

Smoking

- There has been a significant decline in the prevalence of smoking.
- The decline has been more evident among men than among women, so that in 1992 there was only a small difference with 29 per cent of men and 28 per cent of women in Great Britain aged 16 and over who were smokers.
- The highest level of smoking among both men and women is in Scotland.
- Levels of smoking were lower in 1992 than in 1986 in all regions, with the exception of Wales where there was a slight increase in smoking among women.

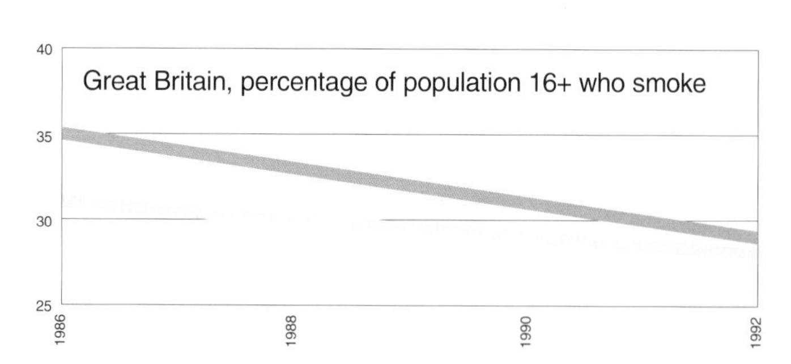

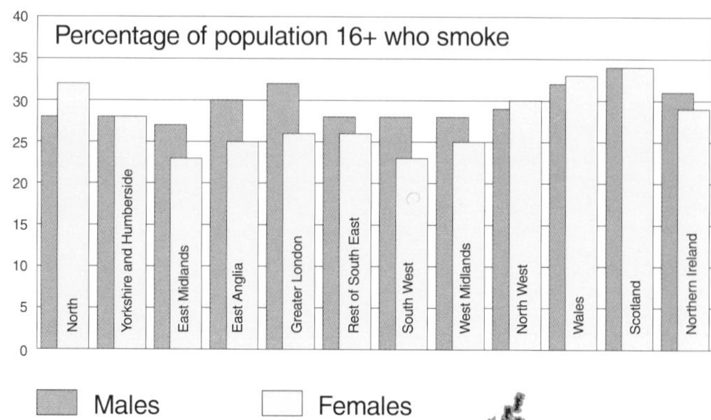

Sources: General Household Survey; Continuous Household Survey, Northern Ireland

Drink

- Spending on alcoholic drink represents the highest proportion of total household expenditure in Yorkshire and Humberside - 6 per cent.
- It is lowest in East Anglia - 3.2 per cent.
- However, East Anglia has the lowest proportion of non-drinkers - 6 per cent of those aged 16 and over.
- The highest proportion of non-drinkers is in Greater London - 15 per cent.

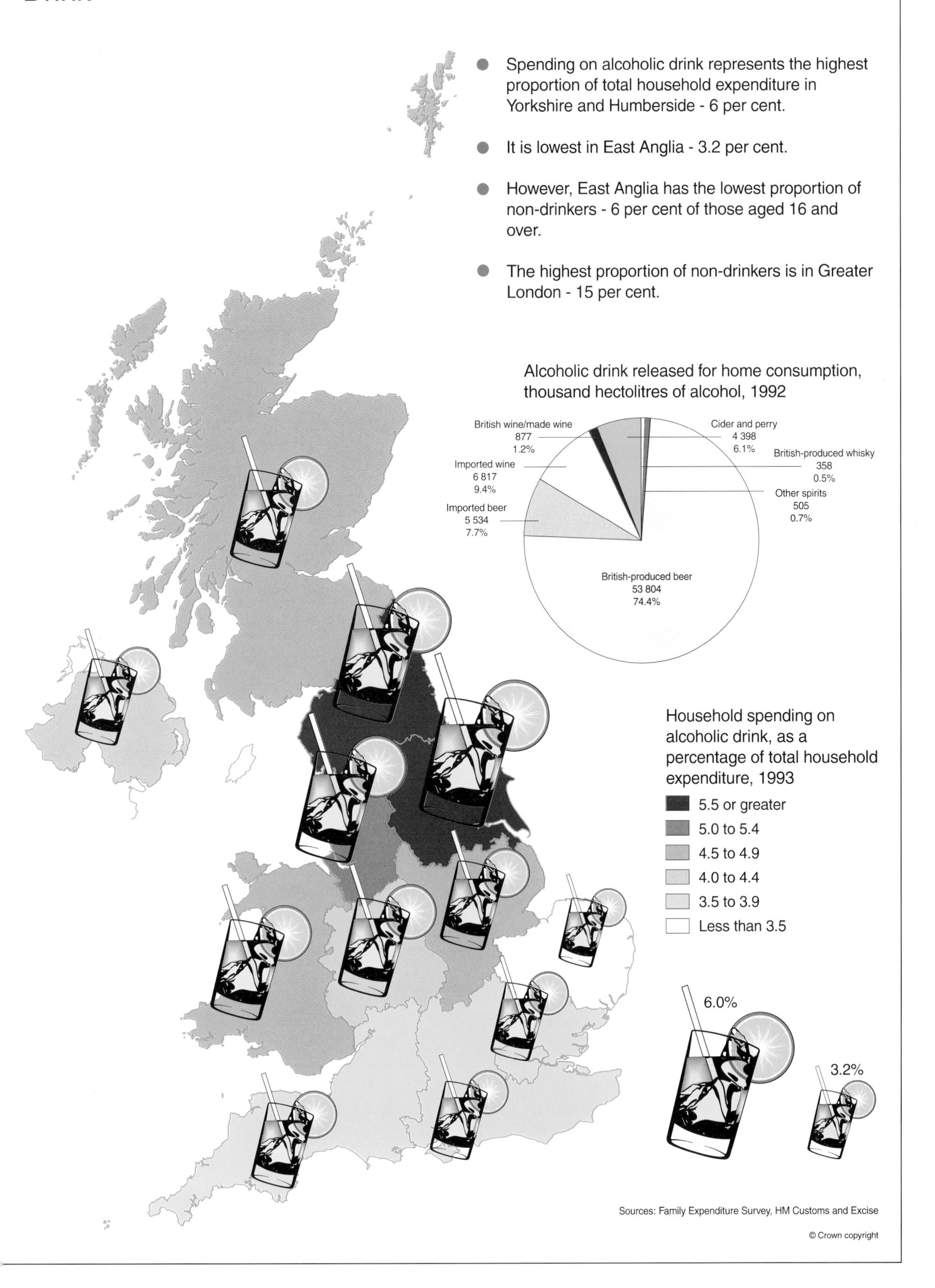

Sources: Family Expenditure Survey, HM Customs and Excise

Children in Care

- The proportion of children looked after by local authorities is generally higher in metropolitan and urban areas.
- Of those areas where figures were available, the highest rates in 1992 were in the area of the South Eastern Library Board for Northern Ireland, Nottinghamshire and Merseyside.
- The lowest rates were in Surrey and Suffolk.
- Around three-fifths of children in care in England, Wales and Northern Ireland are looked after in foster homes.
- The highest proportion by region going into foster homes is in East Anglia (70 per cent).

Children looked after by local authorities per 1 000 population aged under 18, 1992

- 6.0 or greater
- 5.0 to 5.9
- 4.0 to 4.9
- 3.0 to 3.9
- Less than 3.0

Data is unavailable for several local authorities.
Scottish legislation on children in care is different and so no comparable figures are available.
Figures for metropolitan counties include estimates which take account of missing or incomplete data.
Population estimates used are mid-1991.

Sources: Department of Health;
Department of Health and Social Services, Northern Ireland

Elderly People in Residential Accommodation

- The majority of elderly people continue to live in their own homes or in rented accommodation.
- For those in residential accommodation fewer people are now in local authority homes and a higher proportion is in registered private homes.
- By far the highest proportion in registered private homes is in the South West: 26 per 1 000 of those aged 65 and over.
- The South West had the lowest proportion in local authority homes: 6 per 1 000 in this age group.
- The highest proportions in local authority homes are in Yorkshire and Humberside and in the North.
- For Scotland 4 people per 1 000 aged 65 and over were in registered homes.

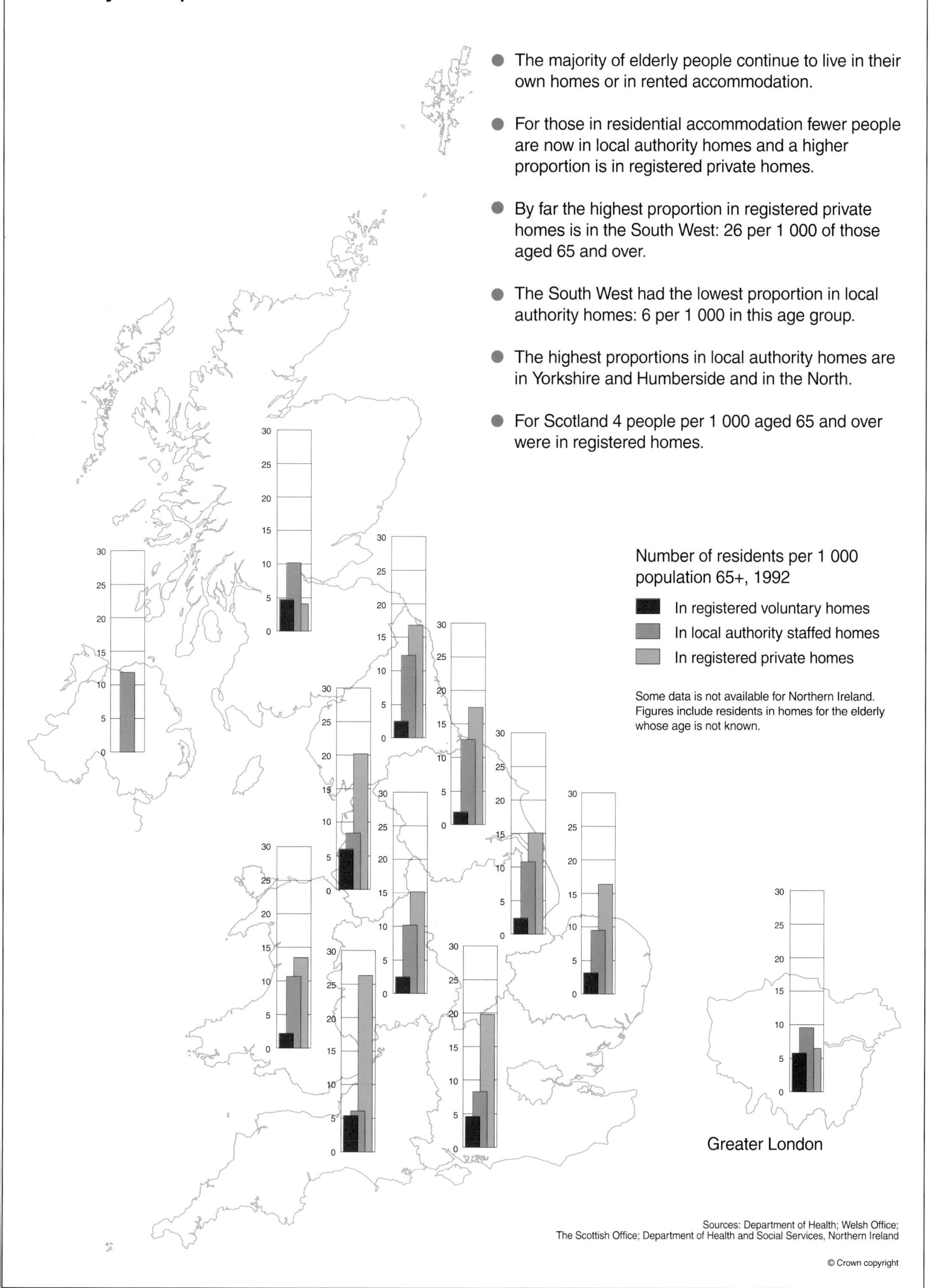

Sources: Department of Health; Welsh Office; The Scottish Office; Department of Health and Social Services, Northern Ireland

Hospitals

- Only a small proportion of the people on hospital waiting lists at 30 September 1993 had been waiting over 12 months for admission, although there was a considerable regional variation in the rates.
- Wales and Northern Ireland had the highest rates among those waiting for ordinary admissions, of over 14 per cent.
- The lowest rate, 0.5 per cent, was in the Mersey Health Authority area.
- The proportion of those waiting over 12 months for day admissions was shorter than for ordinary admissions in all regions for which data was available.
- There is also a considerable variation in hospital cases treated in relation to the population of the area, the highest rates for cases treated being in the North Western Health Authority area and in Scotland.

A Northern
B Yorkshire
C Trent
D East Anglian
E North West Thames
F North East Thames
G South East Thames
H South West Thames
I Wessex
J Oxford
K South Western
L West Midlands
M Mersey
N North Western
O Wales
P Scotland
Q Northern Ireland

Percentage of ordinary admissions waiting 12 months or more

- 12.5 or greater
- 10.0 to 12.4
- 7.5 to 9.9
- 5.0 to 7.4
- 2.5 to 4.9
- Less than 2.5

Cases treated per 1 000 population

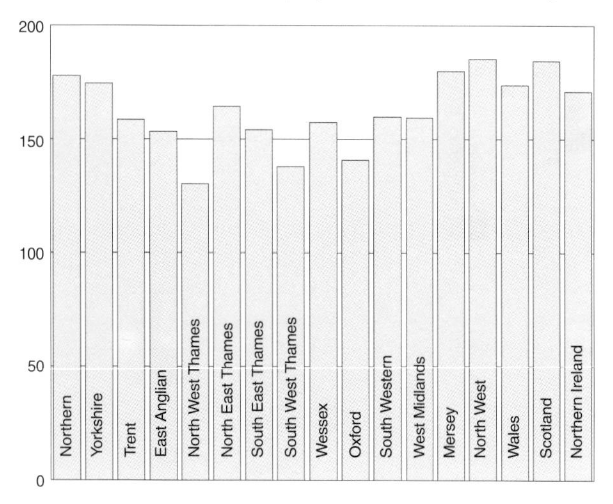

Cases treated is finished consultant episodes for England, discharges and deaths for Wales and Northern Ireland, and discharges only for Scotland.

Sources: Department of Health; Welsh Office; The Scottish Office; Department of Health and Social Services, Northern Ireland

Type of Dwelling

- In most parts of England, around 85 per cent of households live in houses rather than flats.
- A major exception is London, where over half of all dwellings are flats, the majority of them purpose-built rather than converted.
- Terraced houses are especially common in the North and North West, where over one third of all dwellings are of this type.
- Most purpose-built flats are low-rise rather than high-rise.

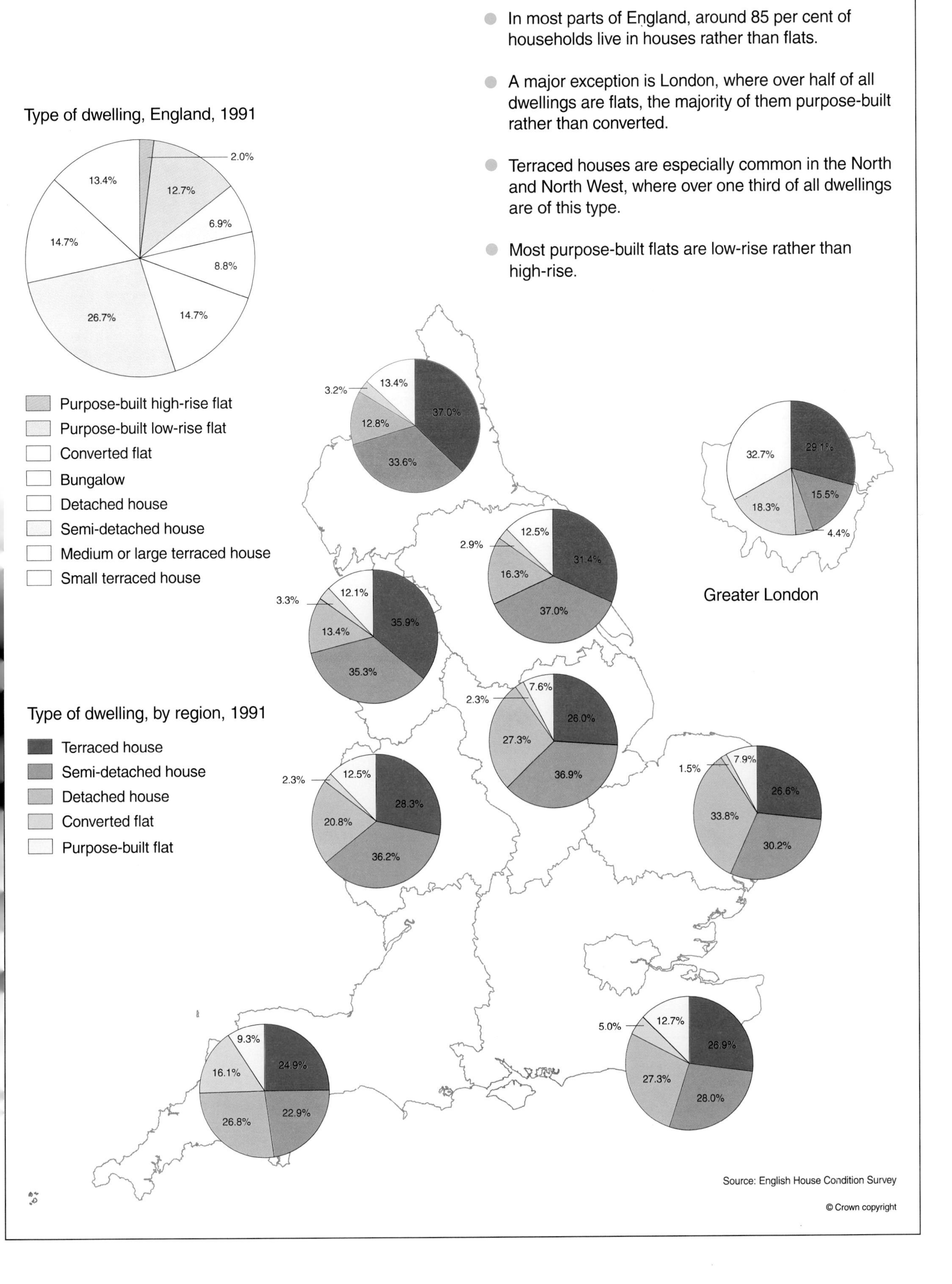

Source: English House Condition Survey

Age of Dwelling

- The part of the country with the highest proportion of post-war dwellings is Northern Ireland (67.6 per cent), followed by the South East outside London and East Anglia.
- The lowest proportion of post-war housing is in Greater London (37.1 per cent).
- The area with the highest proportion of pre-1919 houses is Wales (36.6 per cent), followed by Greater London.

Date of construction of dwellings by percentage of total housing stock in 1993

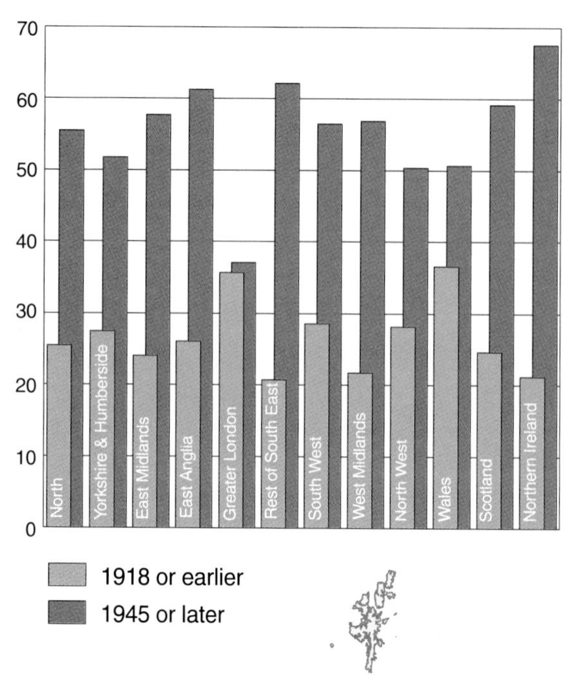

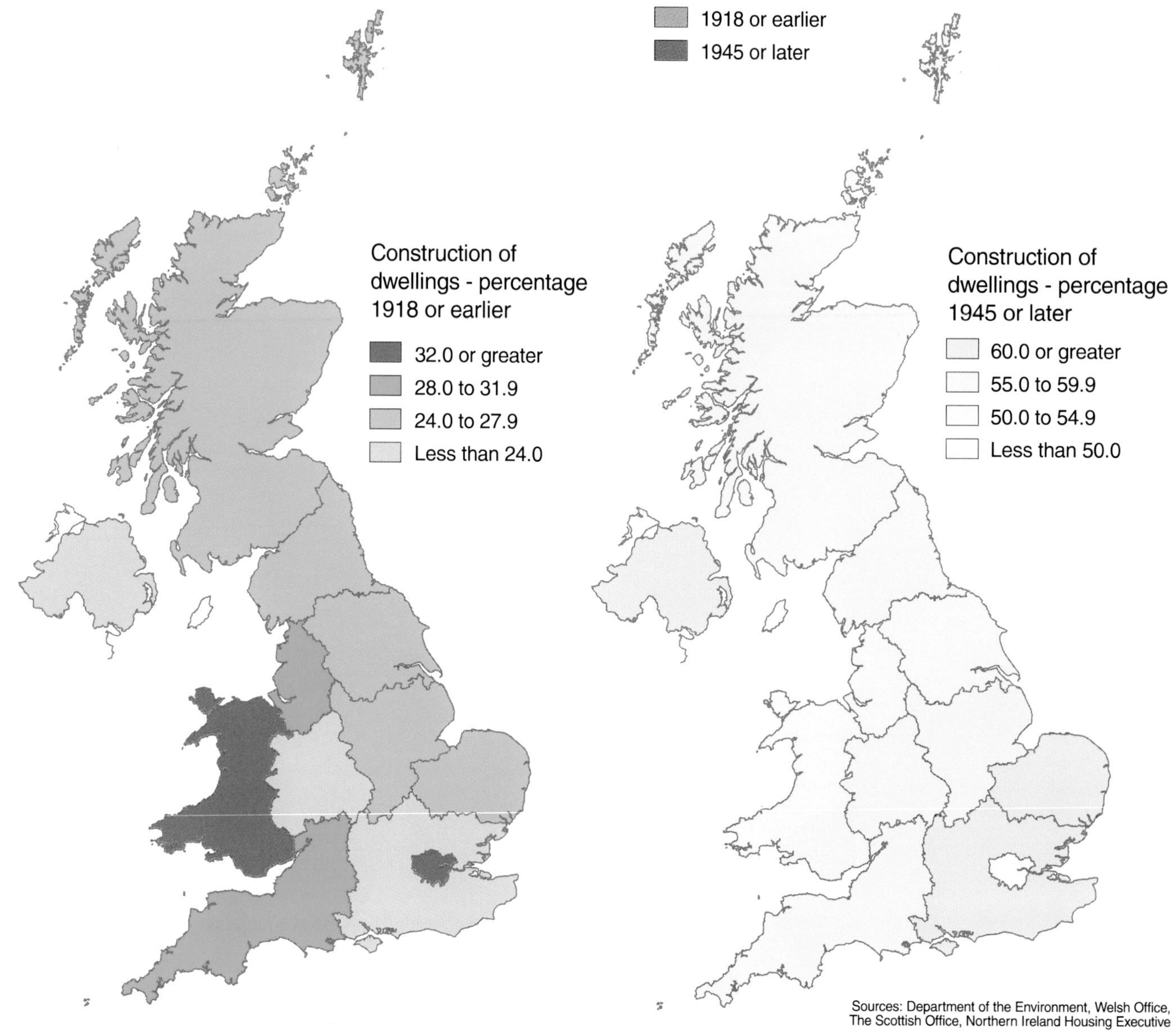

Sources: Department of the Environment, Welsh Office, The Scottish Office, Northern Ireland Housing Executive

Housebuilding

- Relative to the number of households, the number of new dwellings completed was highest in Northern Ireland, followed by East Anglia, both areas of high population growth (see page 17).
- Conversely, the lowest number of dwellings completed was in Greater London, followed by the North, both regions of low population growth or even - in the case of the North - decline.
- The private sector remains the largest builder of new homes; however local authorities have been overtaken by housing associations as the second largest provider.

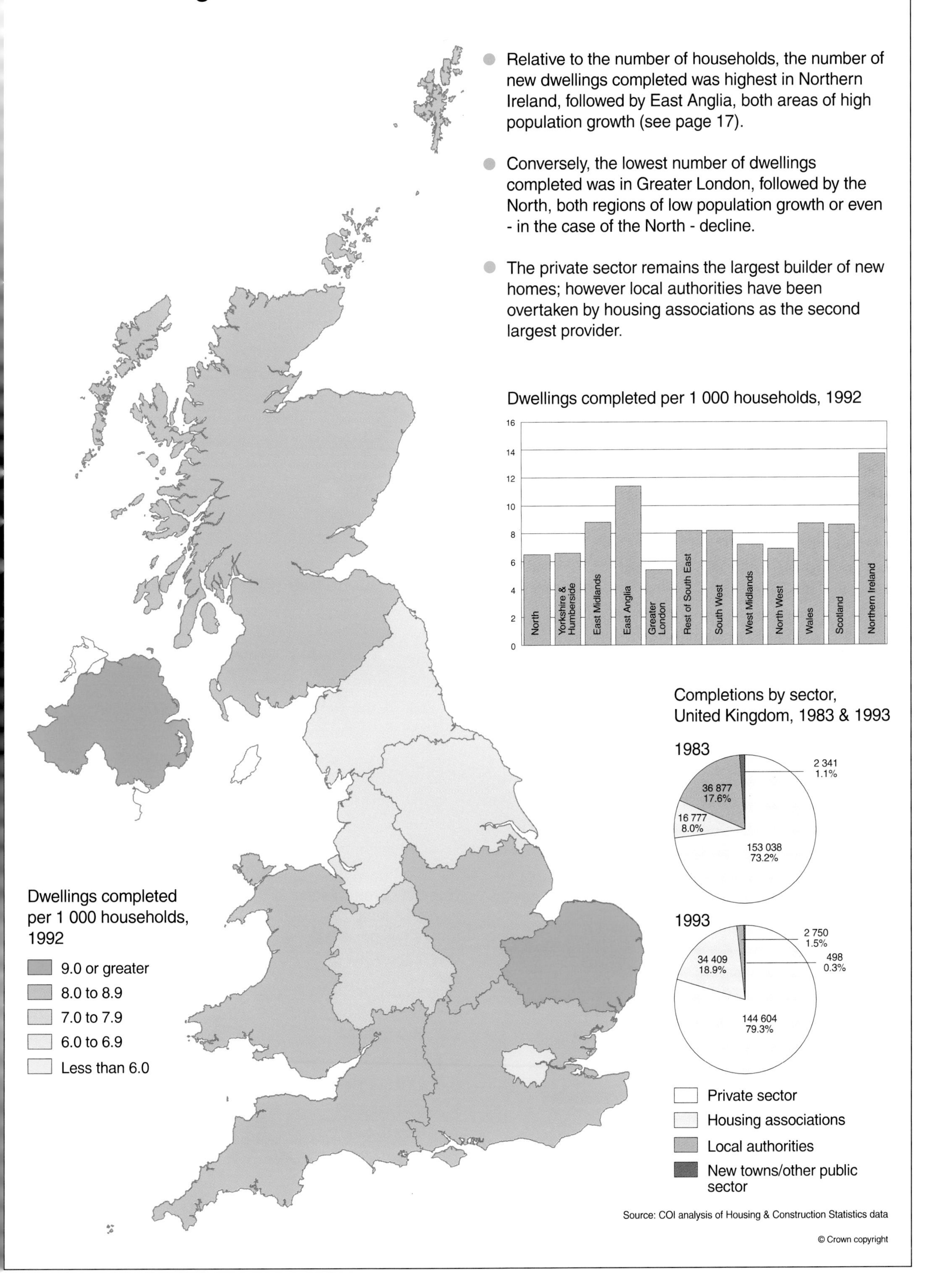

Source: COI analysis of Housing & Construction Statistics data

Housing Renovation

- The law provides for local authorities to pay renovation grants to owner-occupiers, landlords and others for work to bring their houses up to a fitness standard, subject to various circumstances including a means test.
- The number of grants made per 1 000 owner-occupied properties is highest in Wales - by a very considerable margin - followed by Yorkshire and Humberside; Wales in particular has a very high proportion of old houses (see page 34).
- Not all these grants are made to owner-occupiers, but the vast majority of them are - about 89 per cent in England.
- For local authority properties, proportionately the greatest amount of renovation work is also done in Wales.

Sector receiving renovation grants, England, 1992 - 1993

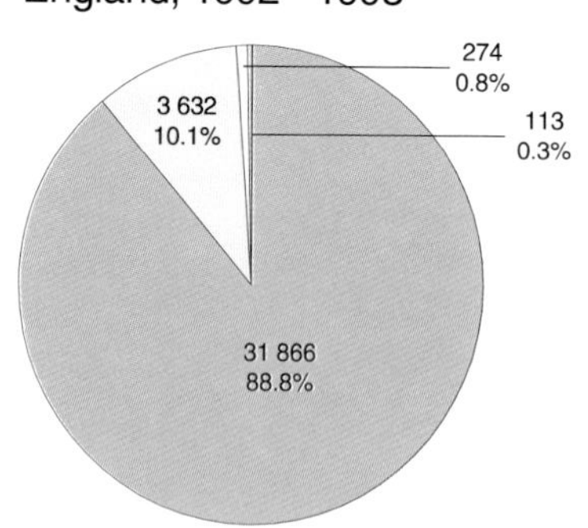

Figures for renovation grants cover grants made under Section 101 of the Local Government and Housing Act 1989, which applies to England and Wales. Not all these grants are made to owner-occupiers, but the vast majority of them are. Housing is not provided by local authorities in Northern Ireland.

Number of renovation grants per 1 000 owner-occupied households, 1993

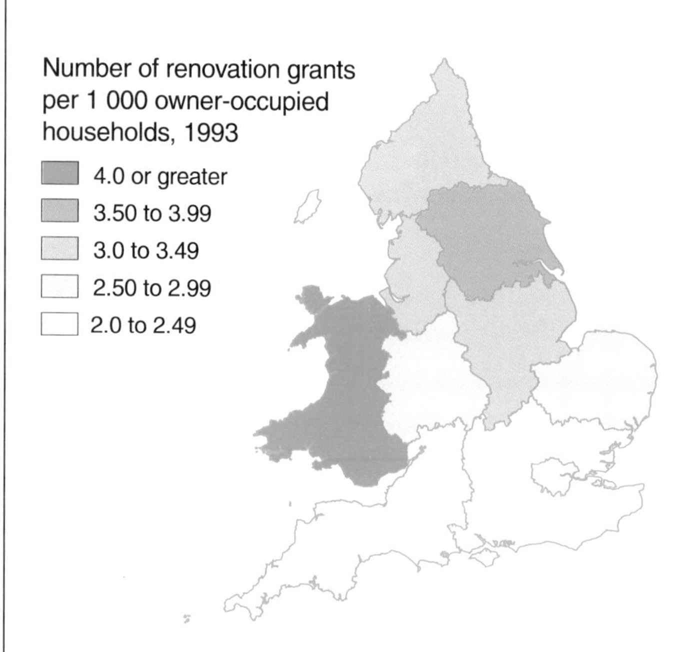

Housing renovation in 1993

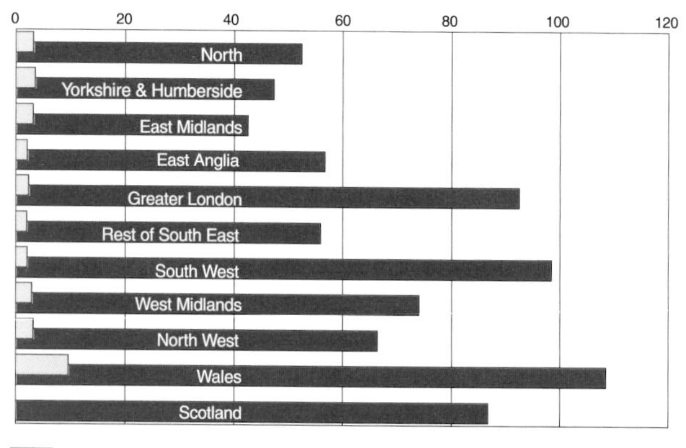

Renovation grants figures for Scotland, and figures for renovation grants and renovation work for local authorities in Northern Ireland are not available.

Number of renovation works for local authorities per 1 000 dwellings, 1993

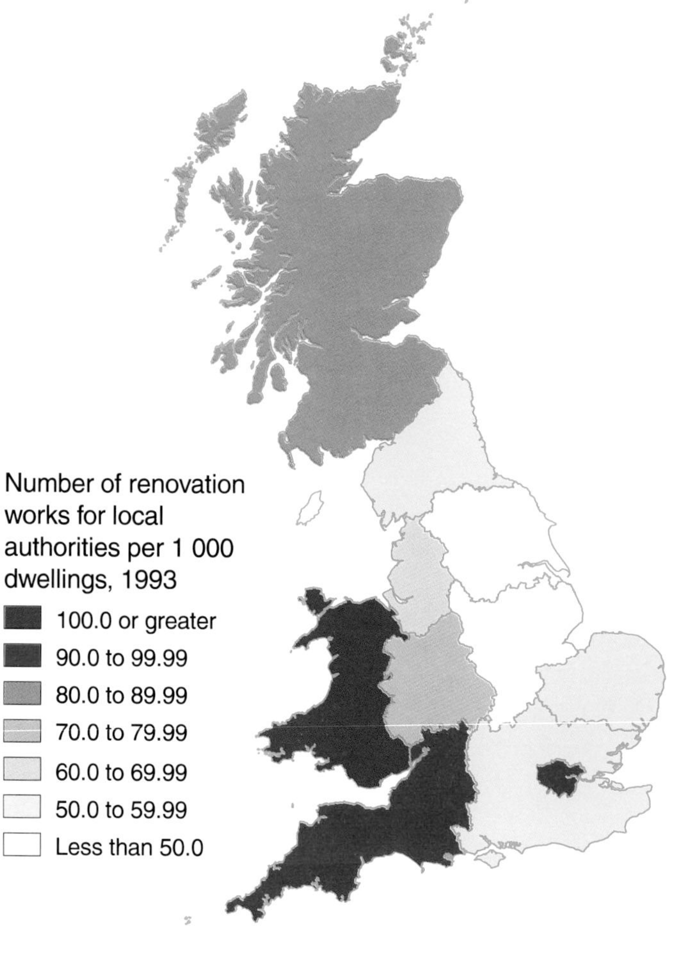

Source: COI analysis of Housing and Construction Statistics data

Tenure of Dwelling

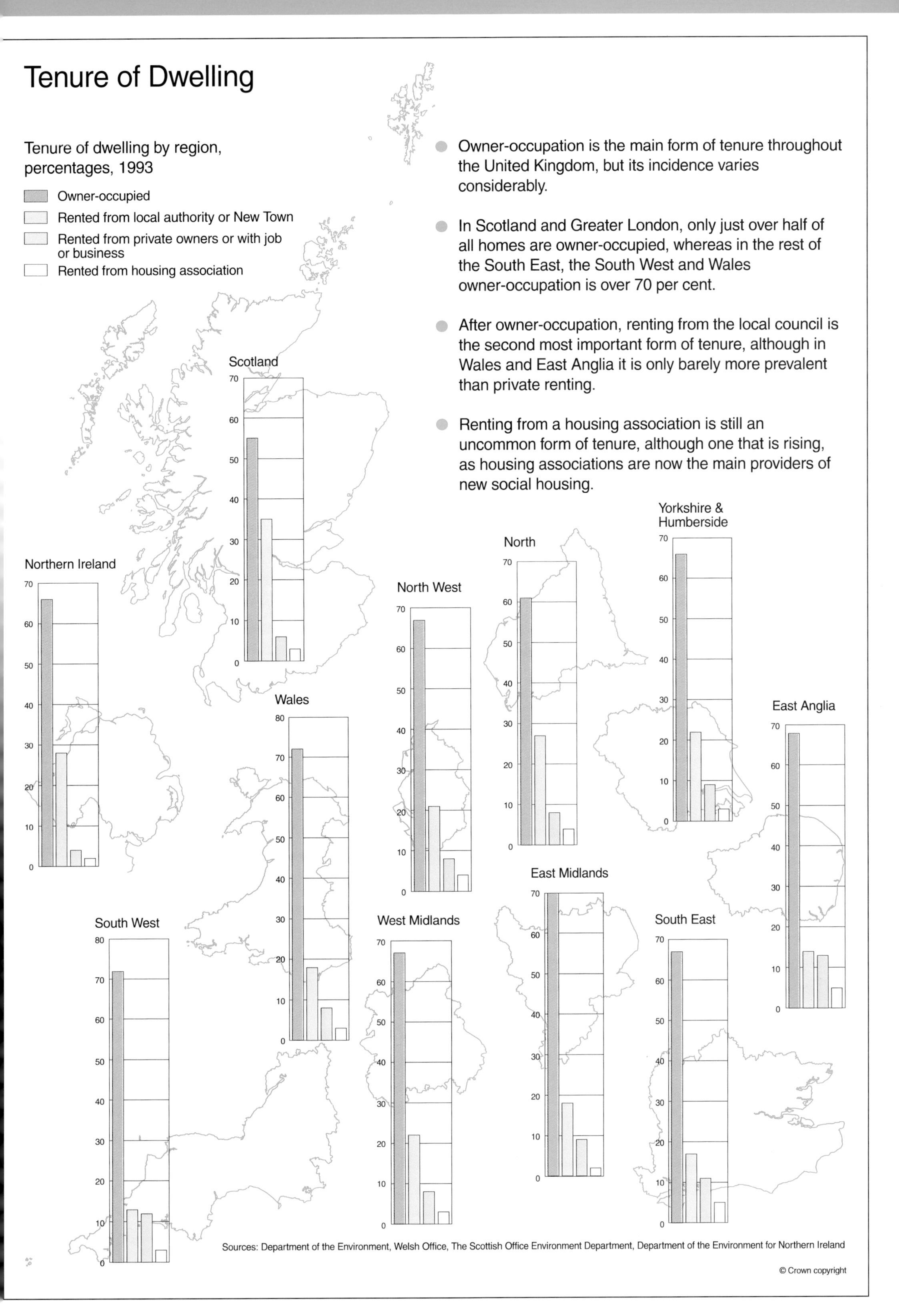

- Owner-occupation is the main form of tenure throughout the United Kingdom, but its incidence varies considerably.
- In Scotland and Greater London, only just over half of all homes are owner-occupied, whereas in the rest of the South East, the South West and Wales owner-occupation is over 70 per cent.
- After owner-occupation, renting from the local council is the second most important form of tenure, although in Wales and East Anglia it is only barely more prevalent than private renting.
- Renting from a housing association is still an uncommon form of tenure, although one that is rising, as housing associations are now the main providers of new social housing.

Sources: Department of the Environment, Welsh Office, The Scottish Office Environment Department, Department of the Environment for Northern Ireland

Owner-Occupation

- Owner-occupation has increased in all parts of the United Kingdom between 1981 and 1993, but this increase has not been at a uniform rate.

- The highest increases were in areas where owner-occupation started the period at a low level - for example in Scotland, it grew by 52 per cent and in the North by 27 per cent.

- By contrast, the growth was low in areas such as the South East outside London and the North West - in both these areas it grew by only 12 per cent over the 1981 - 1993 period.

Northern Ireland figures relate to 1992, not 1993.

Sources: Department of the Environment, Welsh Office, The Scottish Office Environment Department, Department of the Environment for Northern Ireland

Lone Parent Families

Live births outside marriage as a percentage of all births, 1992

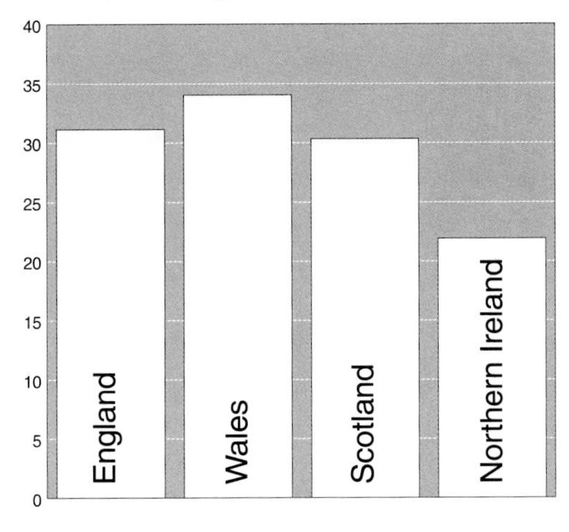

- A significant proportion of households now consist of a single parent with children.
- The highest proportion of lone parent families are in Greater London (11.8 per cent), Merseyside (11.9 per cent) and Cleveland (12.1 per cent).
- The lowest proportions of such households are in West Sussex (7.9 per cent) and Dorset and the Isle of Wight (both 7.7 per cent), although the high proportion of elderly people in these areas will tend to mean that there are relatively fewer households with children, whether with both parents present or not.
- The incidence of births outside marriage is increasing and now forms a very significant proportion of all births; this, however, is not necessarily an indication of single-parent families, as many births outside marriage are registered by both parents, suggesting a stable but non-married relationship.

Lone parent households as a percentage of all households, 1992

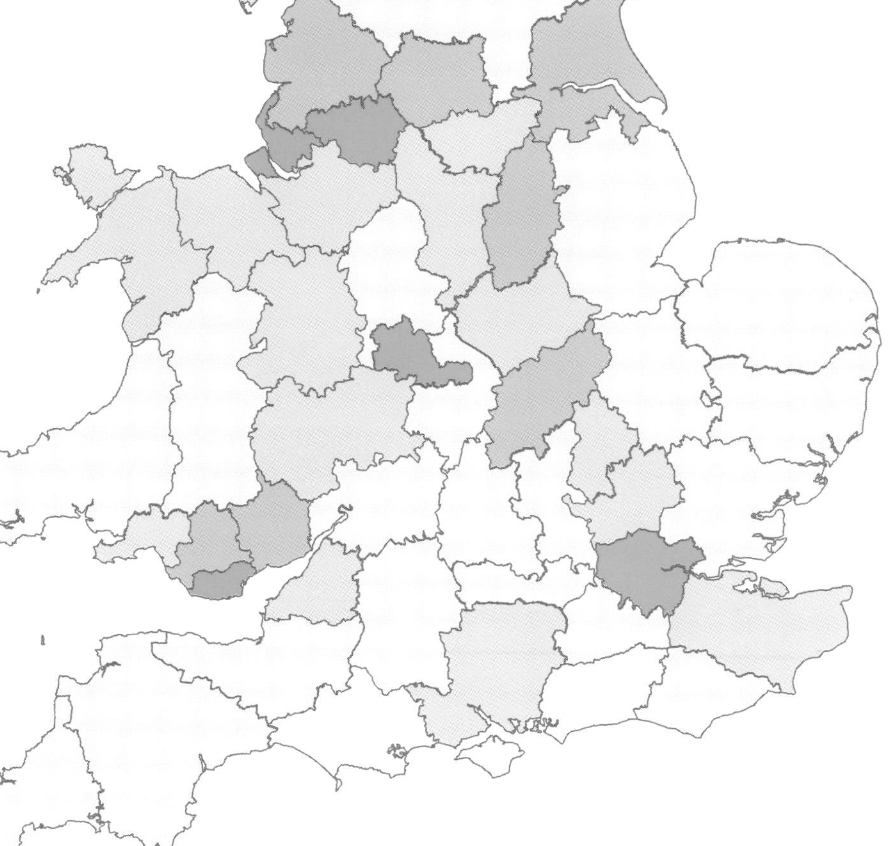

Sources: Department of the Environment; Welsh Office

House Prices

- Average house prices are highest in Greater London and lowest in Northern Ireland.
- The average Greater London price is over twice that of Northern Ireland.
- After Northern Ireland, properties are cheapest in the North of England, followed by Scotland and Wales.
- Average property prices rose steadily in the early 1980s, rapidly in the late 1980s, before falling back in the early 1990s.

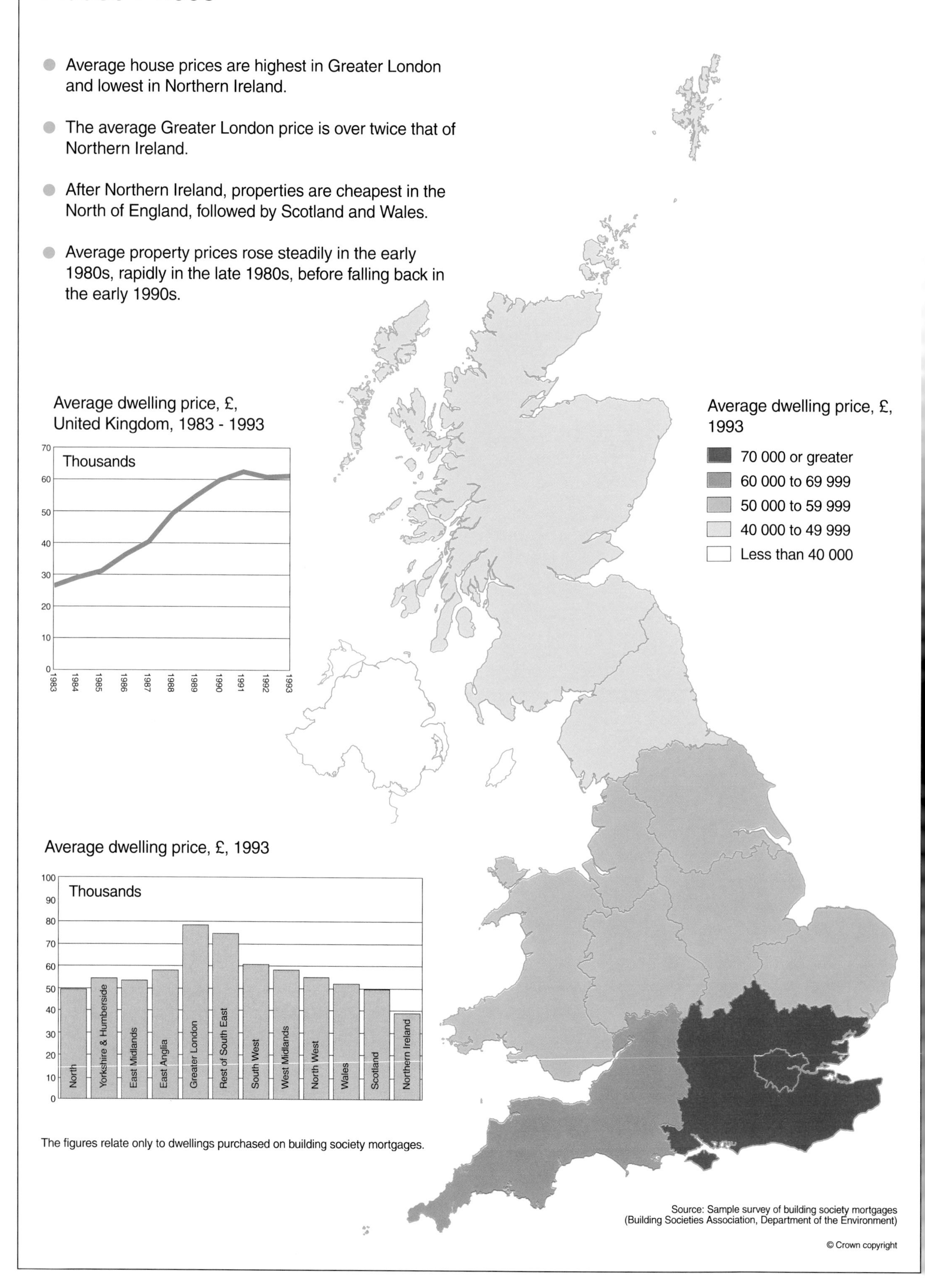

The figures relate only to dwellings purchased on building society mortgages.

Source: Sample survey of building society mortgages (Building Societies Association, Department of the Environment)

Spending on Housing

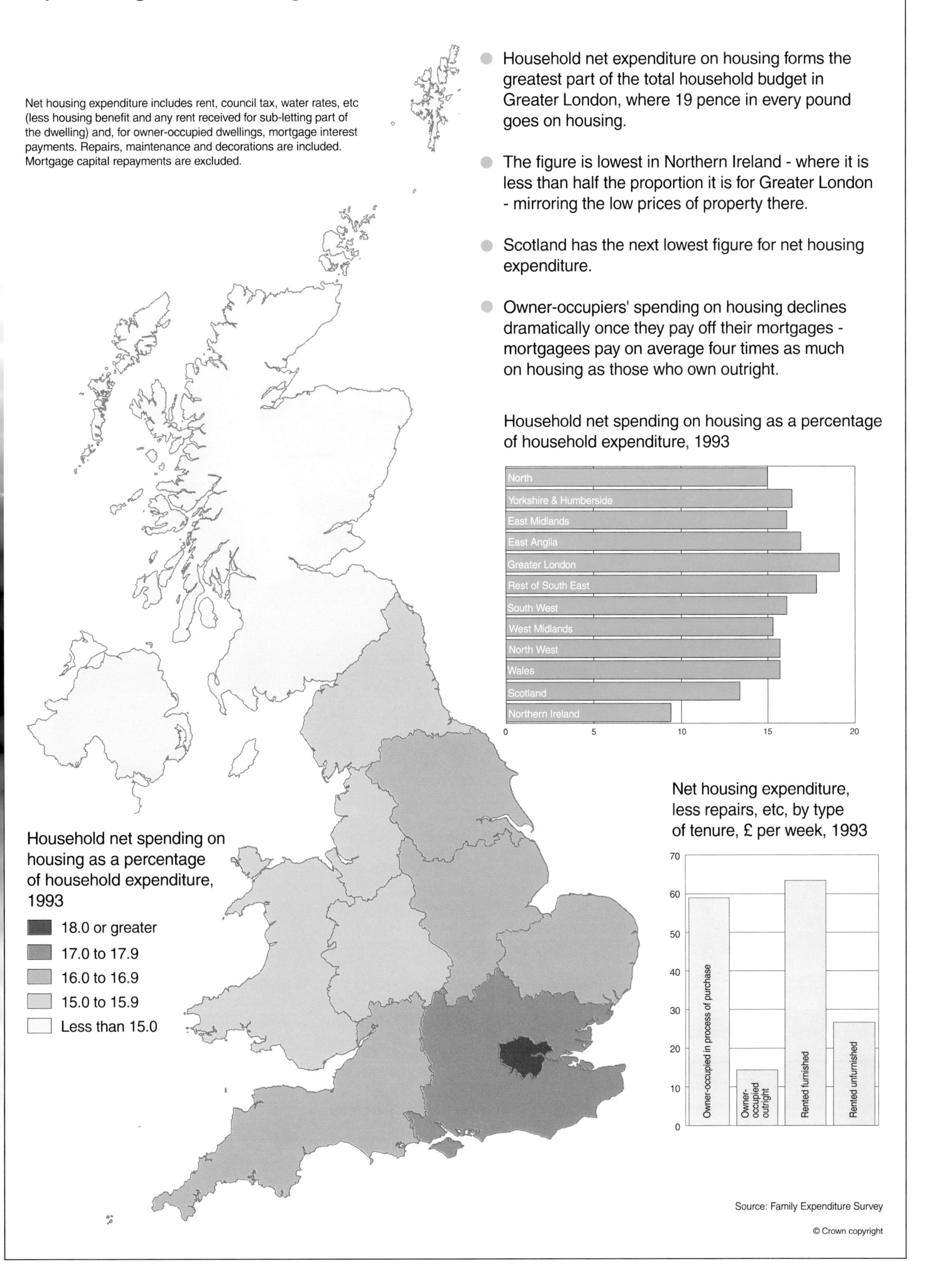

Energy Use

- Average household spending on fuel, light and power is highest in Northern Ireland, where there is no natural gas supply; a large proportion of this spending therefore goes on solid fuel or fuel oil.
- Spending is also high in Wales, the South East outside London and the East Midlands.
- Expenditure on energy is lowest in Greater London, possibly reflecting the tendency of air temperatures there to be slightly warmer than in the surrounding countryside.
- Gas and electricity make up between them the major fuels; only in Northern Ireland is the pattern very different from that in the United Kingdom as a whole.

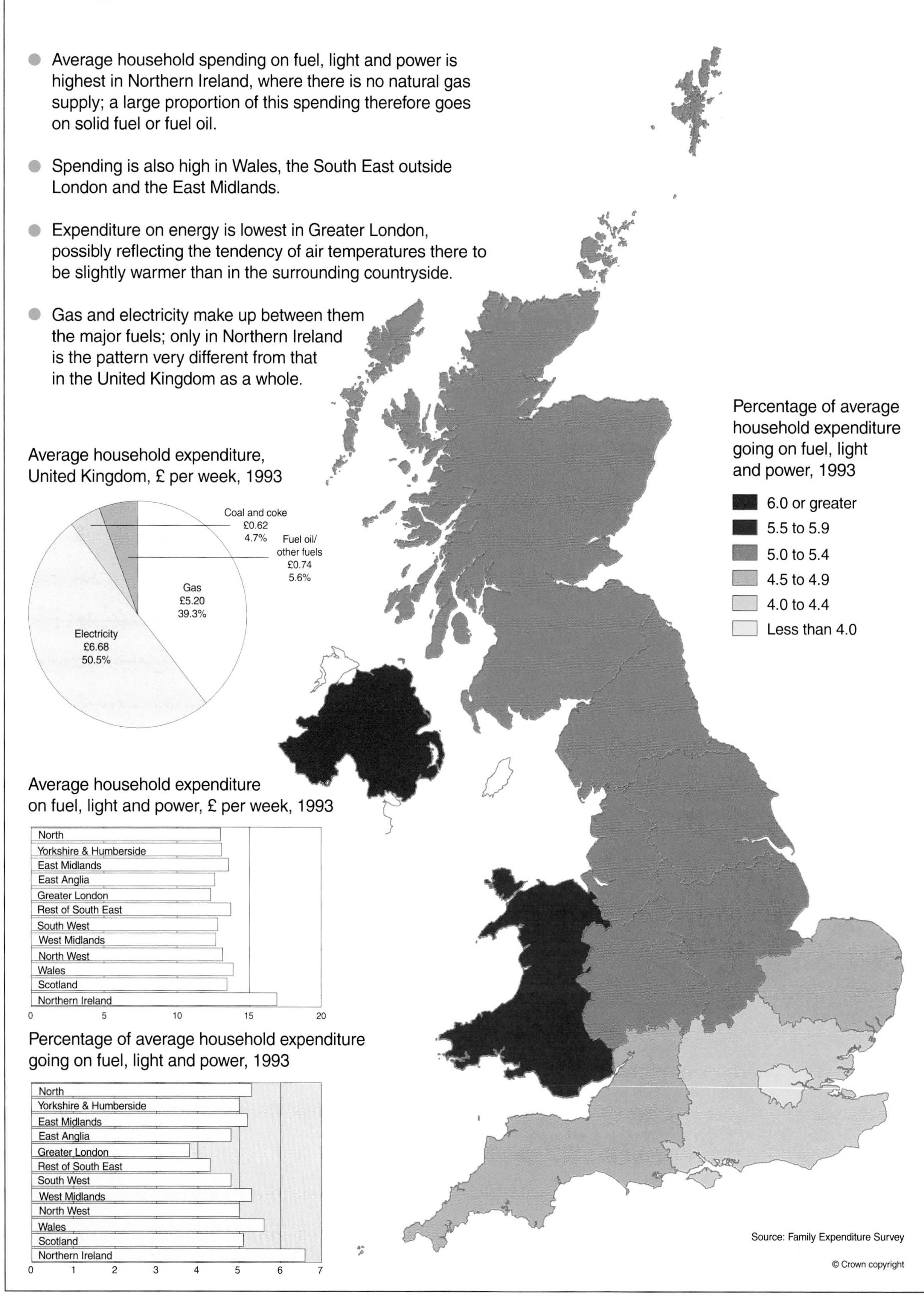

Source: Family Expenditure Survey

Gross Domestic Product per Head of Population

Estimates of GDP include regional estimates of income from employment on a residence basis rather than on where people work.

- Gross domestic product (GDP) - the sum of incomes earned from productive activity - per head varies widely across Britain.
- It was highest in Greater London, with GDP per head over 46 per cent above the average in 1991, followed by Grampian (35 per cent).
- GDP per head was lowest in Mid Glamorgan and the Isle of Wight, both about 30 per cent below the national average.
- The variation by region is less, ranging from 17 per cent above the average for the South East to 19 per cent below in Northern Ireland.

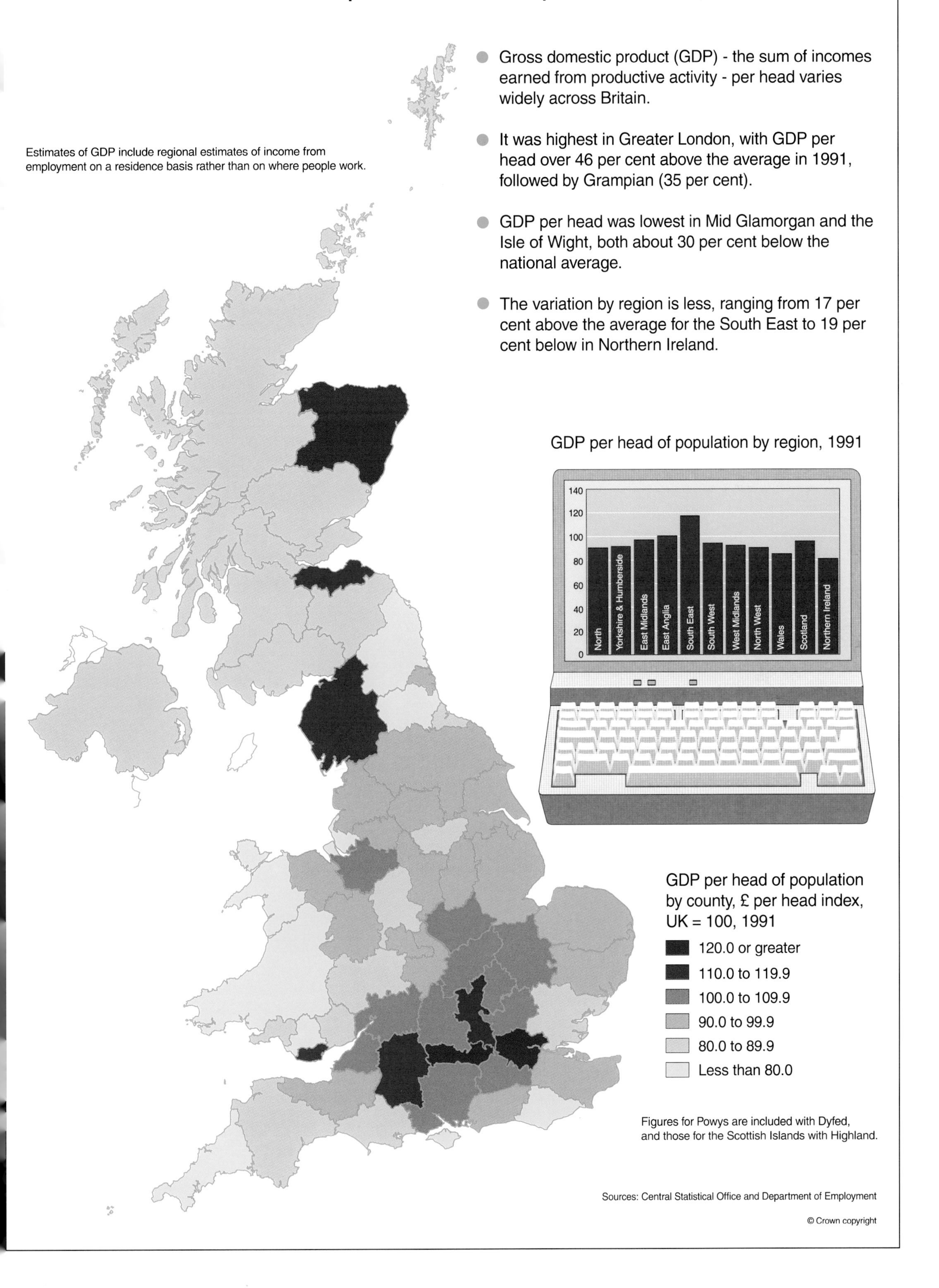

Figures for Powys are included with Dyfed, and those for the Scottish Islands with Highland.

Sources: Central Statistical Office and Department of Employment

Sources of Income

- Wages and salaries still make up almost two-thirds of household income in Britain, but this proportion has declined over the last 15 years.
- Self-employment, investments and annuities and pensions have all become more important as sources of income.
- Wages and salaries are most important in East Anglia and least important in the South West.
- Self-employment is most important in the South East outside London and least important in the North.
- In the North, social security benefits make up almost twice as much of household income as in Greater London - 19.2 per cent as against 10.0 per cent.

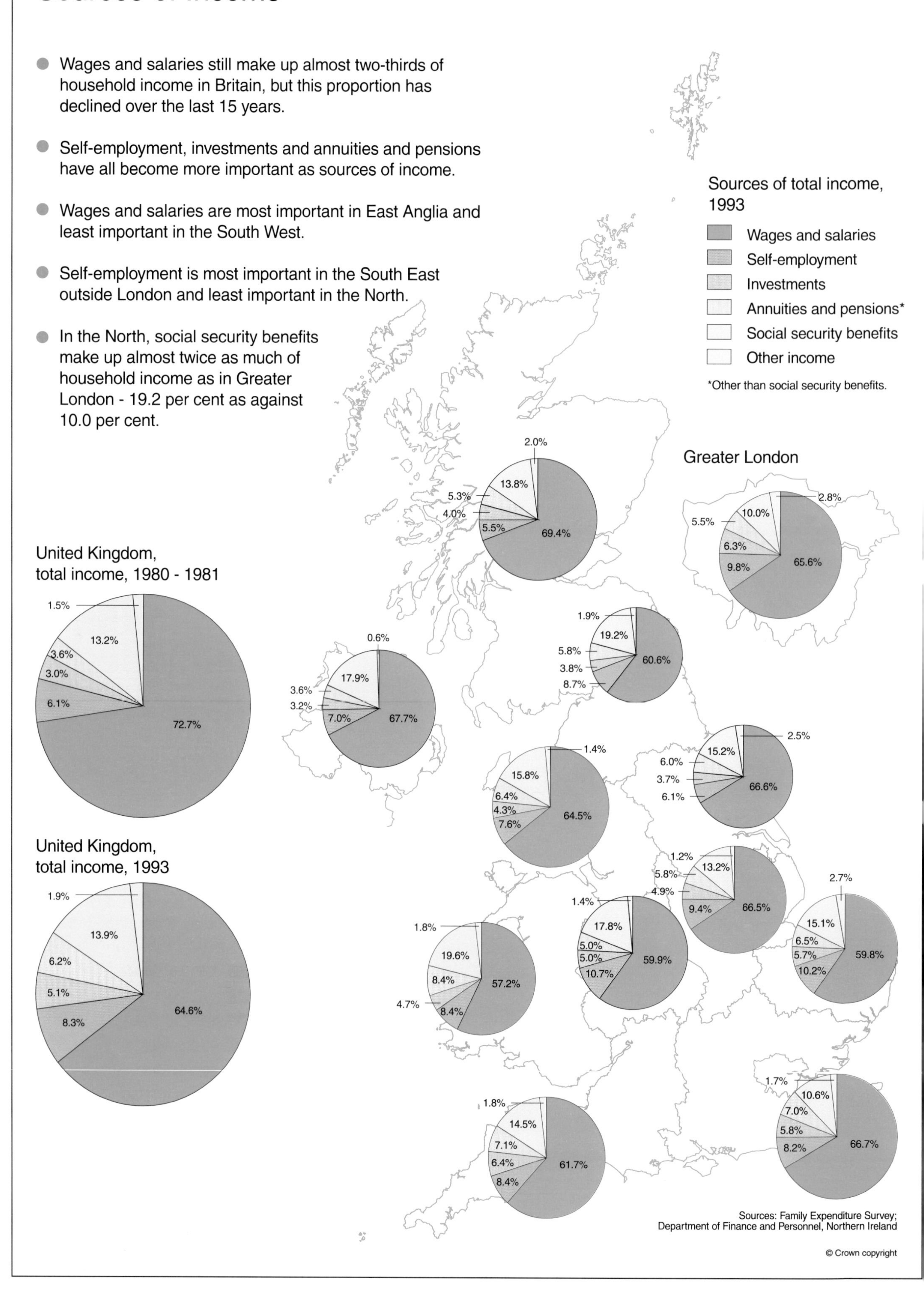

Sources: Family Expenditure Survey; Department of Finance and Personnel, Northern Ireland

Household Disposable Income per Head of Population

- Household disposable income per head in 1991 was highest in the South East, 10 per cent above the national average.
- By county it was highest in West Sussex and Surrey (18.5 and 17.5 per cent above the national average respectively).
- In 1986 the figure for Bedfordshire was around the average; by 1991 it was 13 per cent above the average.
- The lowest level of household disposable income per head in 1991 was in Mid Glamorgan (81 per cent of the average).

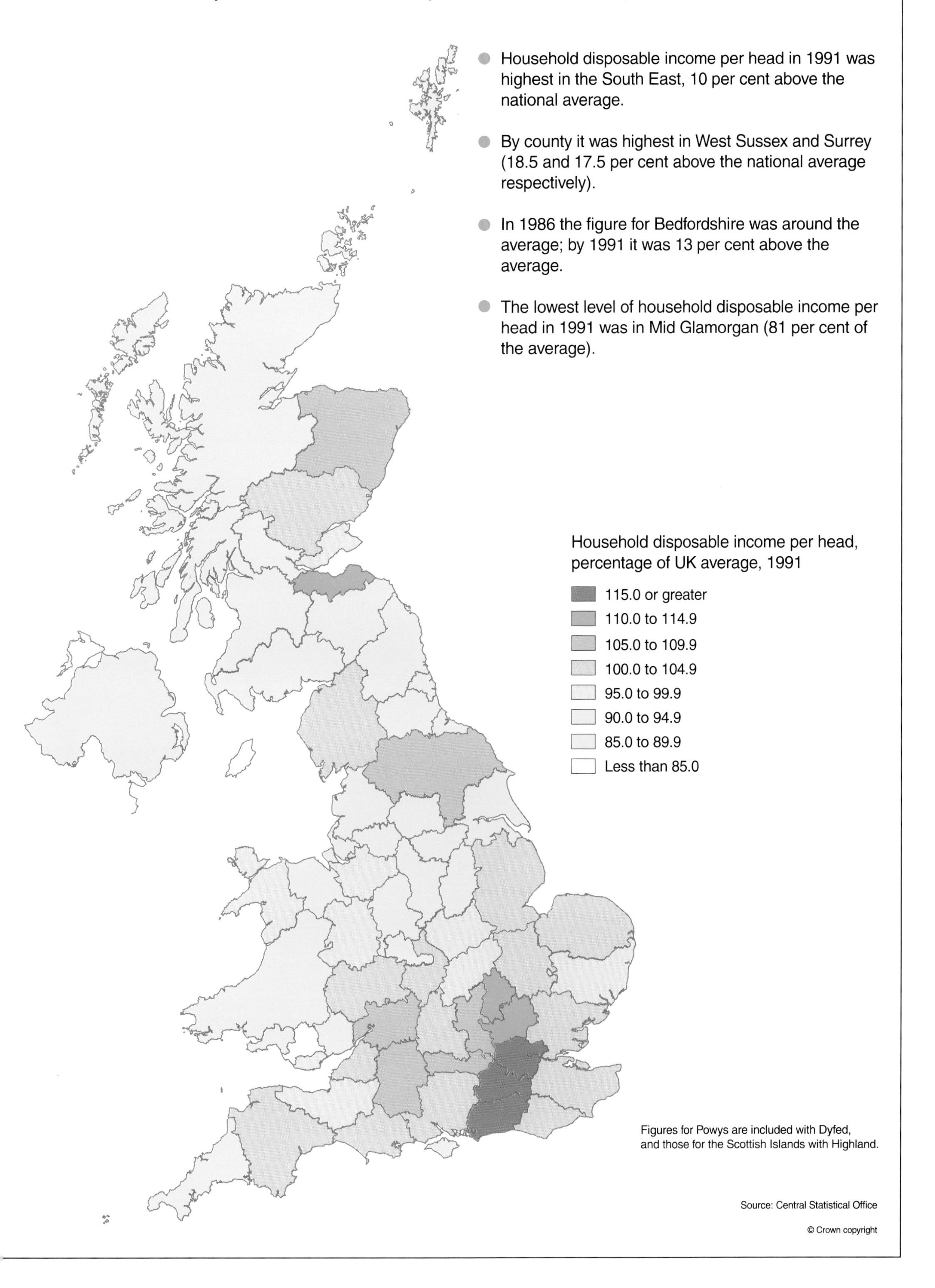

Figures for Powys are included with Dyfed, and those for the Scottish Islands with Highland.

Source: Central Statistical Office

Personal Disposable Income per Head of Population

- Personal disposable income per head in 1992 was £7 543 in Britain, compared with £5 566 in 1988.
- Levels ranged in 1992 from £9 133 in Greater London to £6 442 in Wales.
- From being below the national average in 1988, the level in Scotland was 1 per cent above the average in 1992.

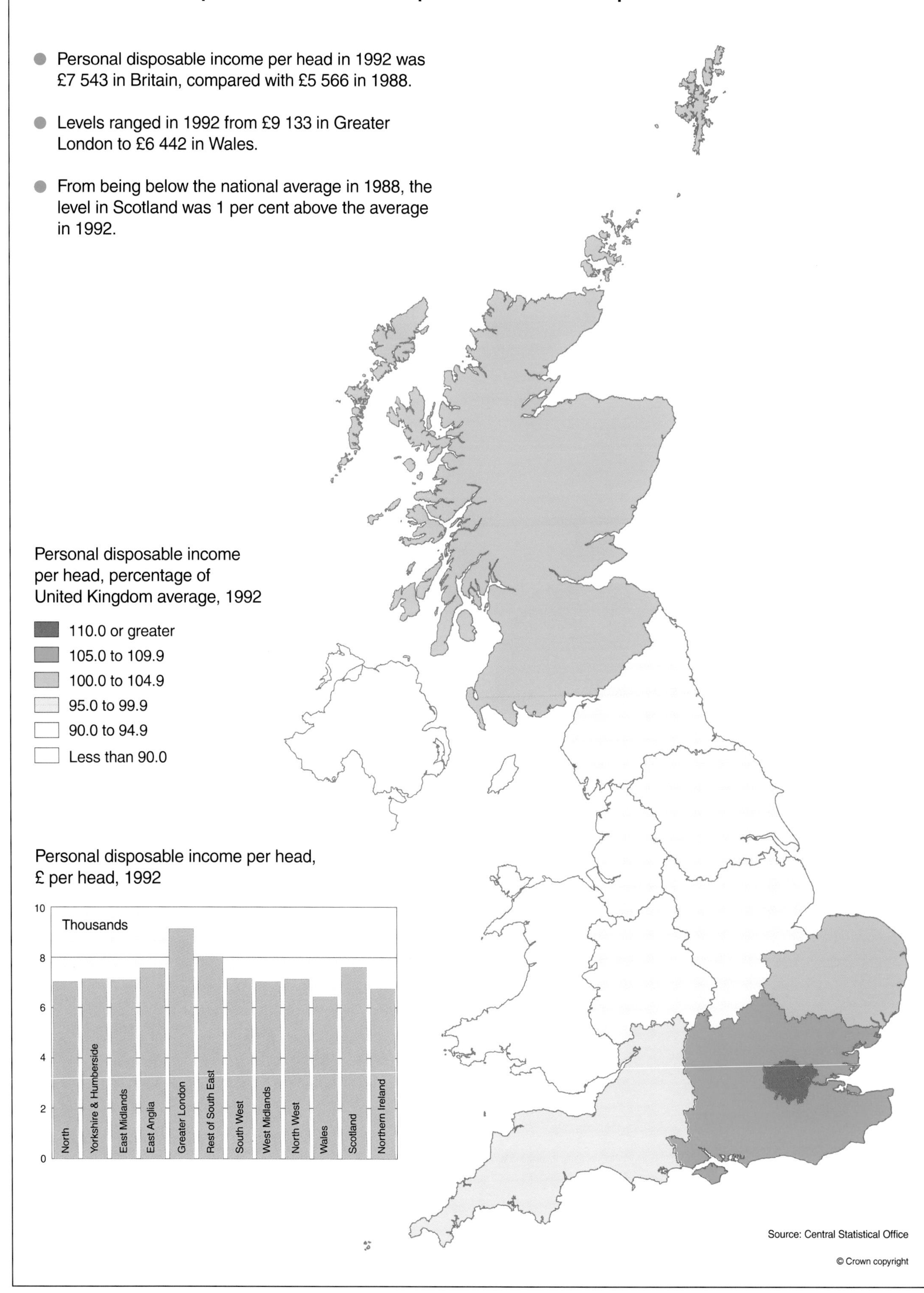

Source: Central Statistical Office

Expenditure

- Food and housing are the most important items of household spending, although motoring costs are also important.
- Alcoholic drink makes up over twice as much of the average household budget as does tobacco - nearly £12 per week as opposed to just over £5.50.
- Expenditure per head is highest in Greater London, where it is 57 per cent higher than Northern Ireland, the lowest spending area in the United kingdom.
- Spending is also low in the West Midlands and Wales.

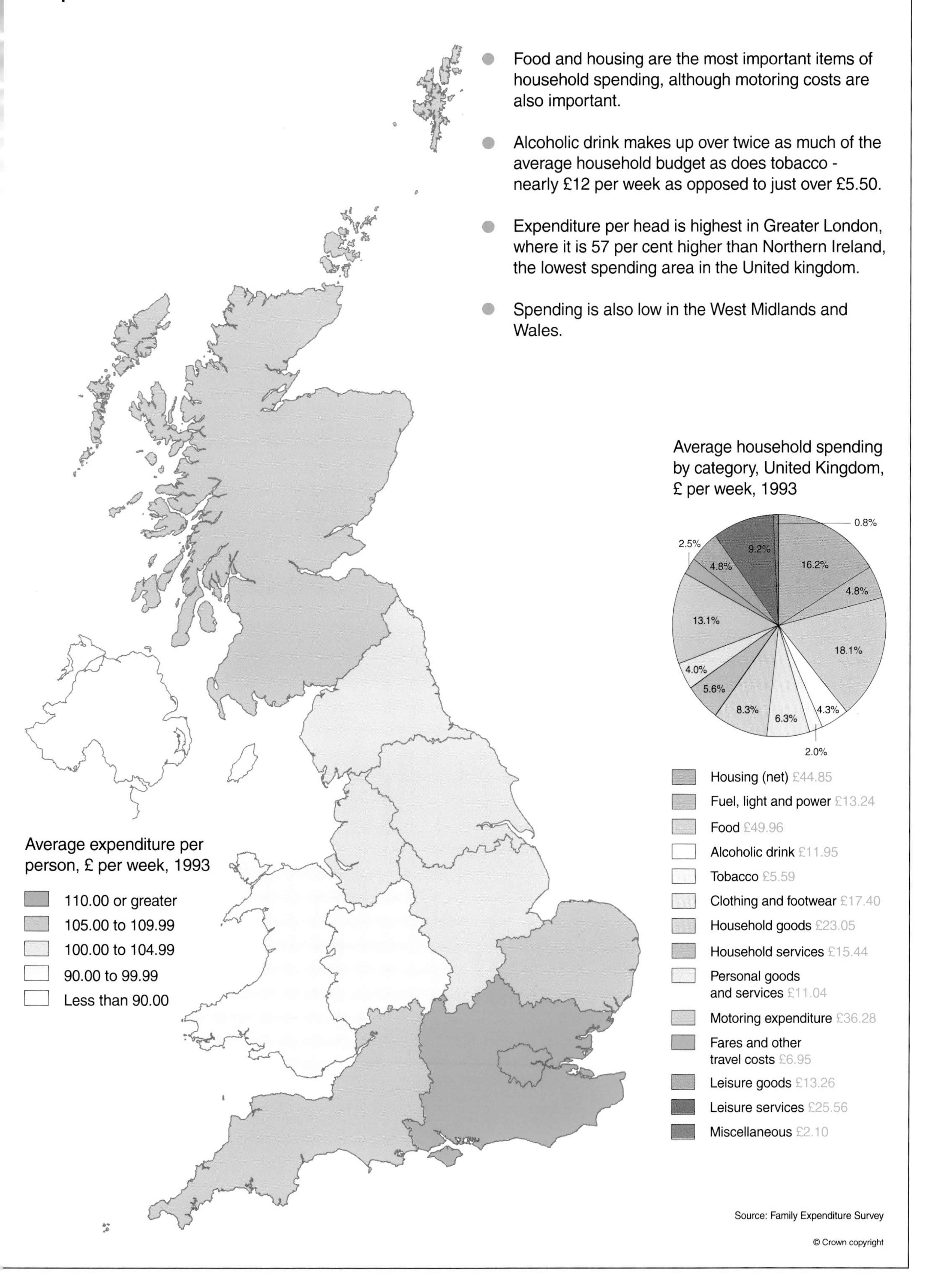

Source: Family Expenditure Survey

Growth In Consumer Durables

- Availability of many durable goods - such as freezers, telephones and videos - has become much more widespread in recent years, with some, such as televisions, being in virtually every house.
- The availability of most types of durable goods is highest in the South East.
- By contrast, the highest level of washing machines is in the North.
- 1991 - 1992 figures for other goods range from:

  central heating - 92 per cent in the North to 72 per cent in Yorkshire and Humberside;

  microwave oven - 62 per cent in Wales to 49 per cent in Northern Ireland;

  compact disc player - 35 per cent in the South East to 18 per cent in Northern Ireland.

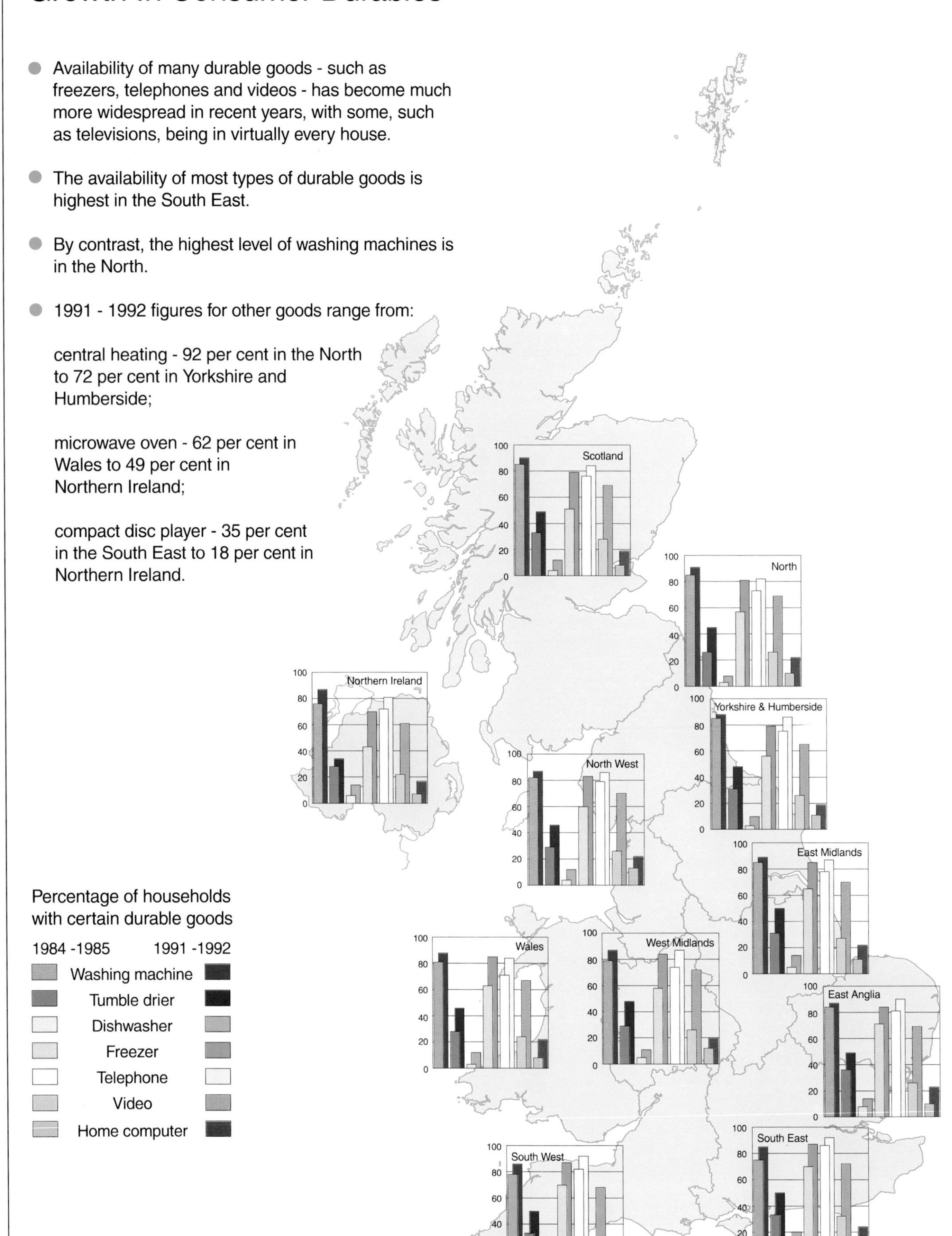

Sources: General Household Survey; Family Expenditure Survey and Continuous Household Survey for Northern Ireland

Weekly Full-time Earnings

- Average gross weekly full-time earnings in Britain in April 1993 were £352.50 for men and £252.10 for women.
- Greater London had by far the highest earnings for both men and women.
- The next highest level of earnings were in Berkshire (for men) and Surrey (for women).

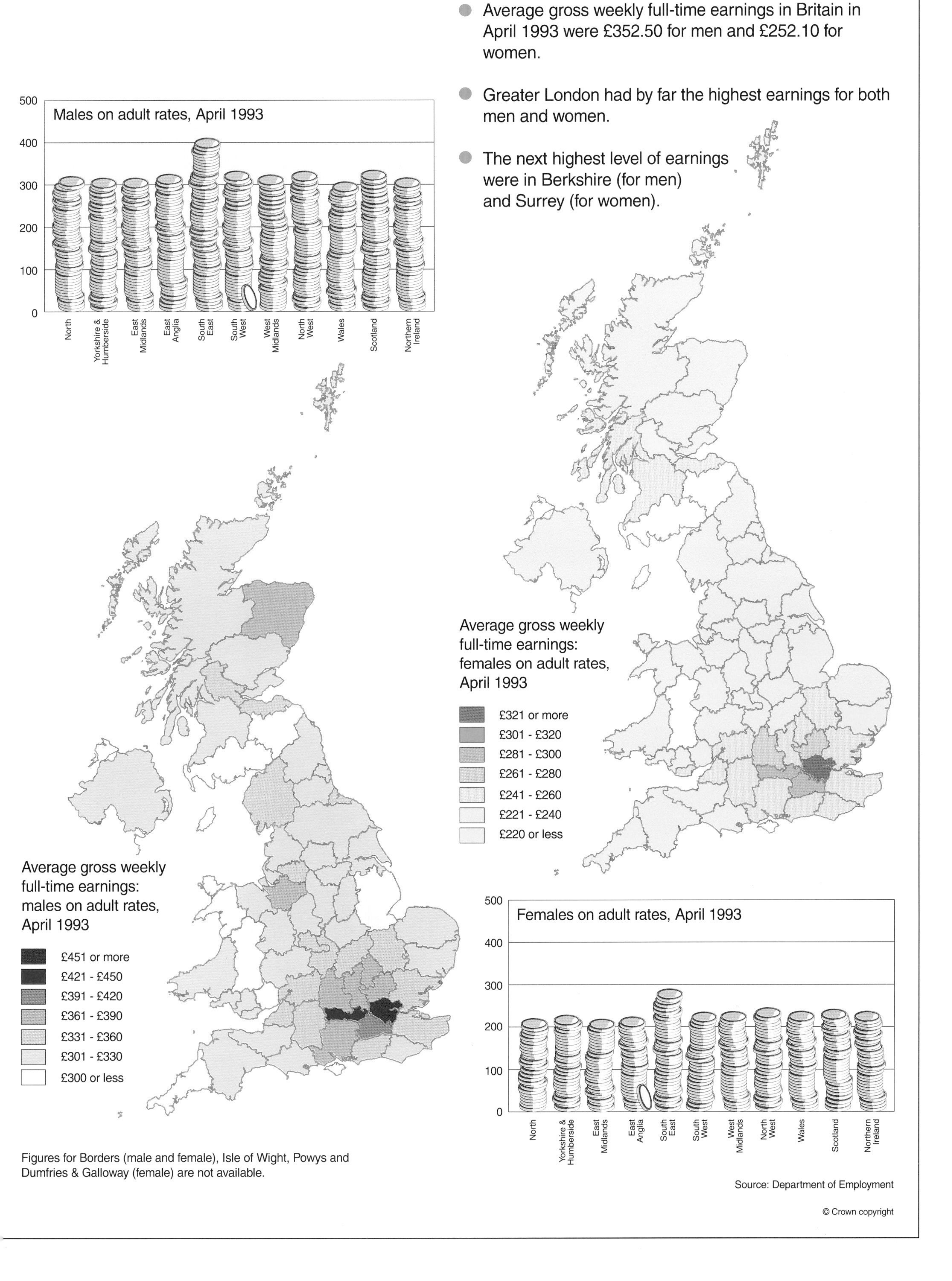

Figures for Borders (male and female), Isle of Wight, Powys and Dumfries & Galloway (female) are not available.

Source: Department of Employment

Employment

- In 1981 there were 21.9 million employees in employment: 12.6 million men (57 per cent) and 9.3 million women (43 per cent).
- By 1993 women represented nearly half the number of employees. Male employees had declined to 10.9 million (under 51 per cent of employees in employment), while the number of women had risen to 10.6 million (over 49 per cent).
- This pattern occurred in all regions, with a narrowing of the gap between the number of men and women employed.
- In the North West the number of female employees exceeded the number of male employees in 1993.

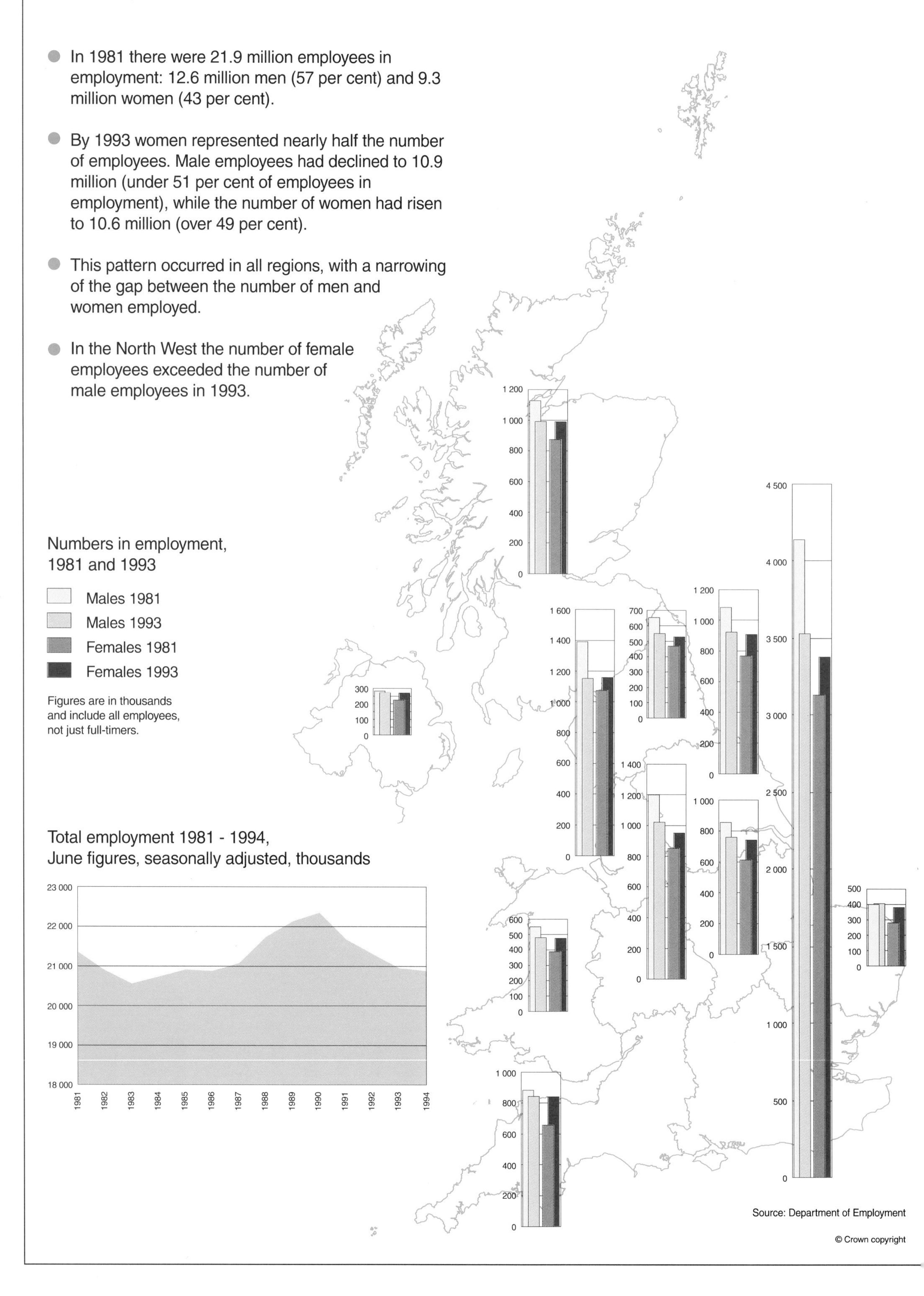

Unemployment

- There has been a decline in unemployment since December 1992 of over 400 000. In November 1994, 2.5 million people were unemployed, 8.8 per cent of the workforce.
- Unemployment has fallen in all regions since December 1992.
- By region unemployment ranged from 4.2 per cent in East Anglia to 13.3 per cent in Northern Ireland.
- Parts of Scotland recorded some of the lowest rates: 2.9 per cent in the Shetland Islands, 4.6 per cent in the Orkney Islands and 4.9 per cent in Borders.

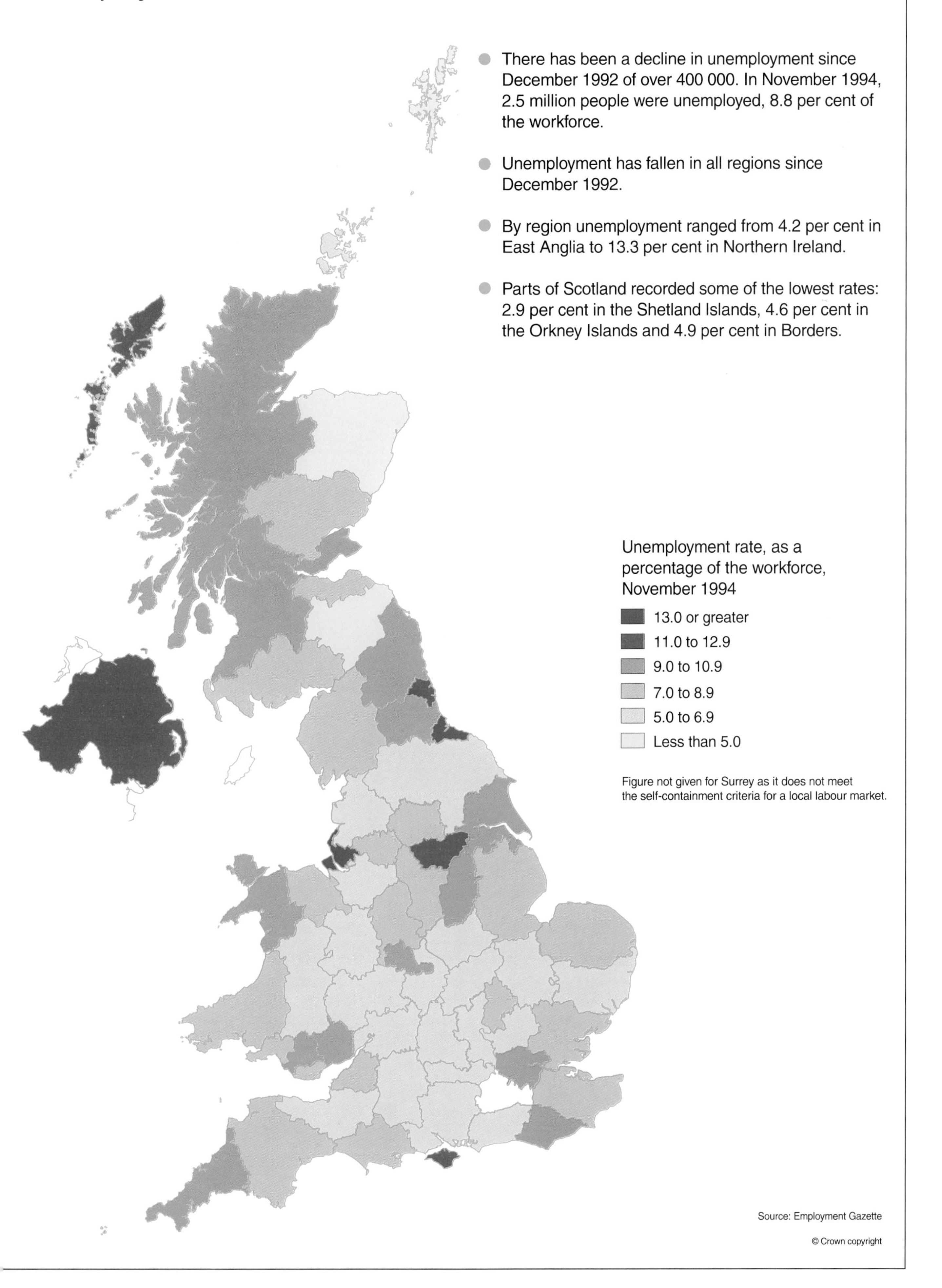

Source: Employment Gazette

Employees by Sector

- An increasing proportion of employees in employment work in the service sector, but there is quite a considerable variation in regional employment patterns.
- The South East has the highest proportion of employees in services - over 80 per cent - and the lowest in manufacturing - now under 15 per cent.
- The two regions where services account for the lowest proportion of employees in employment - the East Midlands and the West Midlands - are those where manufacturing remains most significant, accounting for nearly 30 per cent of employment.
- Northern Ireland has the highest proportion of employees engaged in agriculture, while Scotland has the highest proportion in both construction, and energy and water supply.

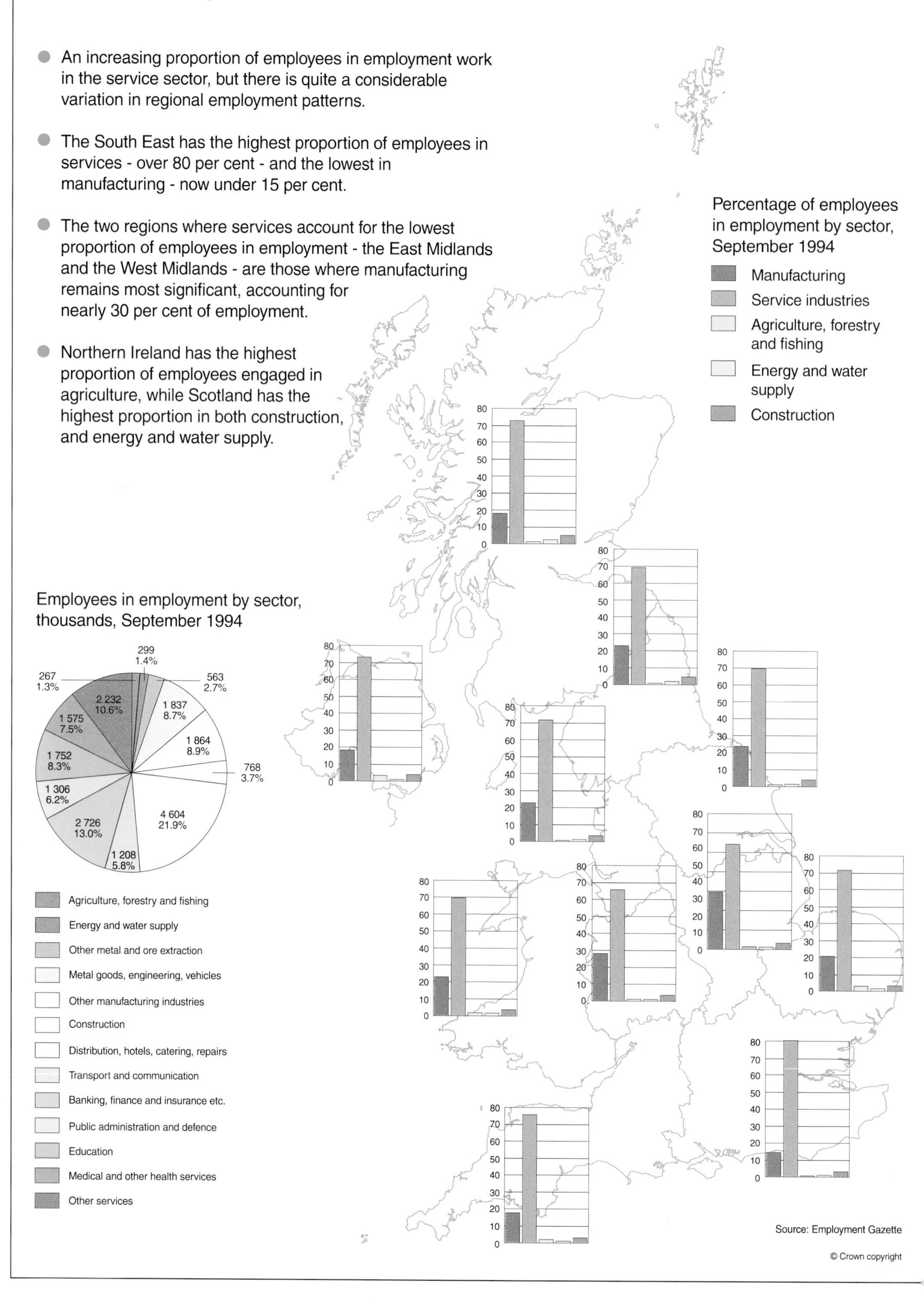

Source: Employment Gazette

Economic Activity

- 'Economically active' people are those who are in work or who are looking for work.
- By region, economic activity rates in spring 1994 ranged from 65.3 per cent in the South East outside London and 64.8 per cent in East Anglia to 56.9 per cent in Wales.
- By far the highest rate was recorded in the Shetland Islands, with over 75 per cent.
- In a few urban areas - for example Liverpool and Swansea - the rate was below 50 per cent.

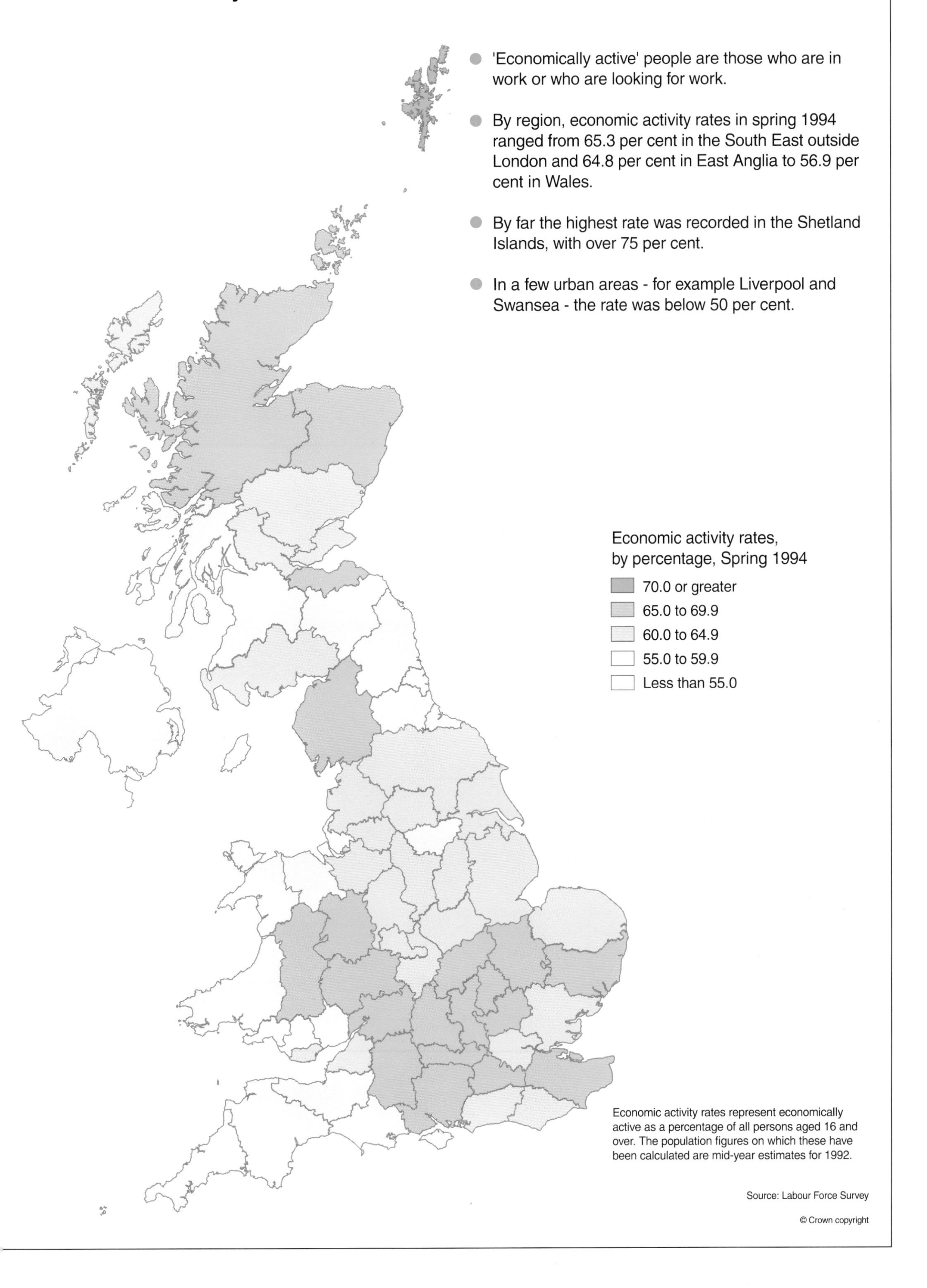

Economic activity rates represent economically active as a percentage of all persons aged 16 and over. The population figures on which these have been calculated are mid-year estimates for 1992.

Source: Labour Force Survey

Share Ownership

- Share ownership has increased in recent years, particularly as a result of privatisation.
- About 10 million people, 22 per cent of adults, now own shares, compared with around 3 million in 1979.

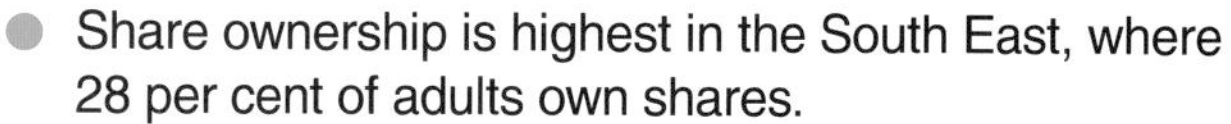

- Share ownership is highest in the South East, where 28 per cent of adults own shares.

- Over 40 per cent of all shares are held in the South East.

Distribution of shares, Great Britain, 1993

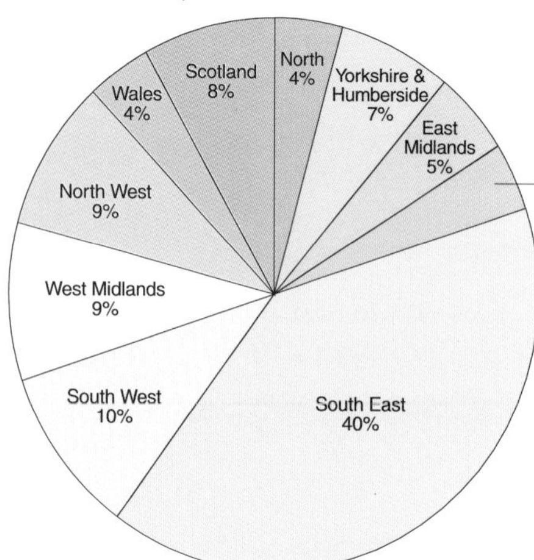

Percentage of people aged 16 and over in region who own shares

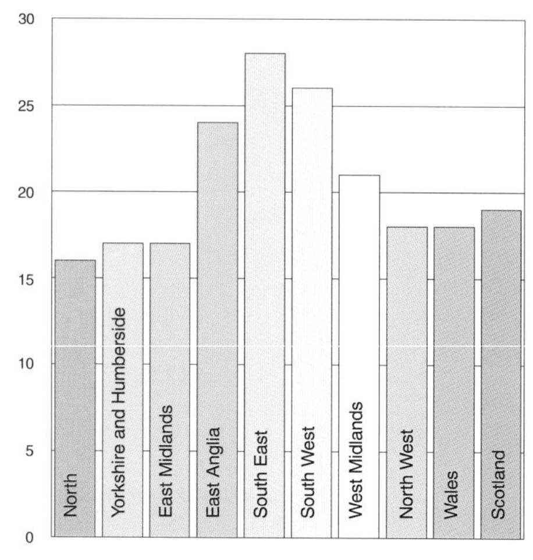

These figures come from a survey conducted for HM Treasury and ProShare. It was carried out only in Great Britain, not Northern Ireland.

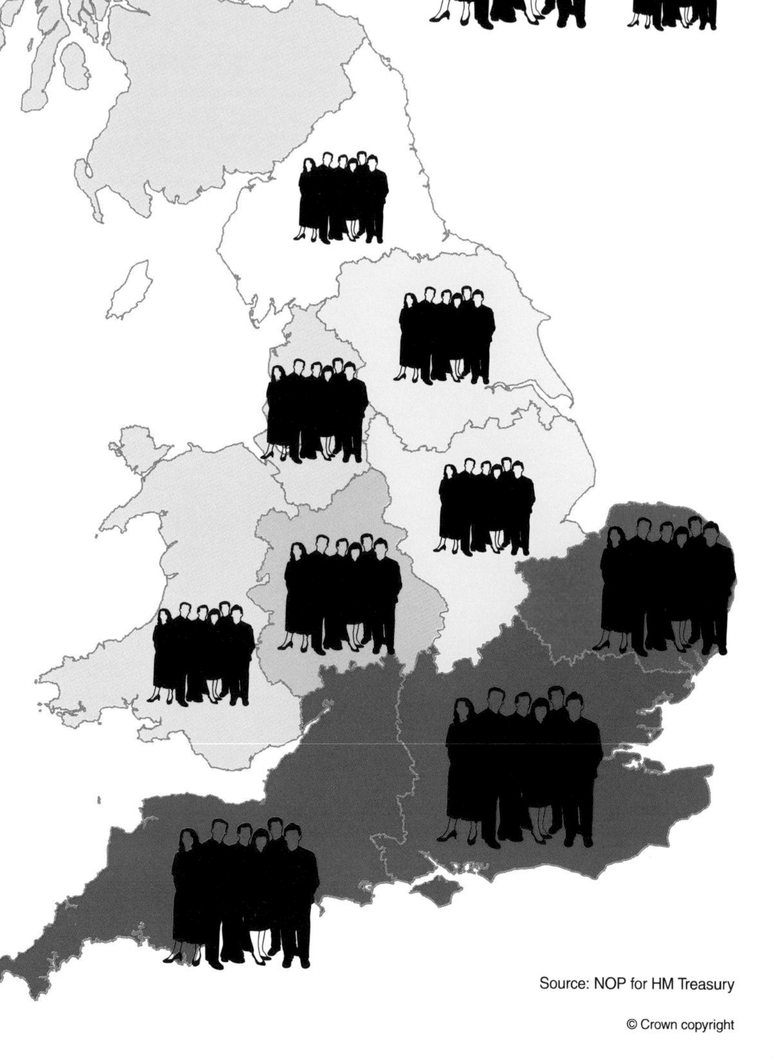

Source: NOP for HM Treasury

Gross Value Added in Manufacturing

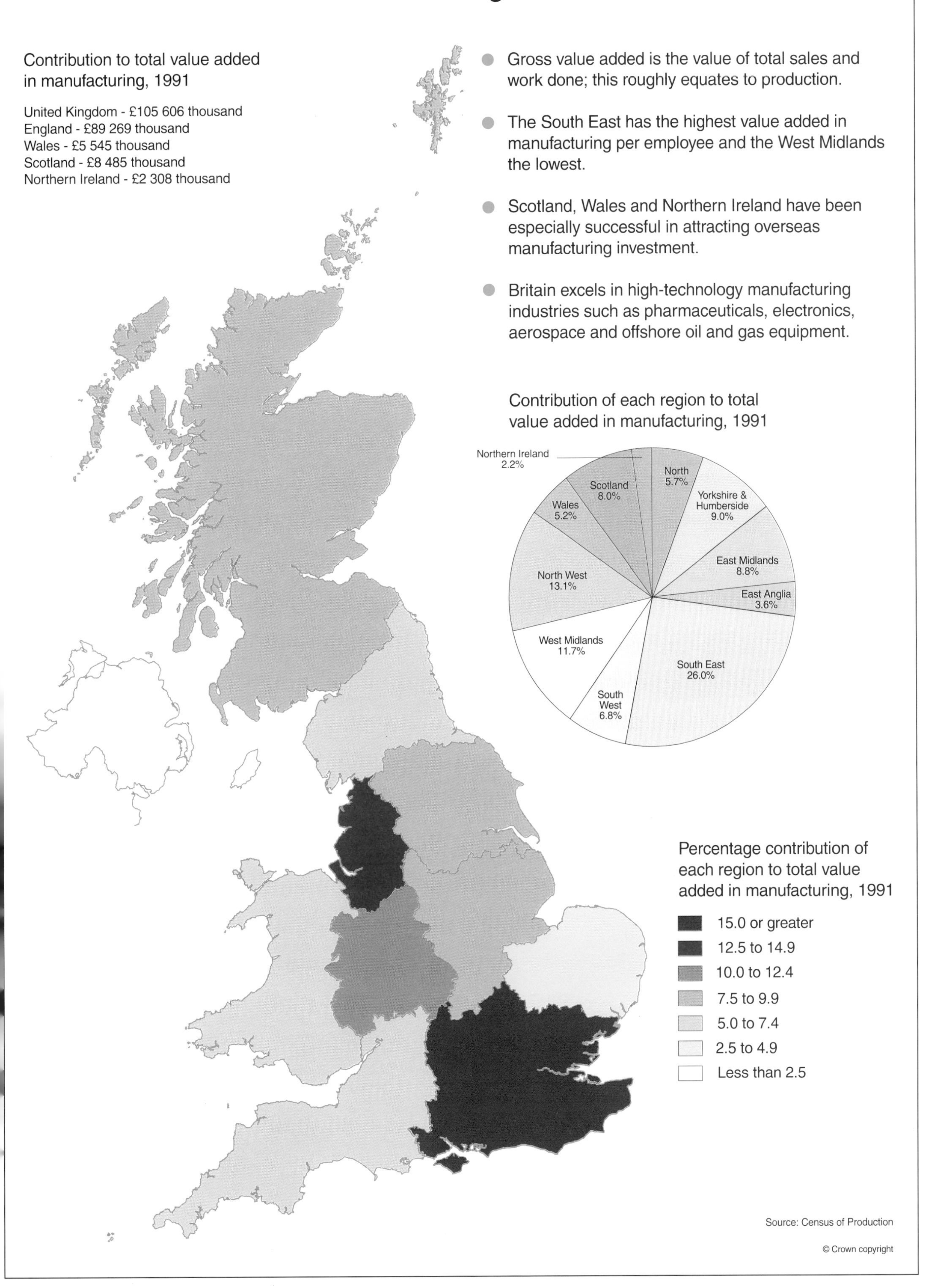

- Gross value added is the value of total sales and work done; this roughly equates to production.
- The South East has the highest value added in manufacturing per employee and the West Midlands the lowest.
- Scotland, Wales and Northern Ireland have been especially successful in attracting overseas manufacturing investment.
- Britain excels in high-technology manufacturing industries such as pharmaceuticals, electronics, aerospace and offshore oil and gas equipment.

Source: Census of Production

Share of Gross Domestic Product

- Manufacturing accounts for over 20 per cent of total gross domestic product (GDP).
- The West Midlands derives more of its GDP from manufacturing than any other region and the South East the least.
- However, the South East has the highest concentration of small manufacturing businesses.
- Some 20 per cent of manufacturing employees in the North and West Midlands work in units employing 1 000 people or more.
- Agriculture contributes 1.4 per cent of GDP in Britain.
- Britain is self-sufficient in 58 per cent of all types of food and animal feed.
- East Anglia derived almost 5 per cent of its GDP from agriculture in 1992, more than any other region, followed by Northern Ireland with 4 per cent.
- The South East and North West derived the smallest percentage of GDP from agriculture.
- Service industries include finance, retailing, tourism and business services.
- The service sector is becoming ever more important and now accounts for 65 per cent of GDP.
- The South East, South West and Northern Ireland derive more of their GDP from services than any other region and the West Midlands the least.

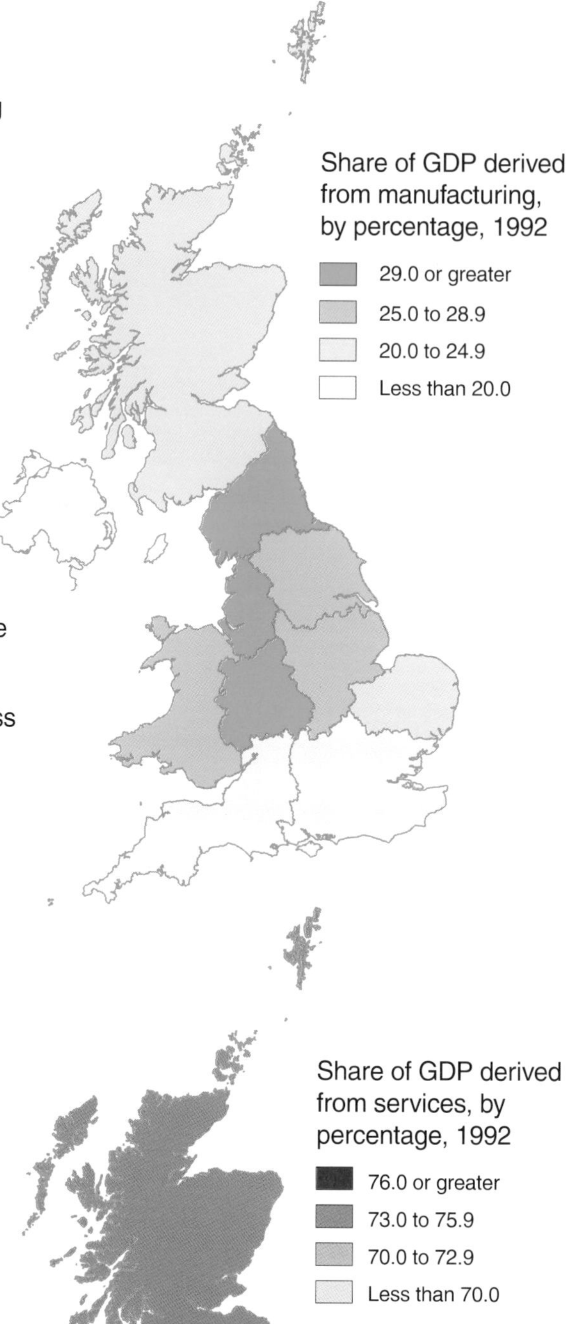

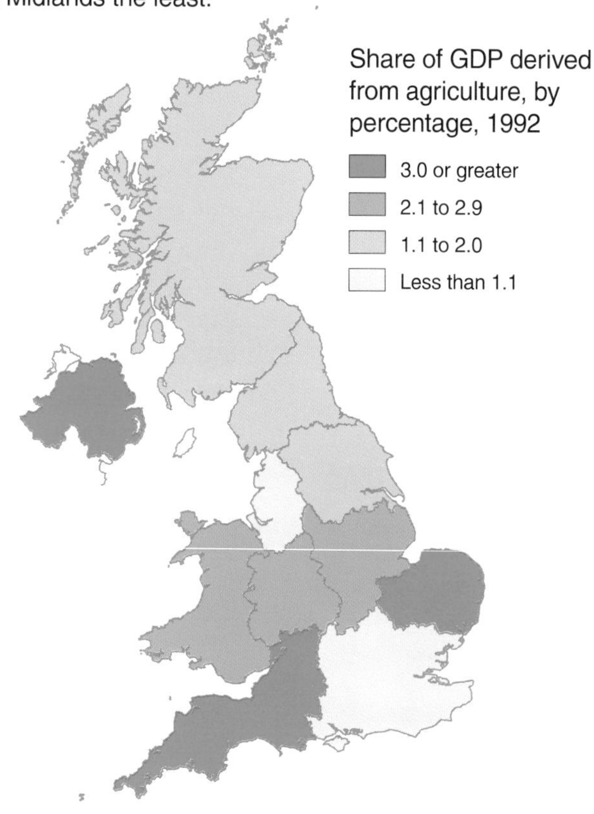

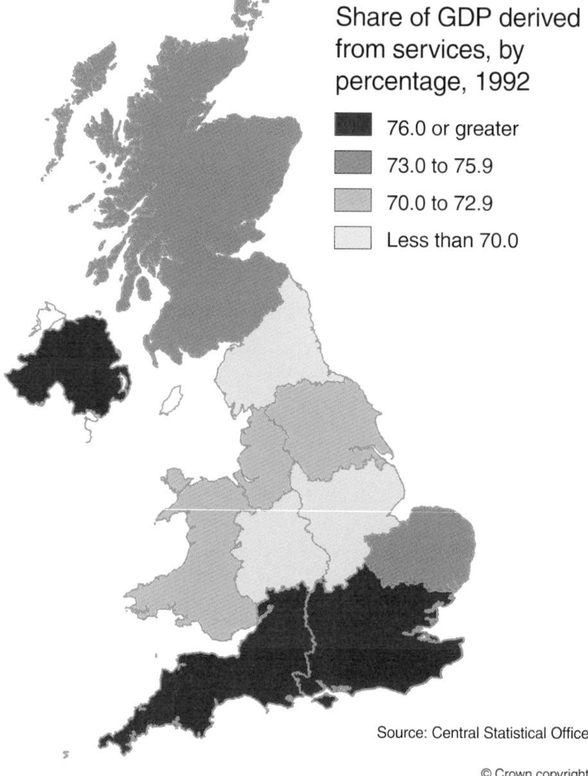

Source: Central Statistical Office

Net Capital Expenditure in Manufacturing

- Total capital investment in manufacturing in Britain amounted to £12 165 million in 1993.
- This comprised £10 146 million in plant and machinery, £1 253 million in new building work and £766 million in vehicles.
- In 1991 levels of capital expenditure ranged from 24.4 per cent in the South East to 2.6 per cent in Northern Ireland.
- London contributed 10.0 per cent of the total and the rest of the South East 14.4 per cent.

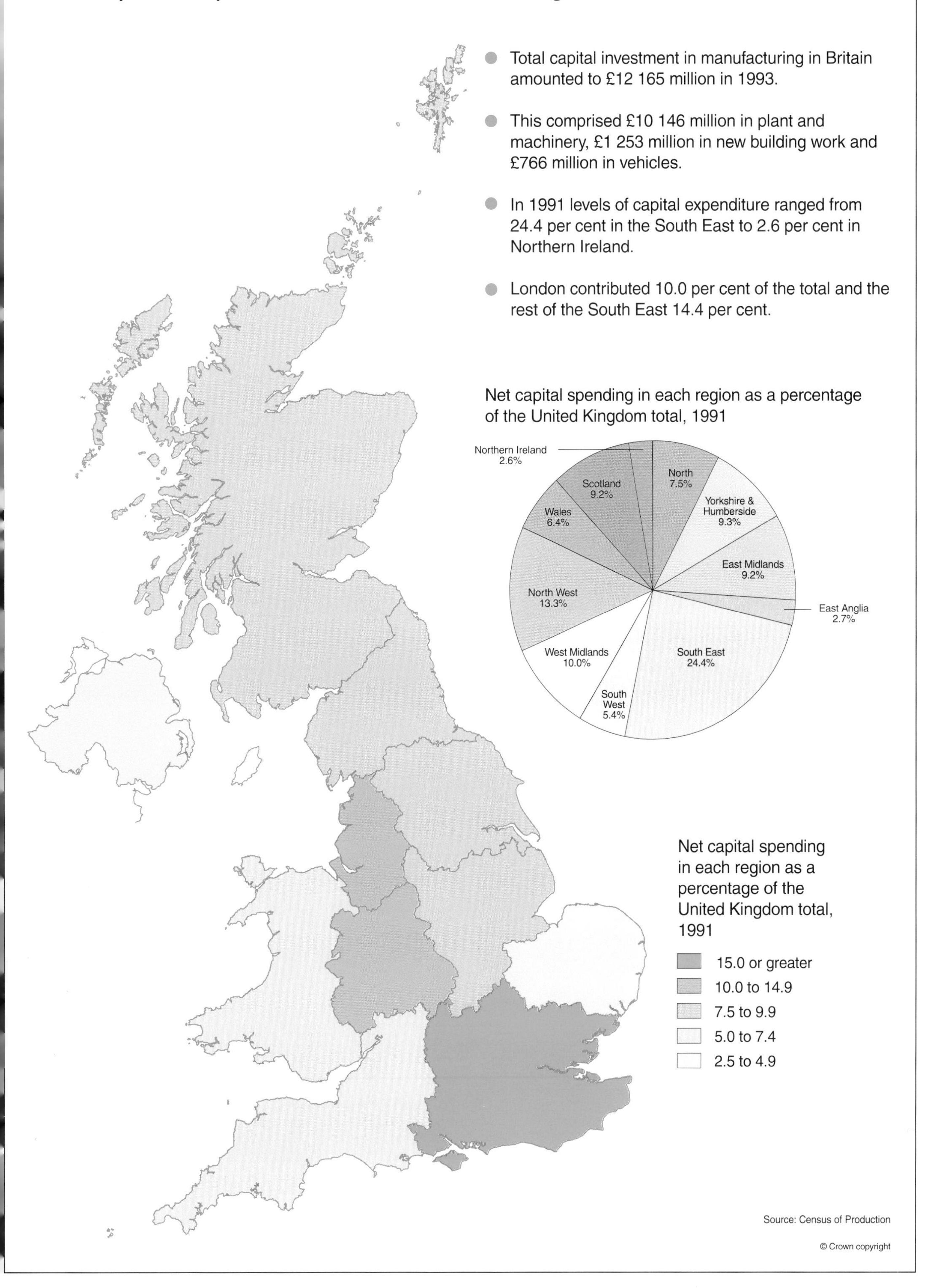

Source: Census of Production

Businesses

- At the end of 1992 there were 1.6 million operational businesses in the United Kingdom.
- Construction, retailing, and finance, property and professional services were the biggest categories.
- In 1992 Northern Ireland was the only region where the number of businesses in operation increased.

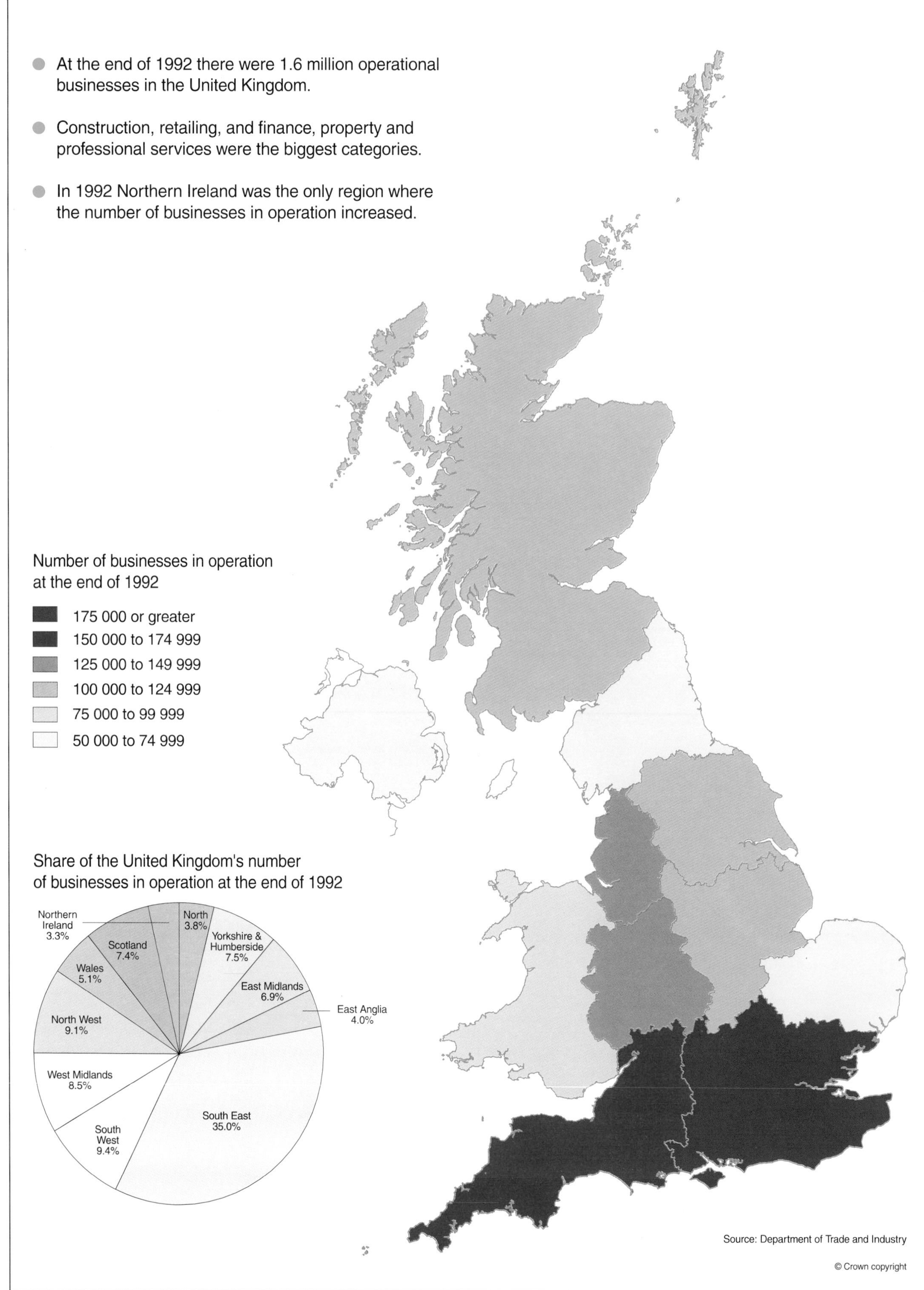

Source: Department of Trade and Industry

Day Nursery Places

- These figures cover places in nurseries that are either provided by the local authority or registered with them, and therefore exclude a small number of places in nurseries that are exempt from the need to register.
- Some of the figures are estimates, and those for Scotland cover only places provided by the local authority - hence the relatively low figures for much of Scotland.
- The greatest availability of day nursery places is in Clwyd, where there are 58.6 places per 1 000 children aged under 5.
- East Sussex, Northamptonshire, Kent, Lancashire and Greater London all also have more than 50 places per 1 000 young children.
- However, day nurseries form a relatively small part of total provision, with playgroups and childminders providing 795 000 places, compared with 135 000 for day nurseries.

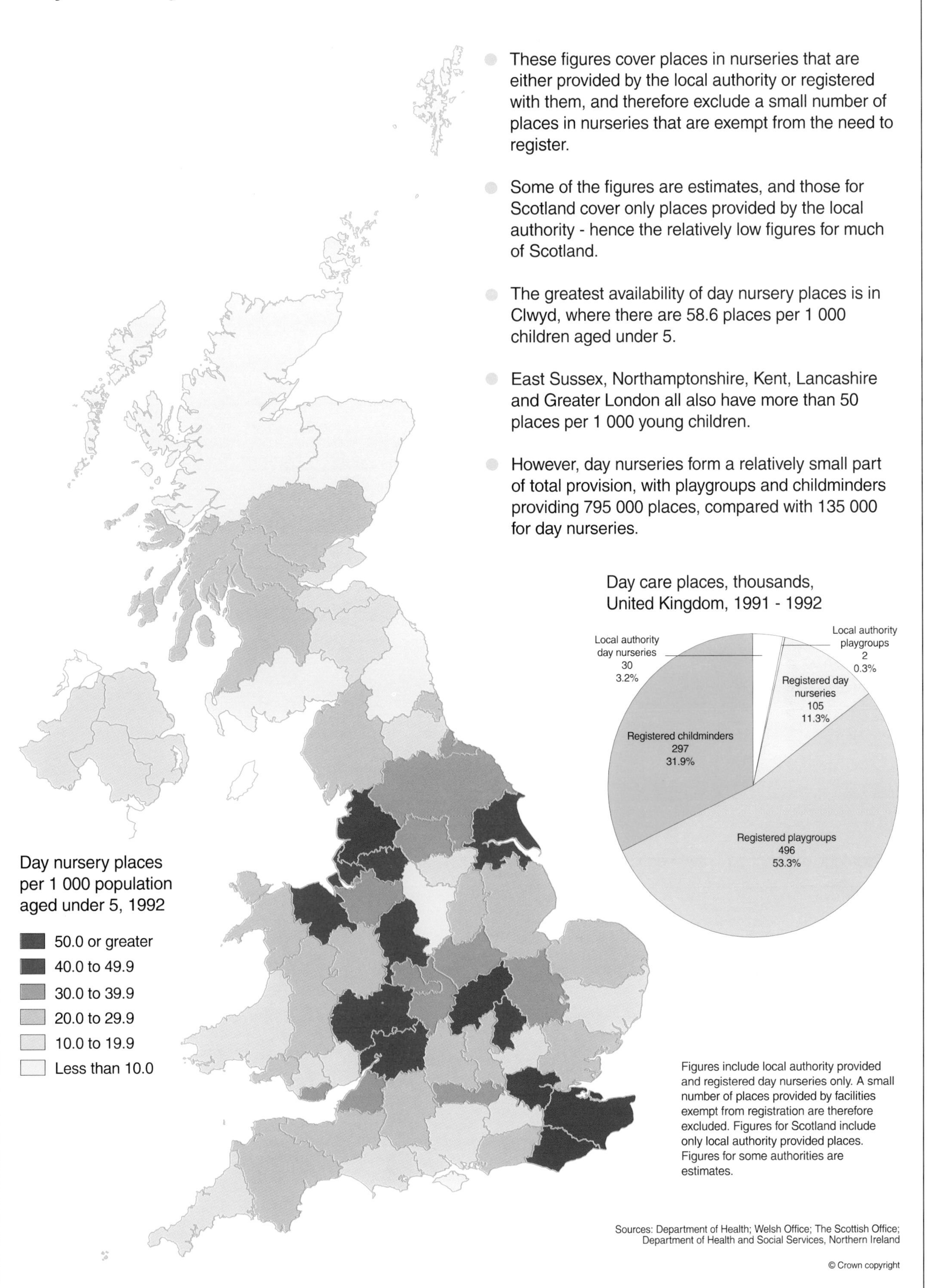

Figures include local authority provided and registered day nurseries only. A small number of places provided by facilities exempt from registration are therefore excluded. Figures for Scotland include only local authority provided places. Figures for some authorities are estimates.

Sources: Department of Health; Welsh Office; The Scottish Office; Department of Health and Social Services, Northern Ireland

Under 5s in State Education

- The figures show the number of children aged under 5 attending maintained nursery or primary schools as a percentage of estimated population aged 3 and 4.
- Half of all these children in the United Kingdom have a place, but the rate varies very considerably across the country.
- The rate is highest in the North, where it reaches 75 per cent, and in one county - Cleveland - 91 per cent.
- It is lowest in the South West, where only 35 per cent of these children have a place.

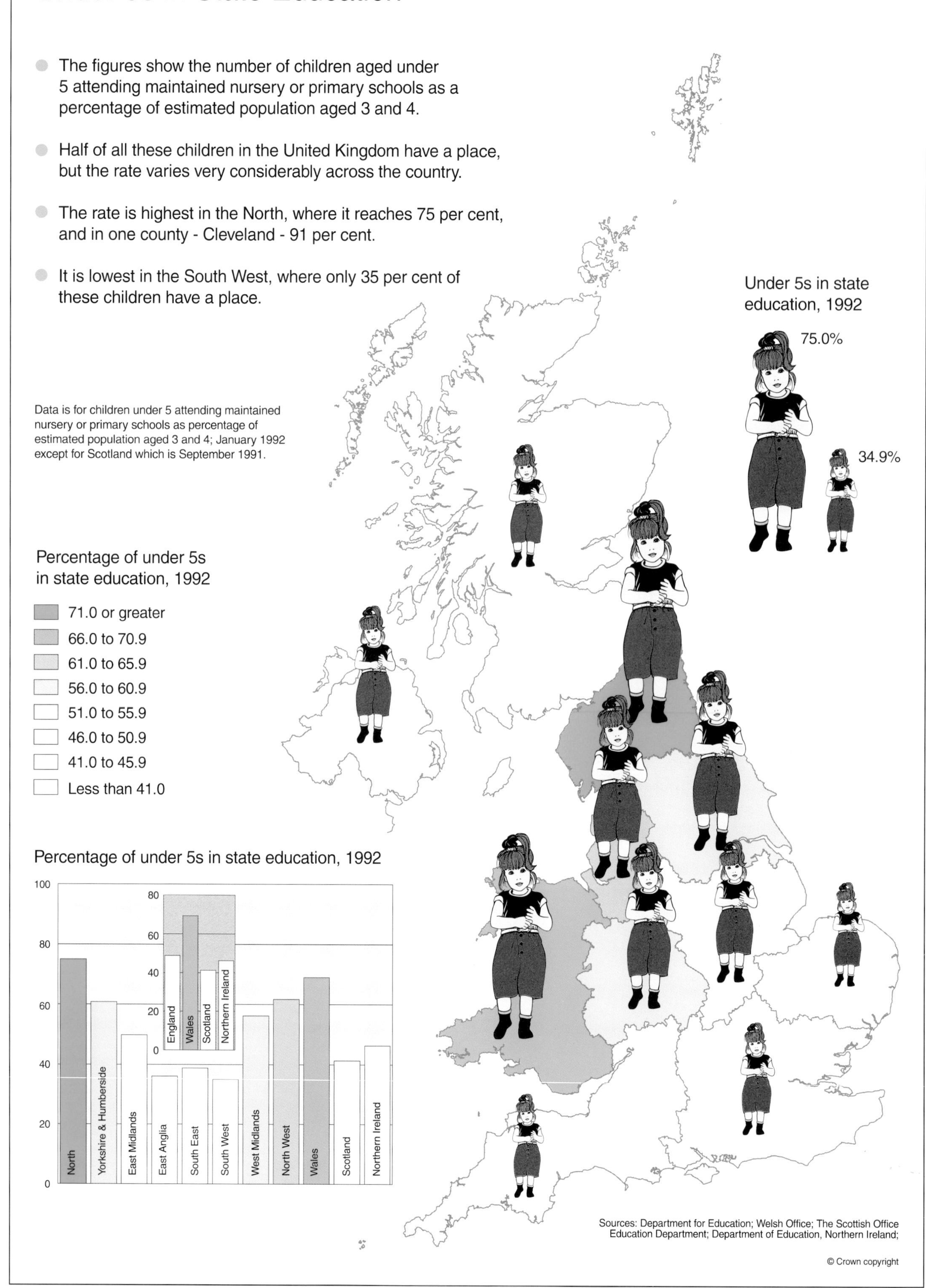

Sources: Department for Education; Welsh Office; The Scottish Office Education Department; Department of Education, Northern Ireland;

School Leavers With GCSEs

- The data covers those pupils who leave school with 5 or more GCSEs graded A-C, or their equivalent.
- Variations are very marked across the country, with neighbouring counties often having very different rates - for example in County Durham 22 per cent of pupils leave school with 5 or more A-C grades, while in Northumberland it is only 9.6 per cent.
- The highest rate was Somerset, with 28.7 per cent.

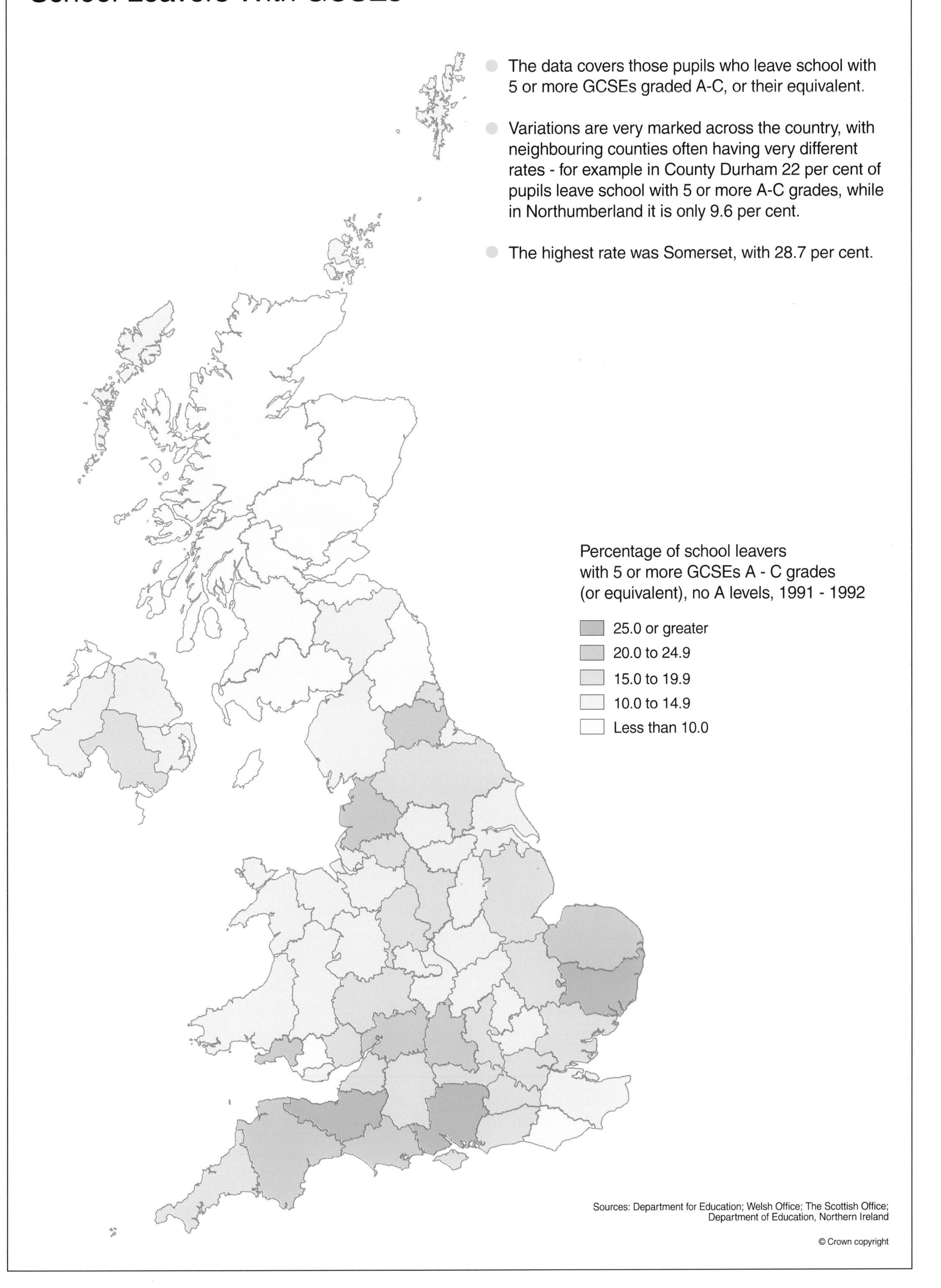

Sources: Department for Education; Welsh Office; The Scottish Office; Department of Education, Northern Ireland

Pupils Aged 16 Staying On in Education

- The number of pupils staying on in education after they reach the age of 16 has increased substantially since the beginning of the 1980s.
- The most dramatic increase was in Northern Ireland, where the staying on rate increased from 53 per cent in 1981 to 88 per cent in 1992.
- There are considerable regional variations in the number of pupils staying on - for example in 1992 it was as low as 66 per cent in Northumberland and Gwynedd.
- By contrast, the rate reached 93 per cent in Hertfordshire.

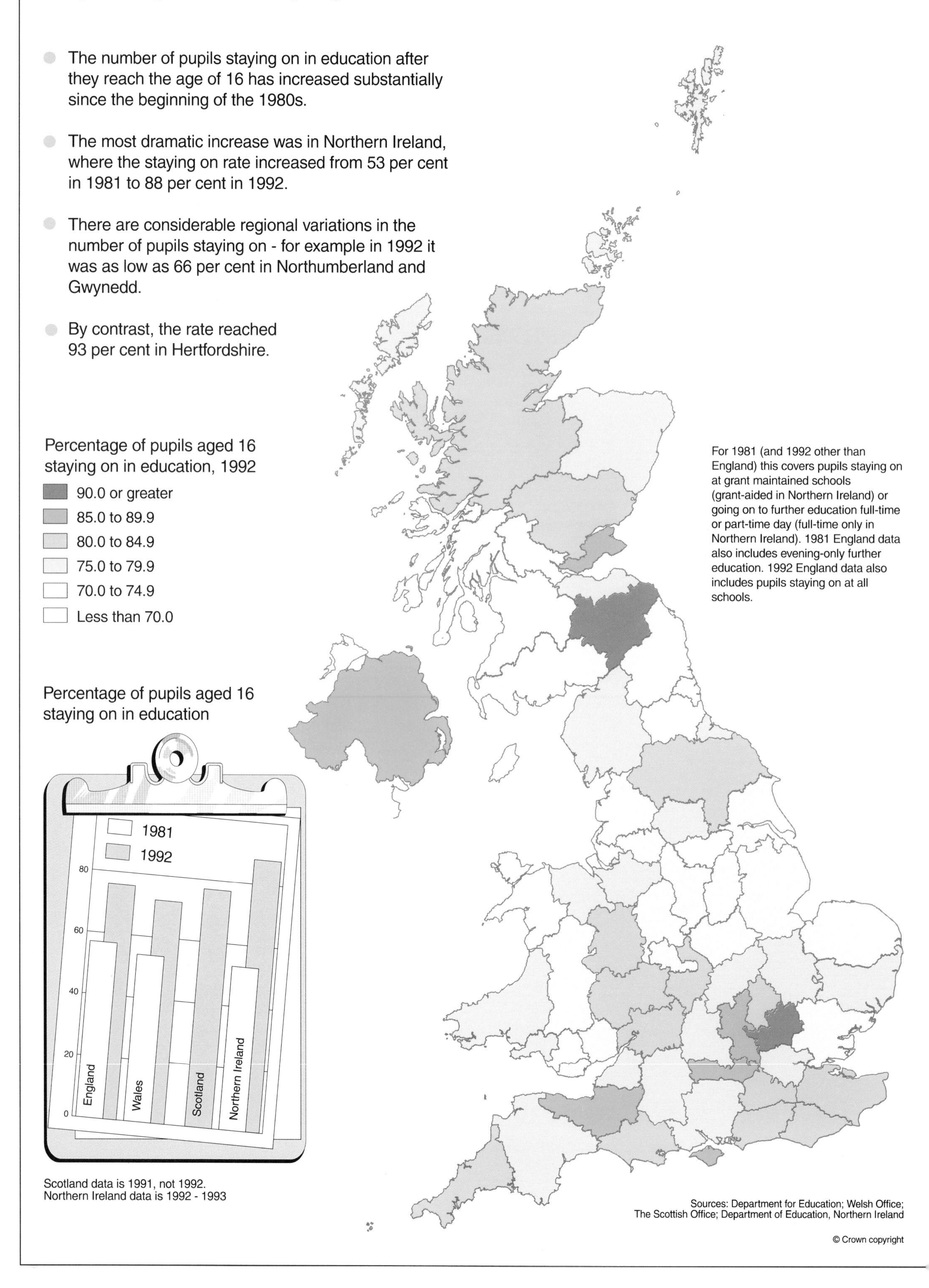

Scotland data is 1991, not 1992.
Northern Ireland data is 1992 - 1993

For 1981 (and 1992 other than England) this covers pupils staying on at grant maintained schools (grant-aided in Northern Ireland) or going on to further education full-time or part-time day (full-time only in Northern Ireland). 1981 England data also includes evening-only further education. 1992 England data also includes pupils staying on at all schools.

Sources: Department for Education; Welsh Office; The Scottish Office; Department of Education, Northern Ireland

School Leavers with A Levels

- The information on the map covers those with two or more A-levels for England, Wales and Northern Ireland; for Scotland, where a different system is used, it covers those with three or more SCE Highers.
- Of the countries in the United Kingdom, Scotland had the highest level of pupils achieving their exams, with 35 per cent of boys and 44 per cent of girls achieving at least one Higher.
- The area with the lowest proportion of pupils getting their A-levels was West Glamorgan, and the highest was the Belfast Education and Library Board area.
- More girls than boys achieve A-levels; the difference is fairly small for England, but for all other parts of the United Kingdom, it is quite marked.

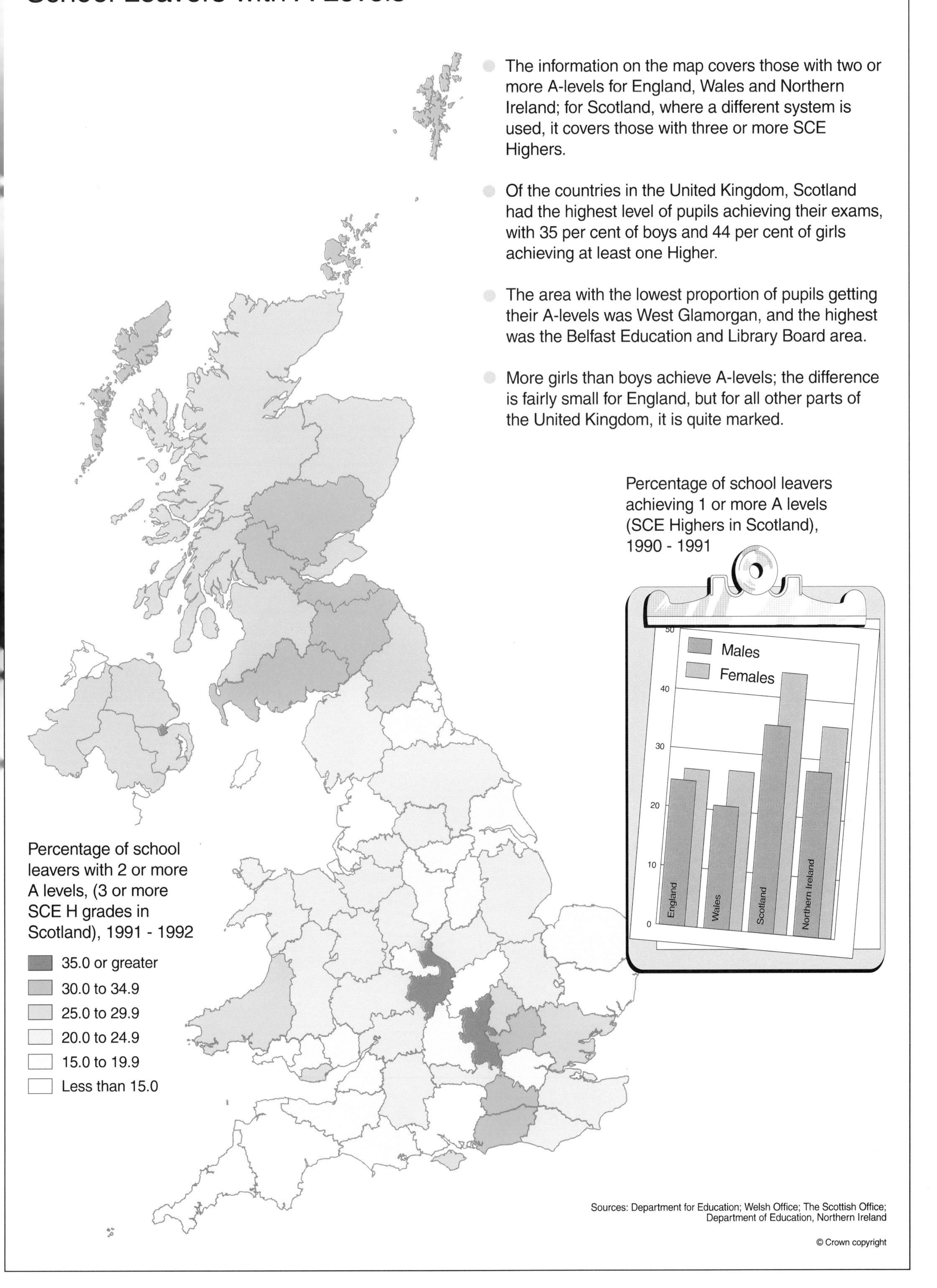

Sources: Department for Education; Welsh Office; The Scottish Office; Department of Education, Northern Ireland

Crime Rate

- The crime rate increased considerably during the 1980s in all parts of the United Kingdom except Northern Ireland, where the increase was fairly slight.
- The region with the lowest mainland crime rate in 1981 - the South West - saw the highest increase.
- By contrast, the region with the highest rate in 1981 - Greater London - saw the second lowest increase on the mainland.
- There is a considerable variation in the overall crime rate, which is about 3 times higher in the North than it is in Northern Ireland (although see note).

Scottish figures are not precisely comparable with those for England, Wales and Northern Ireland because of differences in the legal system. The Northern Ireland figures exclude offences of criminal damage of relatively low value.

Notifiable offences recorded by the police, per 100 000 population, 1992

- 13 000 or greater
- 12 000 to 12 999
- 11 000 to 11 999
- 10 000 to 10 999
- 9 000 to 9 999
- 8 000 to 8 999
- Less than 8 000

Percentage increase in crime, 1981 - 1992

140
120
100
80
60
40
20
0

North
Yorkshire & Humberside
East Midlands
East Anglia
Greater London
Rest of South East
South West
West Midlands
North West
Wales
Scotland
Northern Ireland

Notifiable offences recorded by the police, per 100 000 population, 1992

13 630

4 194

Greater London

Sources: Home Office, The Scottish Office, Royal Ulster Constabulary

Violent Crime

- As with crime overall, there was a large increase in violent crime over the 1980s, although regional variations in the increase were less pronounced than with crime overall.
- Northern Ireland had the lowest increase, thus by 1992 coming to have the lowest rate of violent crime in the United Kingdom.
- The highest increase in violent crime was in Wales, which in 1992 had the third highest level of violent crime.
- Violent offences remain a small proportion of all crime.

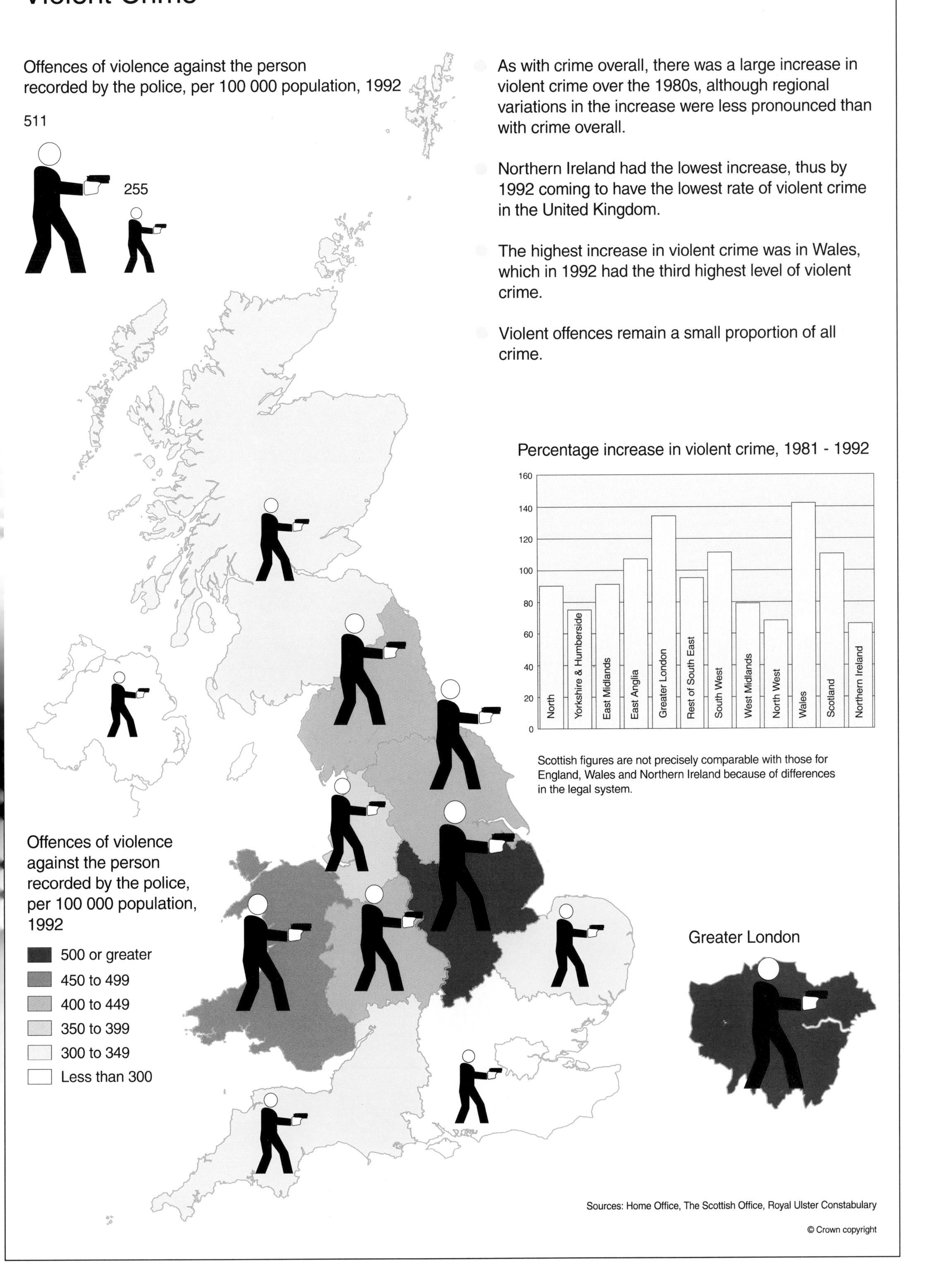

Scottish figures are not precisely comparable with those for England, Wales and Northern Ireland because of differences in the legal system.

Sources: Home Office, The Scottish Office, Royal Ulster Constabulary

Burglary

- Although almost all areas saw an increase in burglary between 1981 and 1992, there was a great deal of variation between regions.
- There were large increases in burglary in some areas, especially the South West and Yorkshire and Humberside.
- The increase in the burglary rate was fairly small in Scotland and Greater London, while Northern Ireland experienced a noticeable decrease.

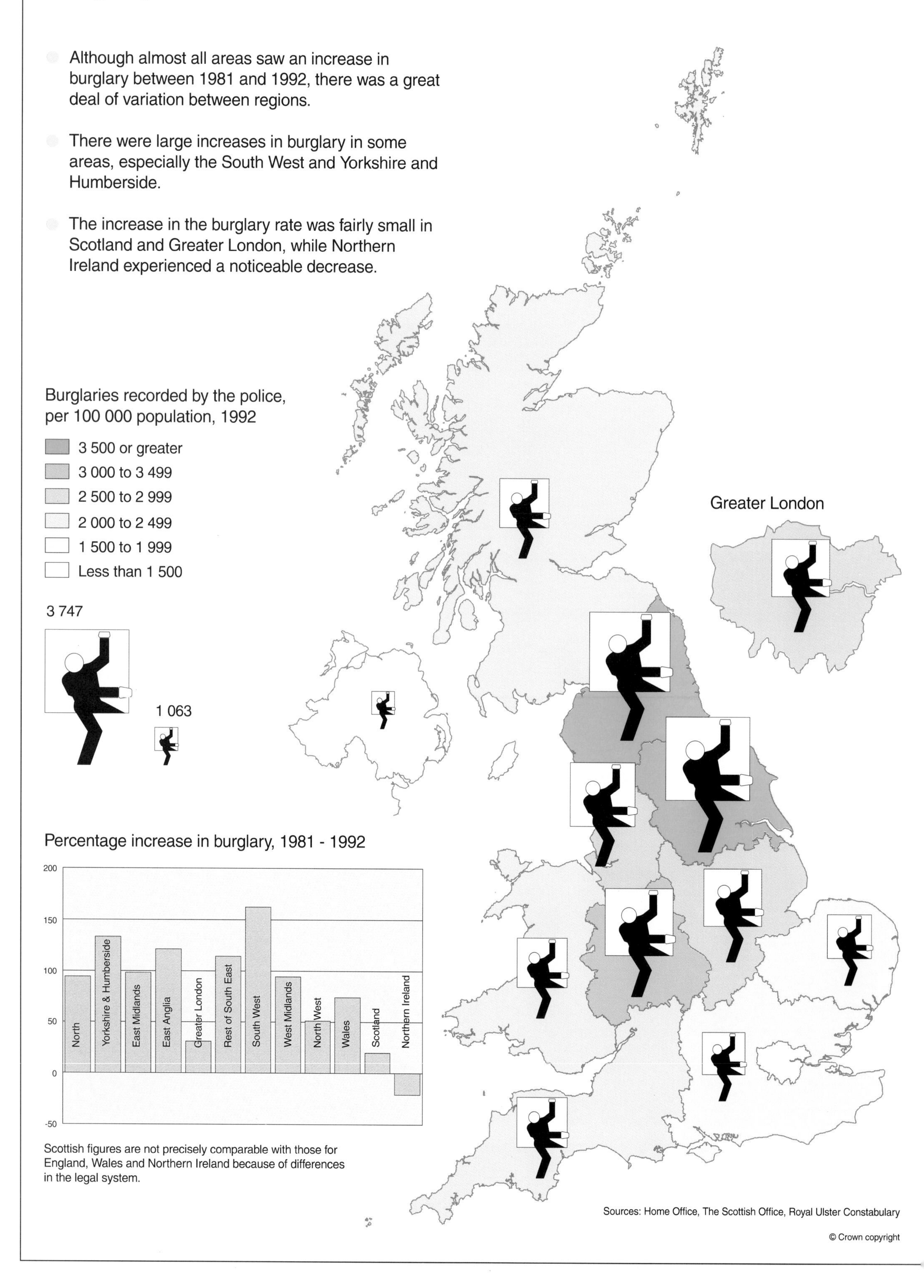

Scottish figures are not precisely comparable with those for England, Wales and Northern Ireland because of differences in the legal system.

Sources: Home Office, The Scottish Office, Royal Ulster Constabulary

Households Burgled

Types of household offence, England, 1991

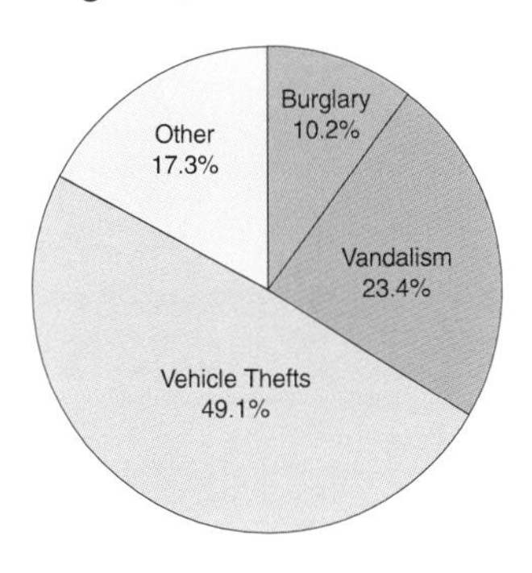

- A government crime survey - which covers England and Wales - asks a sample of people about the level of crime they have suffered from, not all of which will have been reported to the police.
- The proportion of houses that had been burgled in the year of the survey varied from over 8 per cent in Greater London to 3 per cent in East Anglia.
- Motor crime - theft of or from a vehicle - is a particularly common type of offence.

Percentage of households burgled at least once, 1991

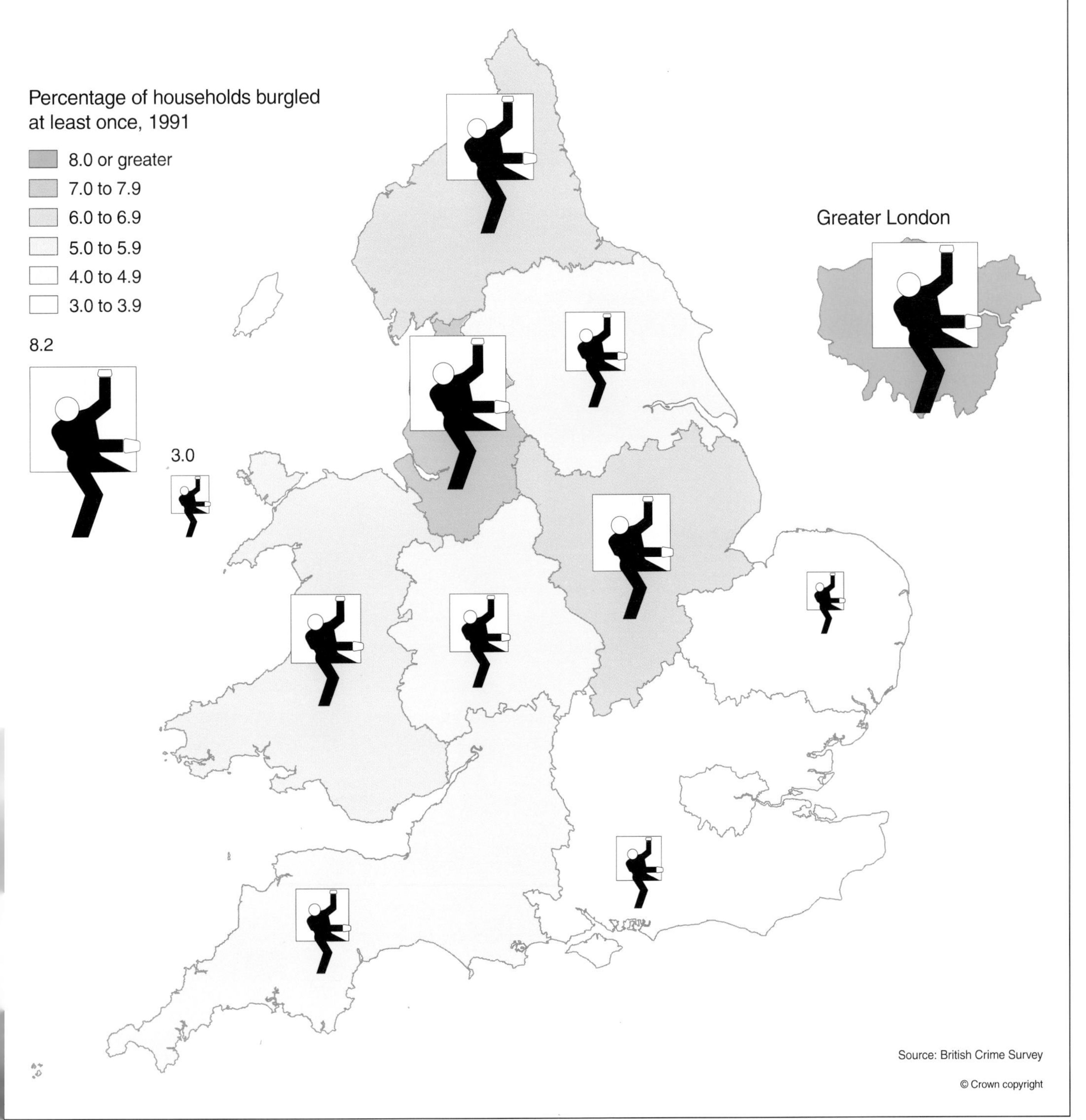

Source: British Crime Survey

Young Offenders

- In most regions, the rate of offending is highest for 17 - 20 year olds, but in the North and Yorkshire and Humberside it is greatest for 14 - 16 year olds.
- The South West has the lowest rate of youth offending in England and Wales right across all 3 age-brackets.
- The highest rate of offending among 10 - 13 year olds is in the North; among 14 - 16 year olds it is in Yorkshire and Humberside and for the 17 - 20 year olds it is in the North West.
- Young offenders are predominantly involved with crimes against property rather than violence, drugs offences or other categories of wrongdoing.

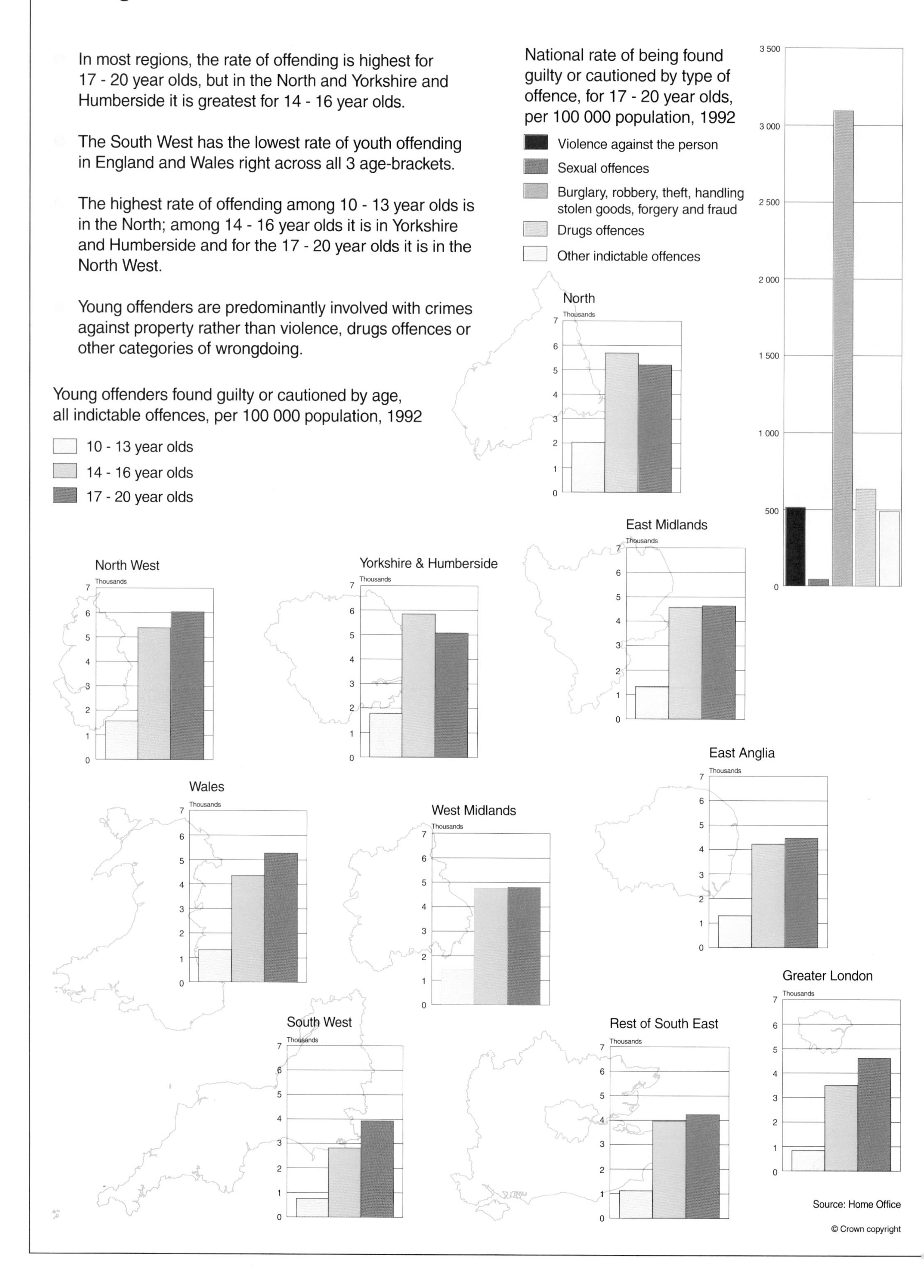

Source: Home Office

Clear-Up Rate

The figure for London is not strictly comparable with other areas owing to a different method of assessing the clear-up rate used by the Metropolitan Police. Scottish figures are not precisely comparable with those for England, Wales and Northern Ireland because of differences in the legal system. The Northern Ireland figures exclude offences of criminal damage of relatively low value.

Generally, cleared up offences are those for which people have been charged, summonsed or cautioned, or which have been taken into consideration on sentencing for another offence, or which have been admitted by prisoners sentenced for other offences.

In most of England between 20 and 30 per cent of crimes are cleared up, although rates vary markedly, being highest in the North West with 36 per cent.

The police are relatively successful in clearing up violence against the person and sexual offences, but less so with offences of criminal damage and burglary.

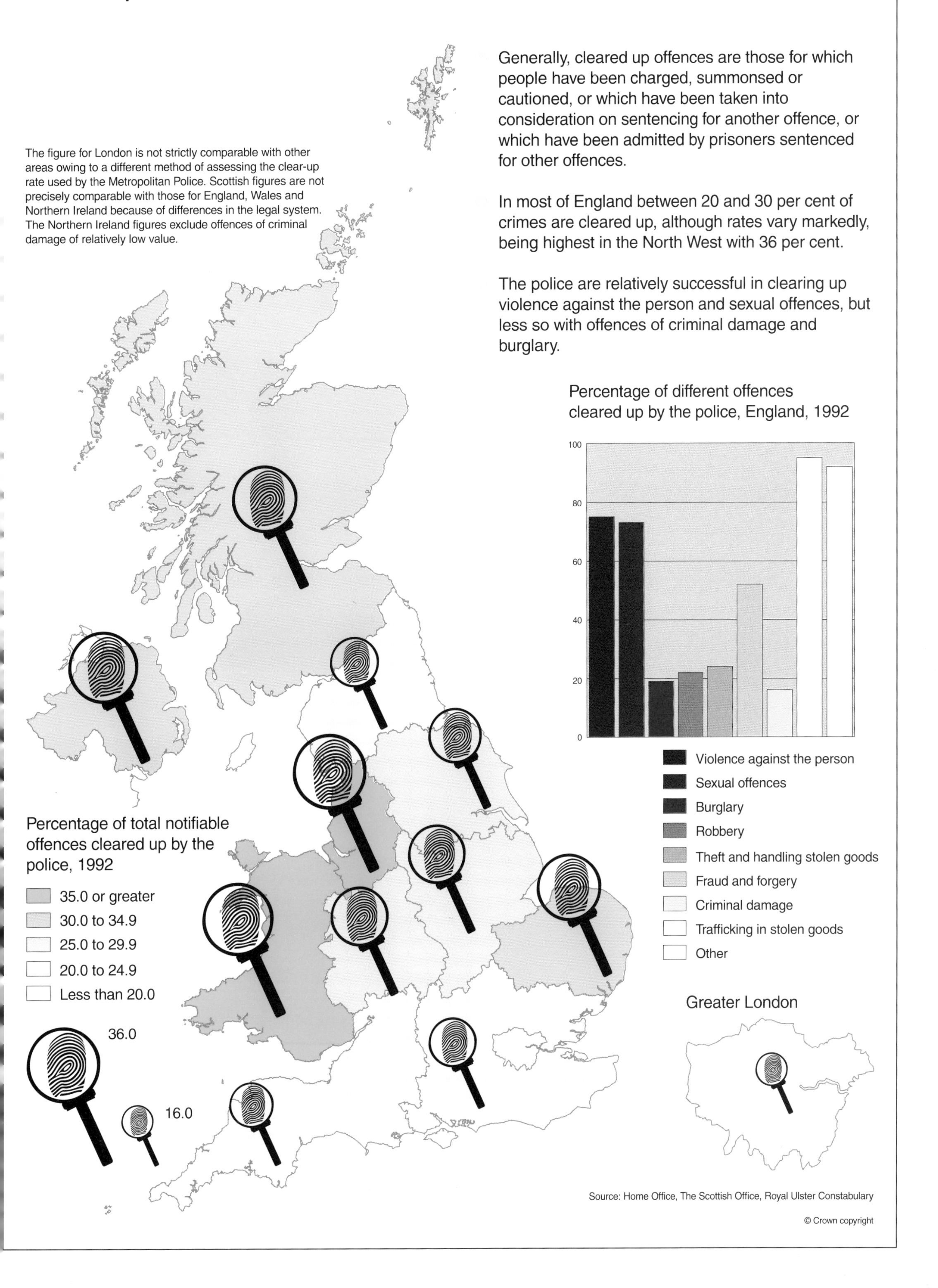

Source: Home Office, The Scottish Office, Royal Ulster Constabulary

Drink-Driving

- Proportionately, the highest number of cases of drink-driving were in Northern Ireland, where in 1992 there were 302 findings of guilt per 100 000 population; however, Northern Ireland also saw the lowest incidence of custodial sentences for these offences.
- The North West and the West Midlands had the next highest rate of drink-driving.
- East Anglia had the lowest rate, at only 144 findings of guilt per 100 000 population, followed by the South West (154).
- The greatest use of custodial sentencing was in the East Midlands, where 6.5 per cent of cases attracted such a penalty.

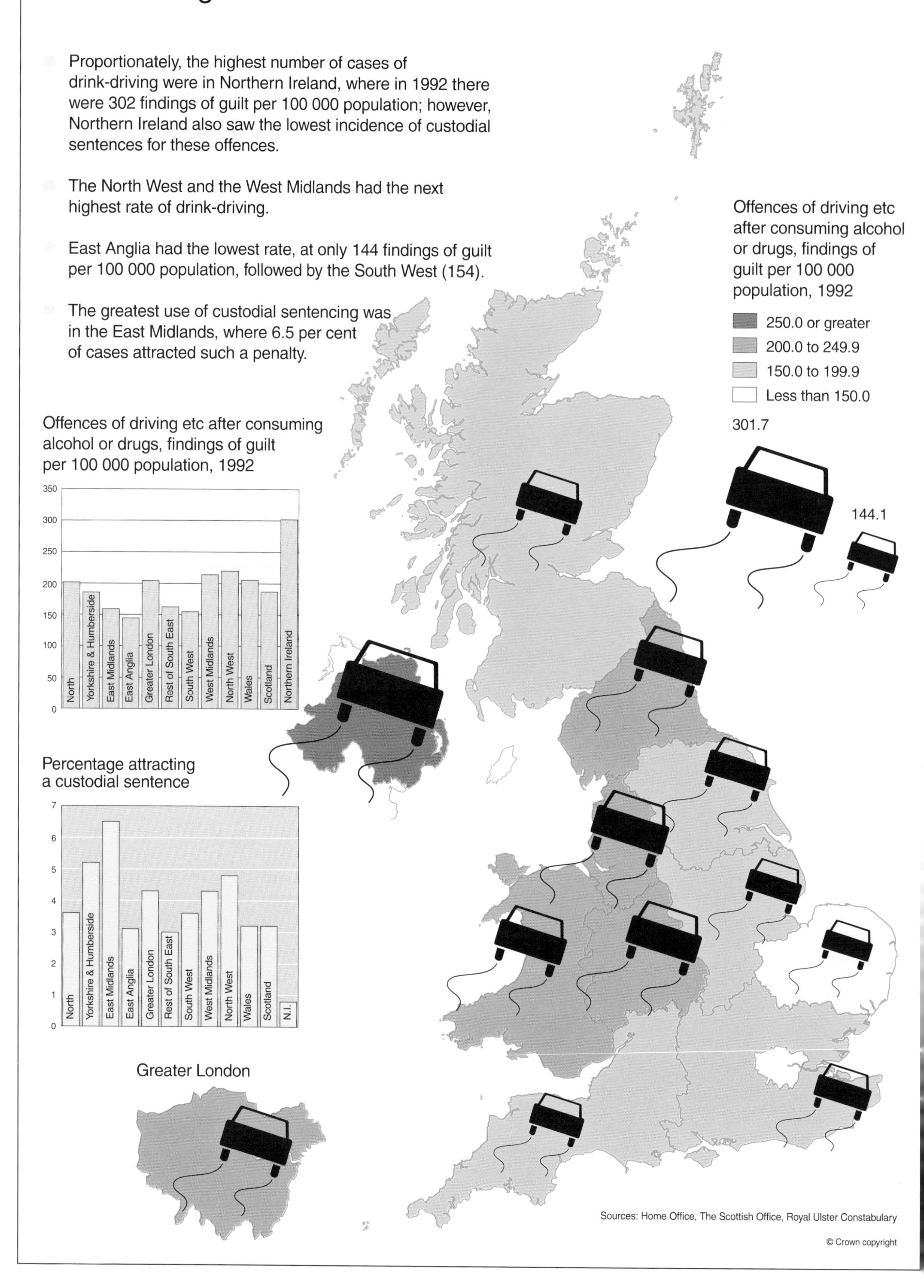

Sources: Home Office, The Scottish Office, Royal Ulster Constabulary

Radiation

The vast majority of radiation to which humans are exposed comes from natural sources - especially from radon, a radioactive gas which is particularly prevalent in parts of the country where granite rocks are common.

The Government has declared several 'radon action areas', within which householders are offered free tests to see if their homes have high levels of radon needing remedial action.

Most 'artificial' radiation sources come from medical uses, such as X-rays and radiotherapy, rather than from other uses such as nuclear power.

Radiation doses are monitored automatically by the RIMNET system, a large network of sensors around the country.

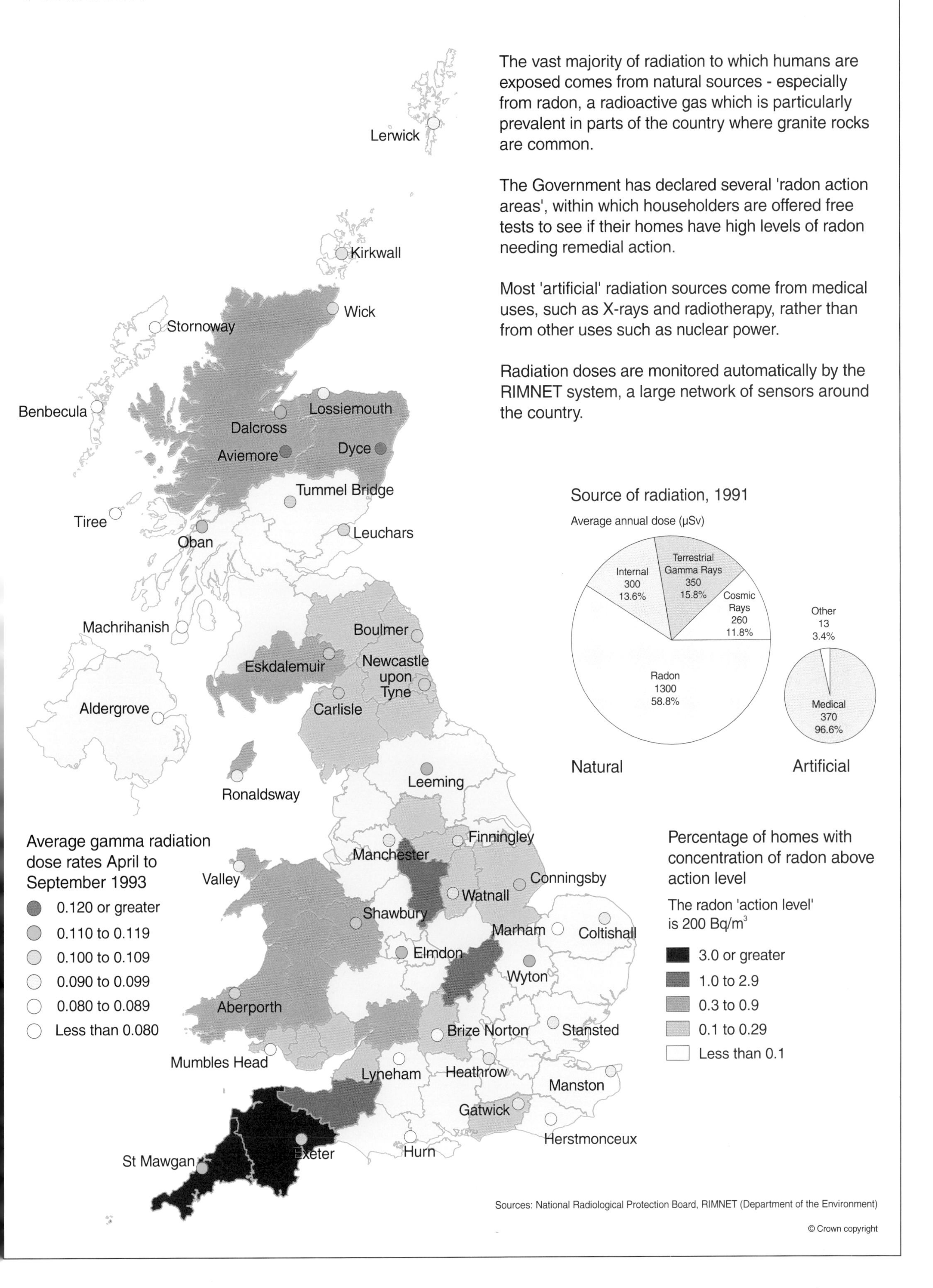

Sources: National Radiological Protection Board, RIMNET (Department of the Environment)

Agricultural Land Use

Arable uses for farmland are most prominent in East Anglia - with about three-quarters of land used for crops - followed by the East Midlands and the South East.

Wales, Scotland and Northern Ireland have the highest proportion of farmland given over to long-established grazing - more than four-fifths in the case of Wales.

The South East has the greatest amount of land - 159 000 hectares - 'set aside'; that is, taken out of production under the EU Common Agricultural Policy to reduce food surpluses.

Scotland has the greatest area of farmland given over to forestry and other uses - 163 000 hectares.

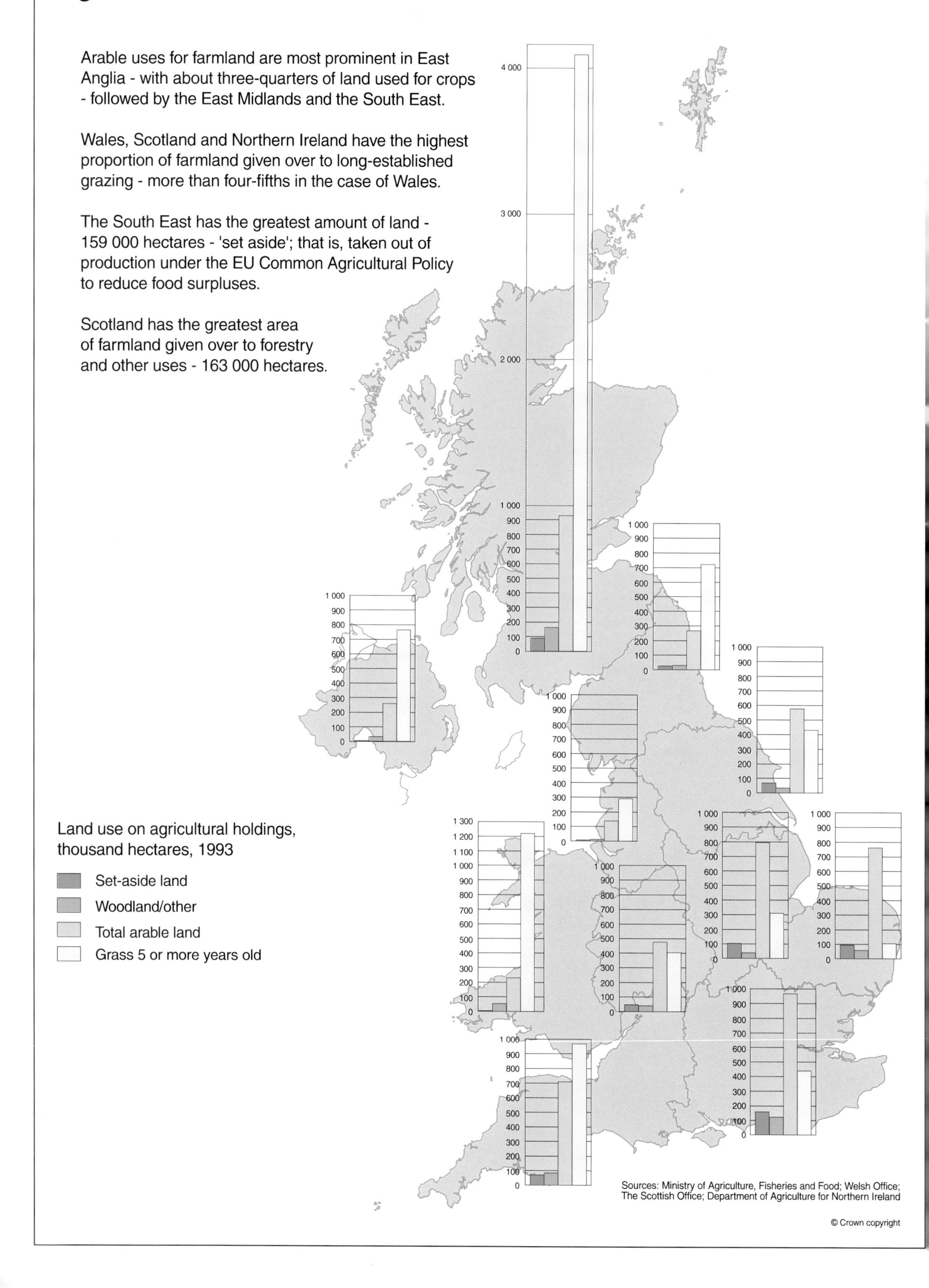

Land use on agricultural holdings, thousand hectares, 1993

Sources: Ministry of Agriculture, Fisheries and Food; Welsh Office; The Scottish Office; Department of Agriculture for Northern Ireland

Urbanisation

A large proportion of land with new urban uses is now previously developed - as much as 83 per cent in Greater London.

However, in other parts of the country significant amounts of 'green field' land is still being developed.

The information relates to map changes recorded by Ordnance Survey between 1988 and 1992. The figure for Wales is affected by one very large change which accounts for over 20 per cent of the Welsh total.

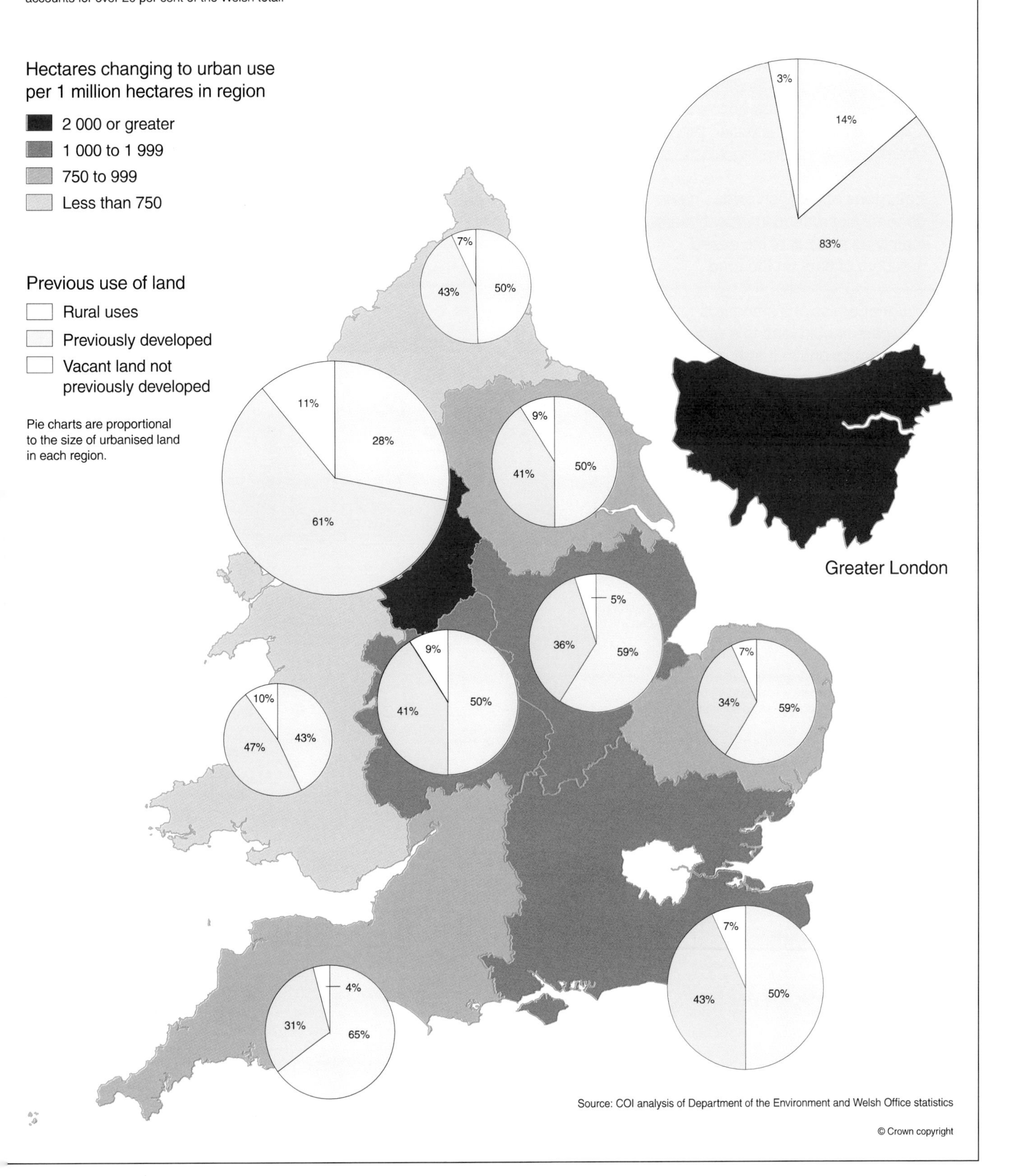

Source: COI analysis of Department of the Environment and Welsh Office statistics

Air Pollution

Emissions of sulphur dioxide and black smoke have been reduced sharply in recent years, partly as a result of reduced use of coal as a domestic fuel.

The recent increased use of gas for electricity generation will also lead to further falls in these emissions.

Concentrations of these pollutants are higher in big cities such as London and Manchester than in smaller places such as Slough and Norwich; Plymouth has very low concentrations of sulphur dioxide in particular, probably benefiting from prevailing winds.

Emissions of nitrogen oxides have generally increased in recent years, mainly as a result of increased numbers of cars on the road.

Tougher emissions standards for new cars should lead to a reduction in these emissions in future as older, dirtier cars are scrapped.

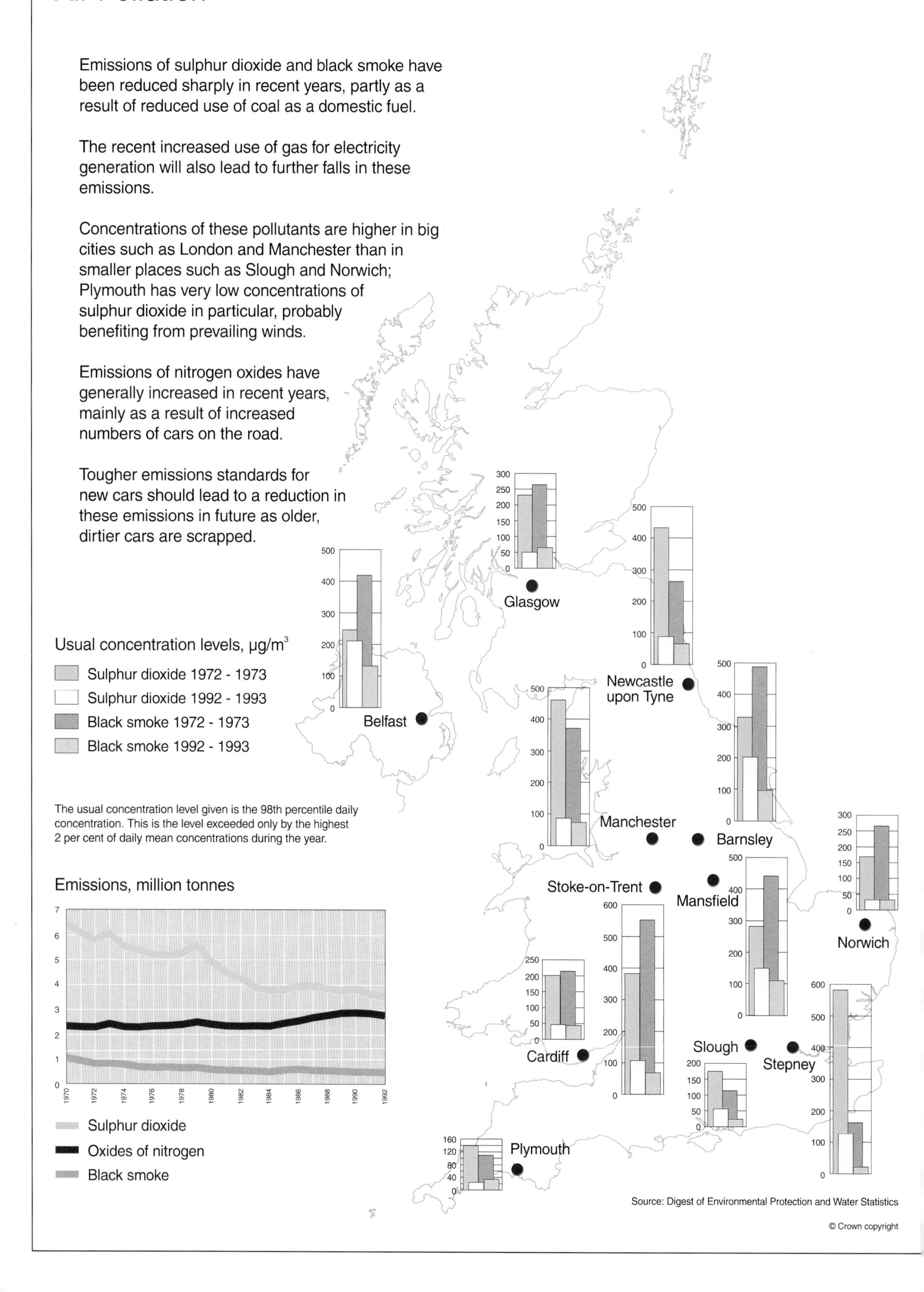

The usual concentration level given is the 98th percentile daily concentration. This is the level exceeded only by the highest 2 per cent of daily mean concentrations during the year.

Source: Digest of Environmental Protection and Water Statistics

River Quality and Water Pollution

Statistics for river quality are collected in slightly different ways in the different parts of the United Kingdom, so that the figures are not strictly comparable.

However, it is clear that river quality is exceptionally high in much of Scotland, and to a lesser extent in Wales and Northern Ireland, while it is much lower in heavily industrialised areas such as Severn Trent and North West.

On a per capita basis, Wales and North West had the highest number of water pollution incidents that could be substantiated.

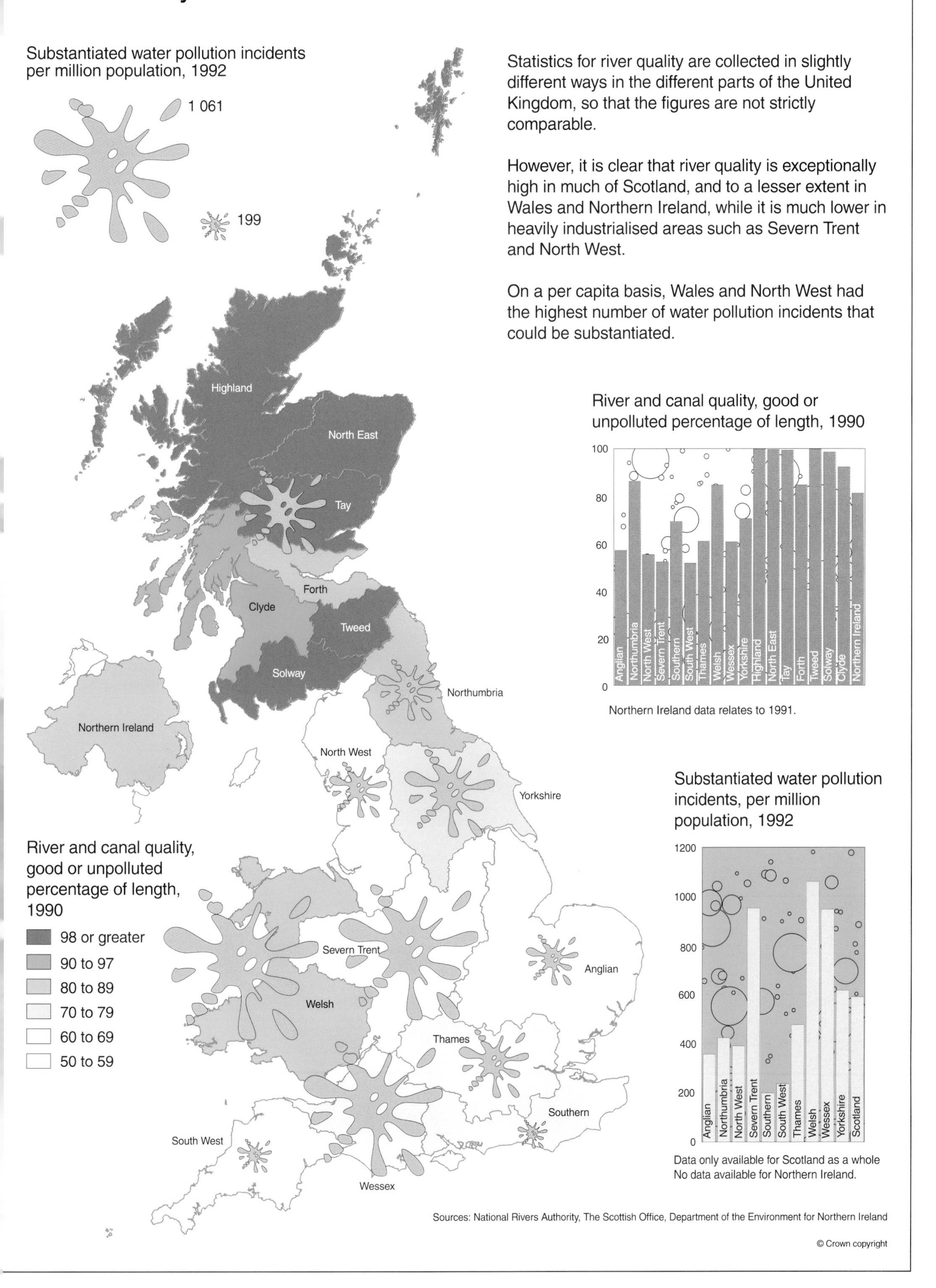

Sources: National Rivers Authority, The Scottish Office, Department of the Environment for Northern Ireland

Bathing Waters

Under a European directive, the cleanliness of recognised bathing waters is measured against the 'coliform standard' - the number of *e.coli* bacteria in a sample of a given volume - to indicate the degree of sewage contamination.

Since the mid-80s there has been a marked drop in the proportion of beaches failing this test - down from 45 per cent in 1987 to 18 per cent in 1994 - reflecting considerable spending by the water companies on improved treatment.

The best beaches are in the Wessex region, followed by Northern Ireland and Yorkshire, while Thames had the poorest, despite considerable strides in cleaning up the river.

Percentage of beaches passing coliform standards in the EC Bathing Waters Directive, 1994 bathing season

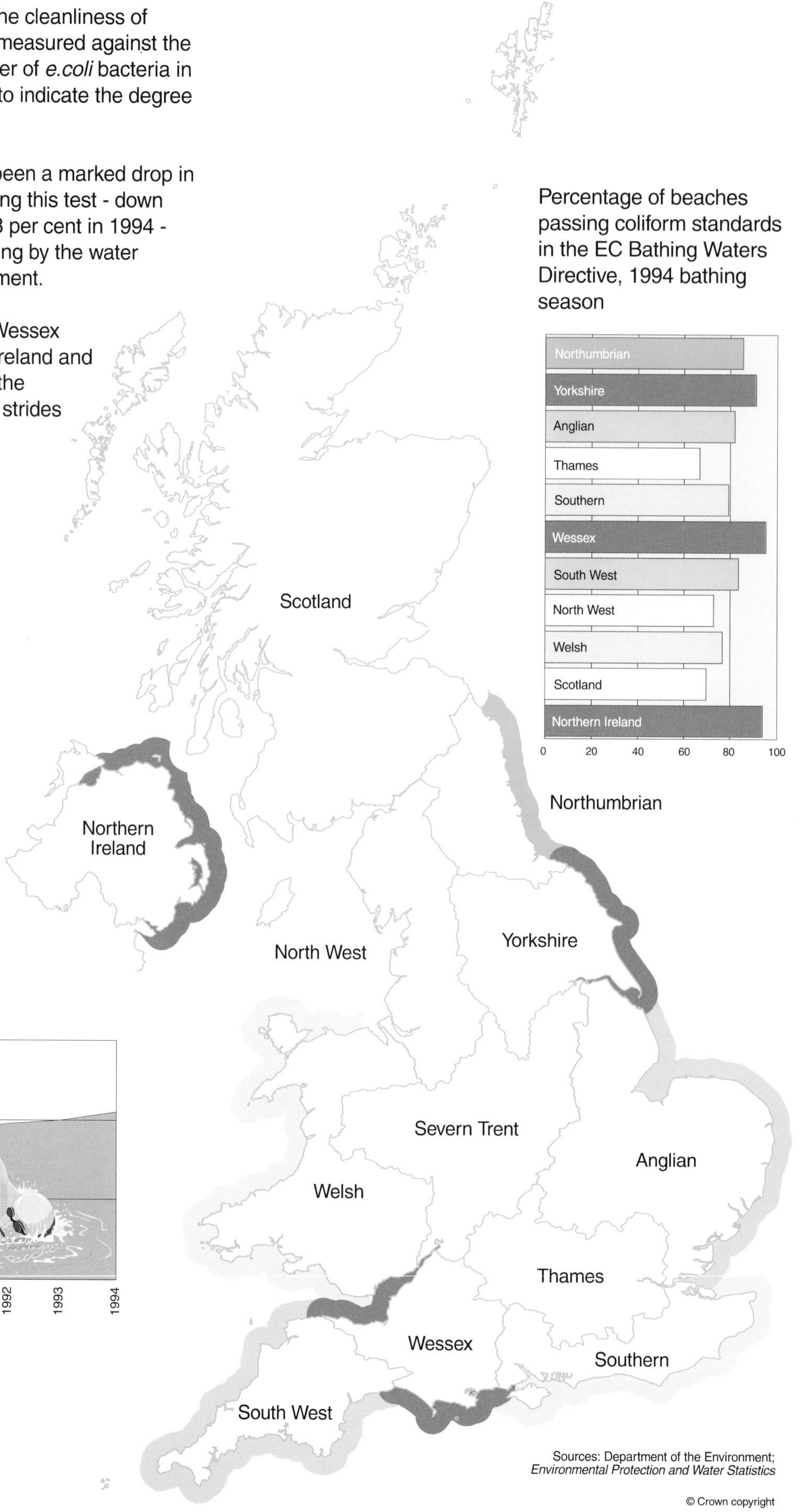

- 90.0 or greater
- 85.0 to 89.9
- 80.0 to 84.9
- 75.0 to 79.9
- 70.0 to 74.9
- Less than 70.0

Compliance, United Kingdom

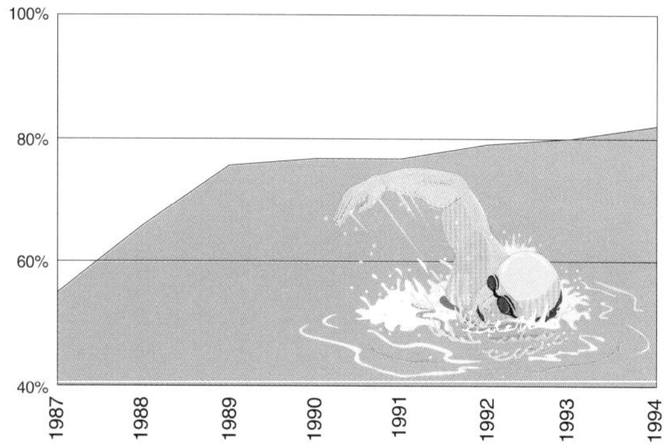

Percentage of beaches passing coliform standards in the EC Bathing Waters Directive, 1994 bathing season

Sources: Department of the Environment; *Environmental Protection and Water Statistics*

Growth in Motor Vehicles

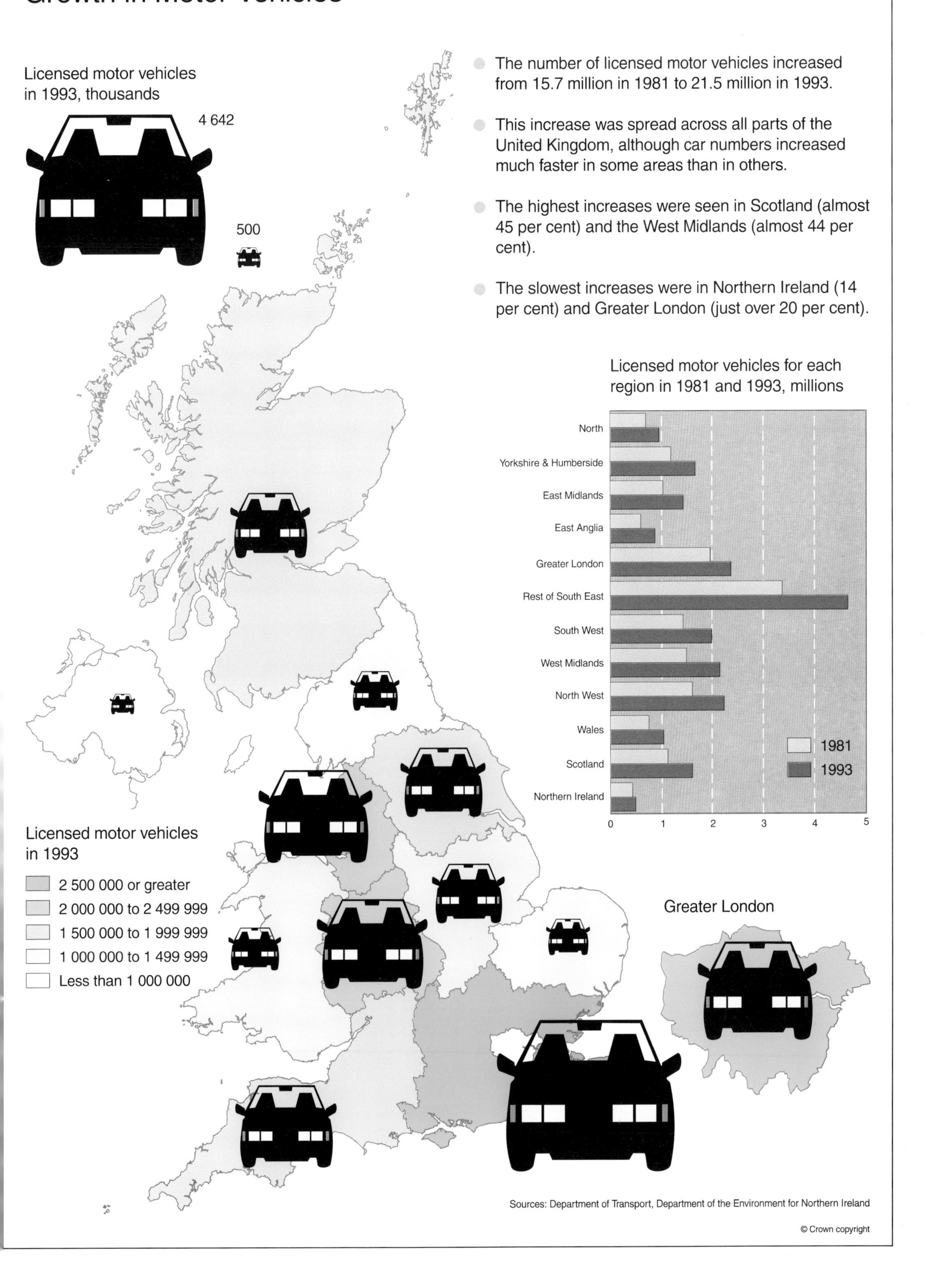

Car Ownership

- The proportion of households without regular use of a car has declined as the number of cars has risen, down in Great Britain from 45 per cent in 1981 to 33 per cent in 1992.
- Scotland and the North remain as the areas with the highest proportion of households without cars; for both this was 49 per cent in 1981 and 43 per cent in 1992.
- The South West is the region with the greatest proportion of car-owning households; 77 per cent in 1992.
- The number of households with two or more cars has increased quite strongly, from 15 per cent in Great Britain in 1981 to 23 per cent in 1992.
- There is a substantial variation between the regions in the number of two-car households; this was 15 per cent in Scotland in 1992, but no fewer than 31 per cent in the South East outside London.

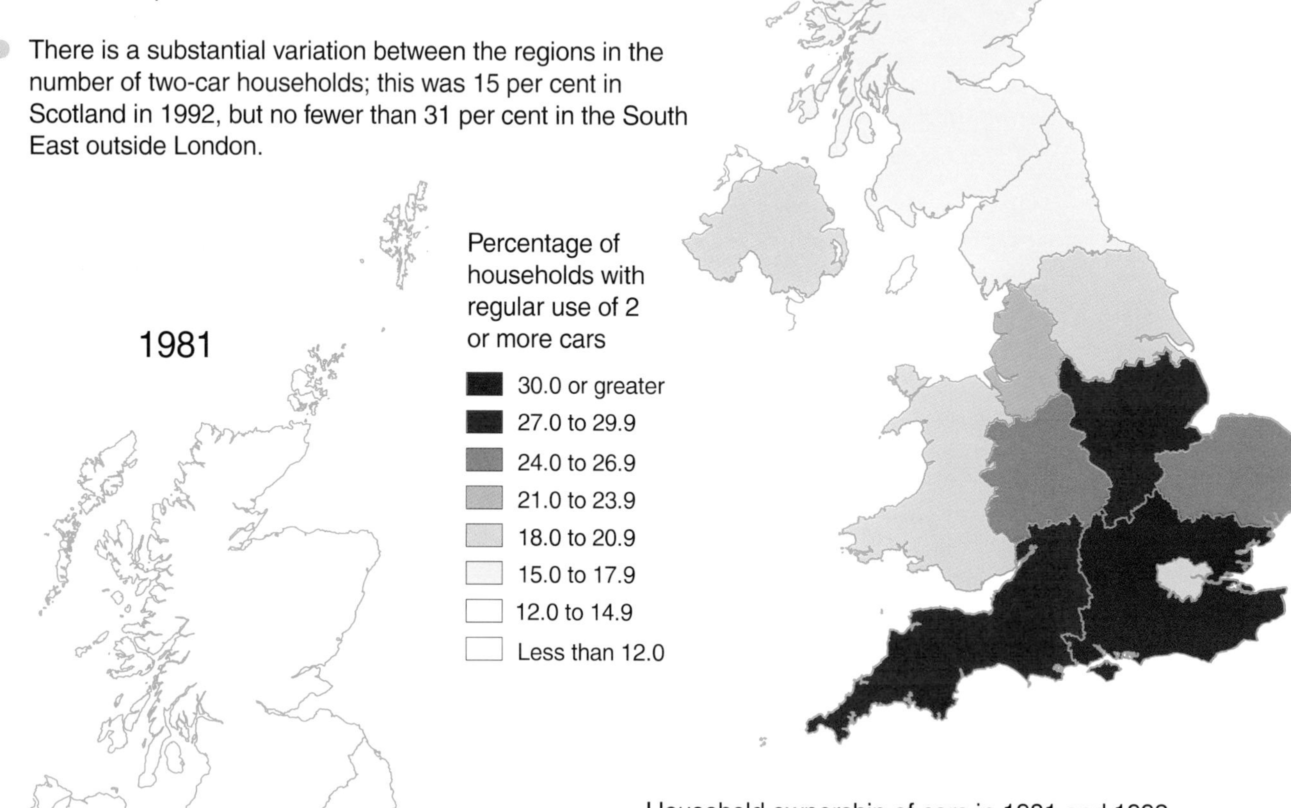

Household ownership of cars in 1981 and 1992

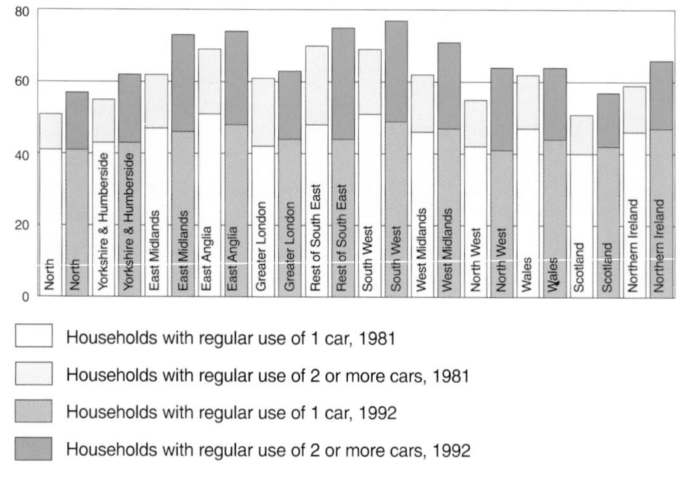

Sources: Department of Transport, Department of Finance and Personnel for Northern Ireland

Car Travel

- Average car travel as a driver is highest in the South East outside London, where it is almost twice what it is for London (the area with the lowest average car travel).
- Car travel as a passenger is highest in non-metropolitan England and Wales outside the South East.
- The main purposes of car driving are commuting to work or on business travel, although visiting friends and shopping are also important.

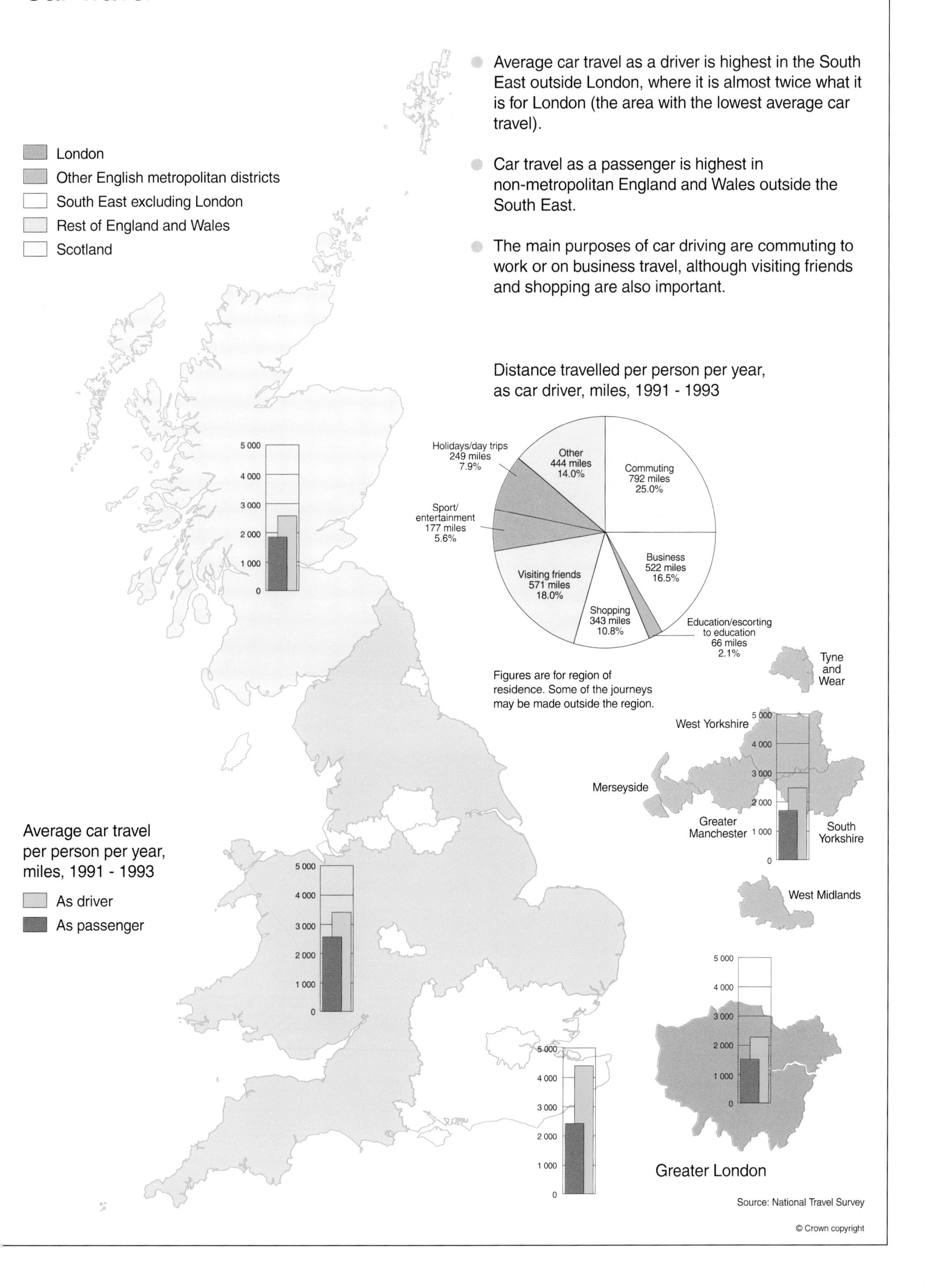

Source: National Travel Survey

Bus Travel

- Bus travel is most important in Scotland, followed by the English metropolitan districts other than London.
- It is least important in the South East outside London, where on average people travel by bus only 40 per cent as much as Londoners do.
- Shopping is the most important single reason for bus travel, although commuting to work is also significant.

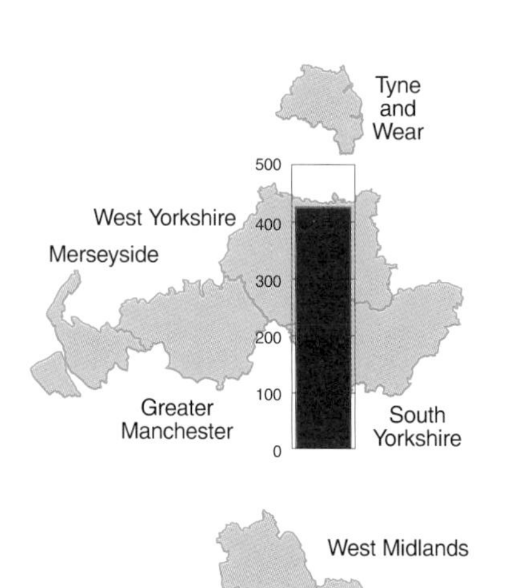

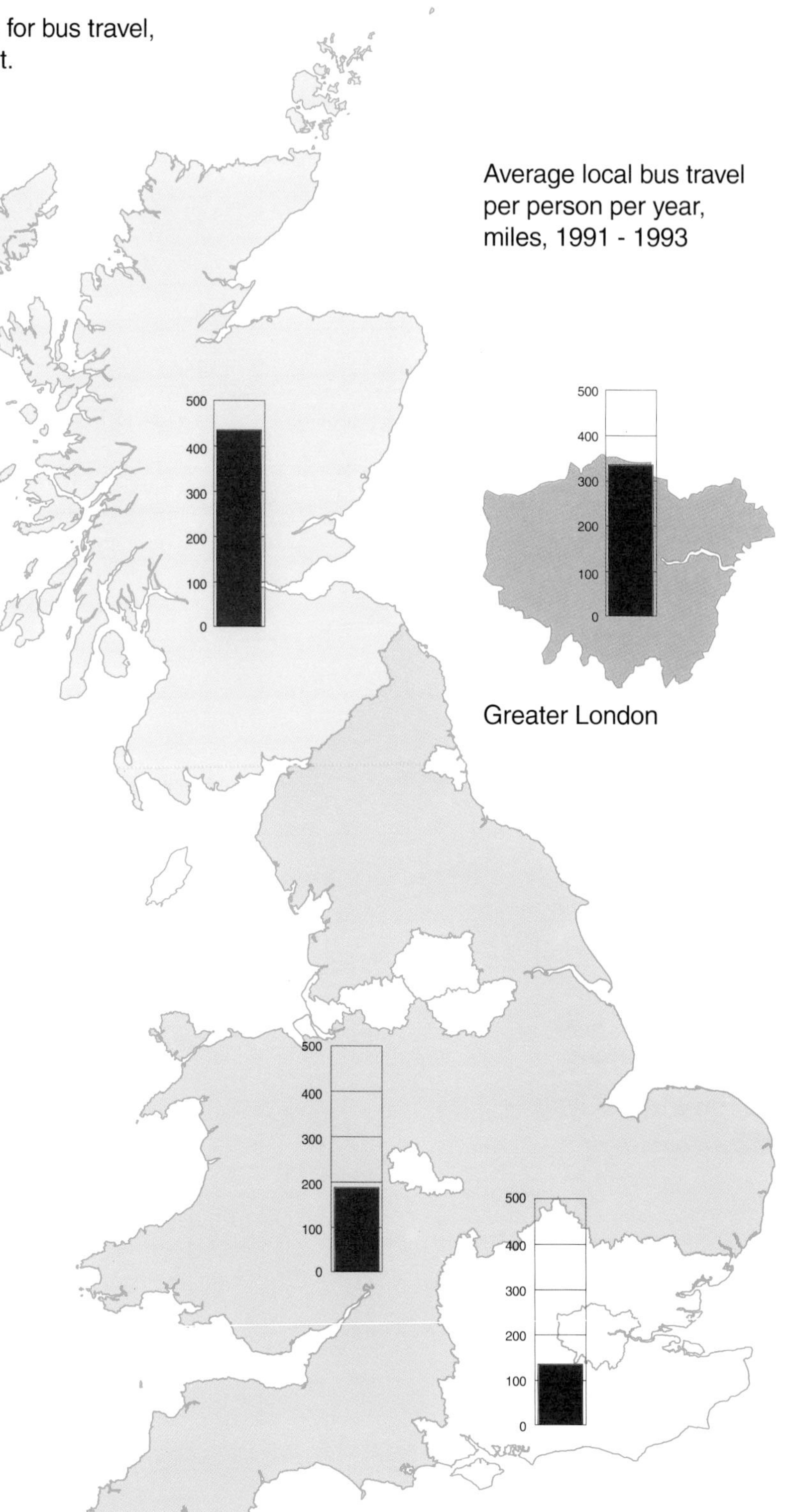

Distance travelled per person per year, by local bus, miles, 1991 - 1993

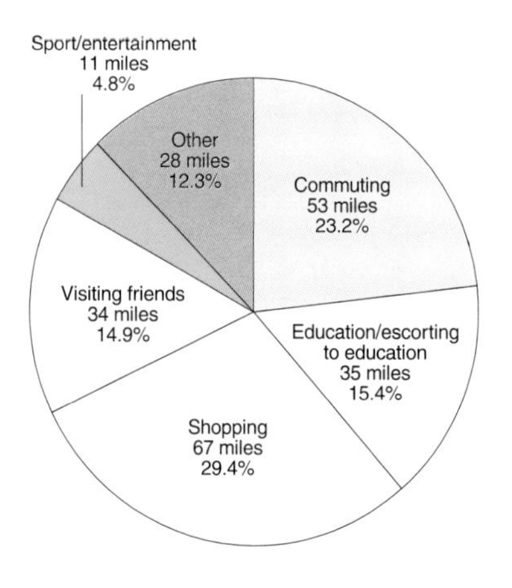

Figures are for region of residence. Some of the journeys may be made outside the region.

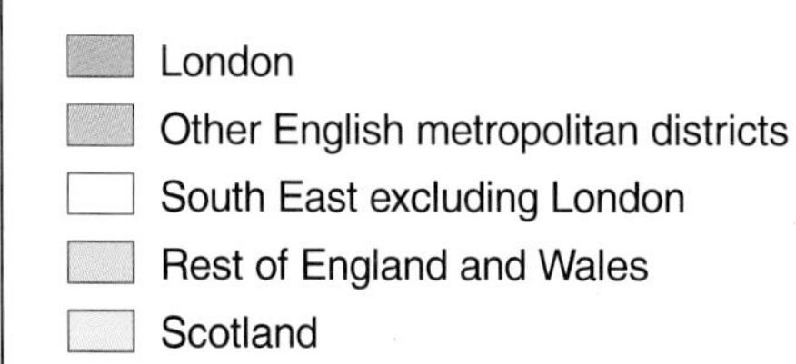

Source: National Travel Survey

Rail Travel

- The area with the highest rate of average travel on the main railway network is the South East outside London, presumably reflecting the importance of the railways as a means of getting people to work in London.
- However, in London, rail travel is even higher than this if one looks both at journeys on the Underground and on the main rail network.
- Average rail travel is lowest in non-metropolitan England and Wales outside the South East.
- Commuting to work is the main reason for travelling on the railways, although visiting friends and going on holidays or a day trip are also important.

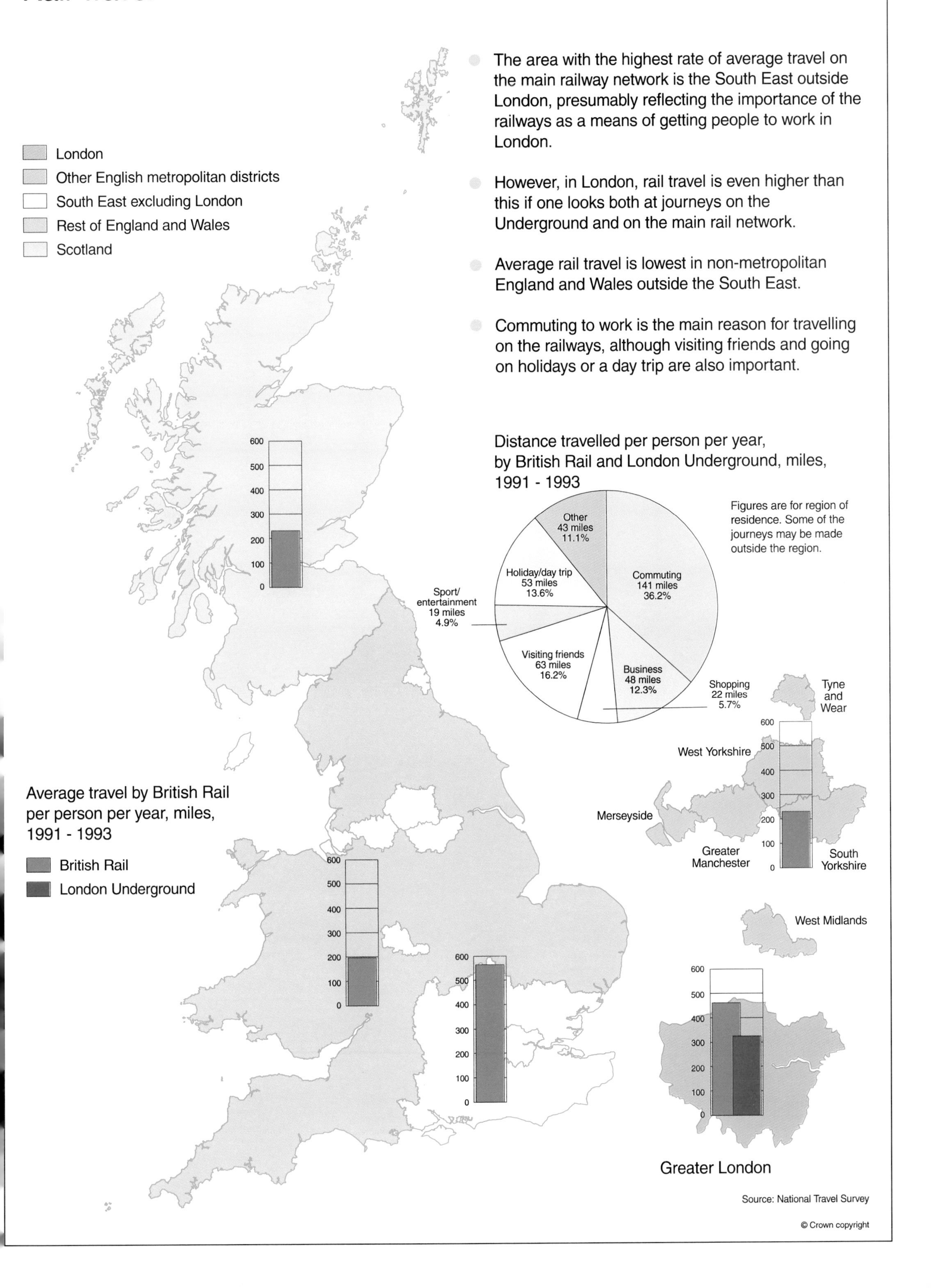

Source: National Travel Survey

Airports and Air Travel

- Heathrow is Britain's busiest airport - in 1993 it handled more passengers than the next five busiest combined.
- The only two other British airports to handle more than 10 million passengers a year were Gatwick and Manchester.
- International air passenger movements to the United Kingdom almost doubled between 1983 and 1993, despite a drop-off in travel in the recession of early 1992.

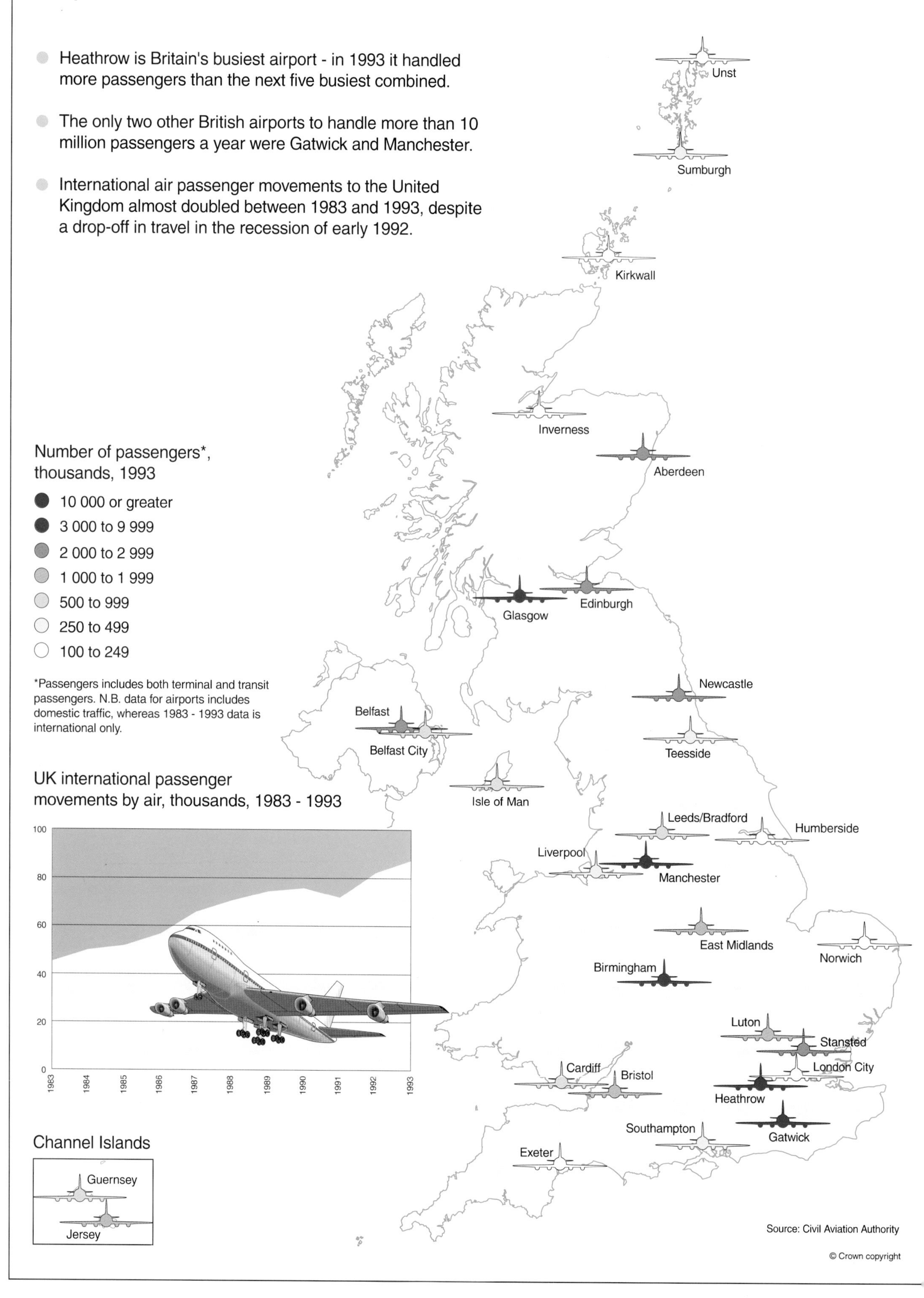

Source: Civil Aviation Authority

Traffic at Major Ports

- London remains the main port of the United Kingdom, followed by Tees & Hartlepool.
- Also especially important are Grimsby & Immingham, Sullom Voe, Milford Haven, Southampton, Liverpool, Forth and Felixstowe.
- The different types of bulk traffic account for the majority of movements, the single most important being crude petroleum.
- Container and roll-on traffic is also quite significant, whereas more traditional forms of traffic ('conventional traffic') are now transported in fairly small quantities.

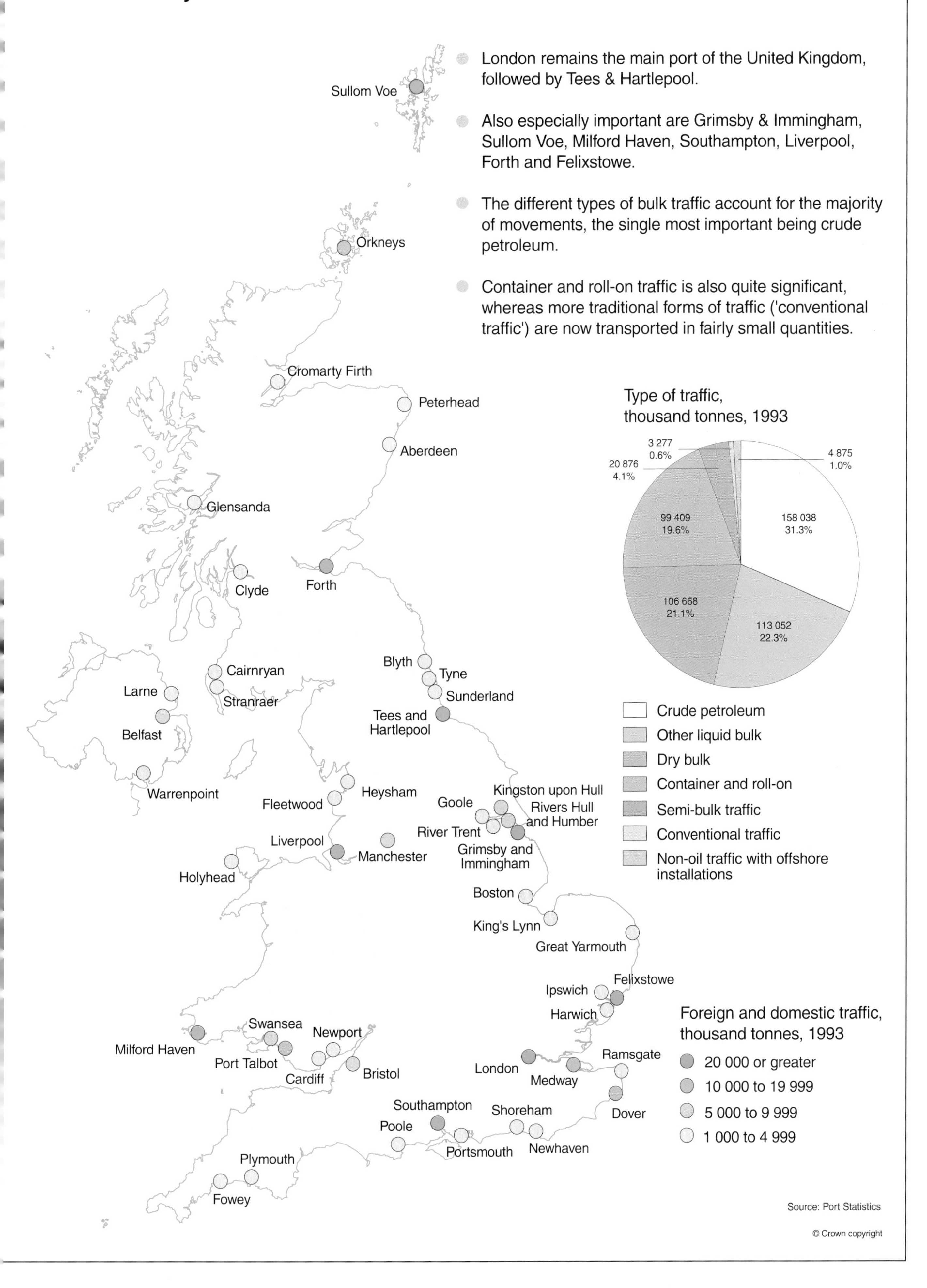

Source: Port Statistics

Travel Spending

- Travel takes up its biggest share of household spending in Greater London, where it accounts for 4 per cent of expenditure.
- It accounts for half this - 2 per cent - in Scotland and only 1 per cent in Northern Ireland.
- Spending on fares is divided fairly evenly between trains, buses and coaches and air travel.

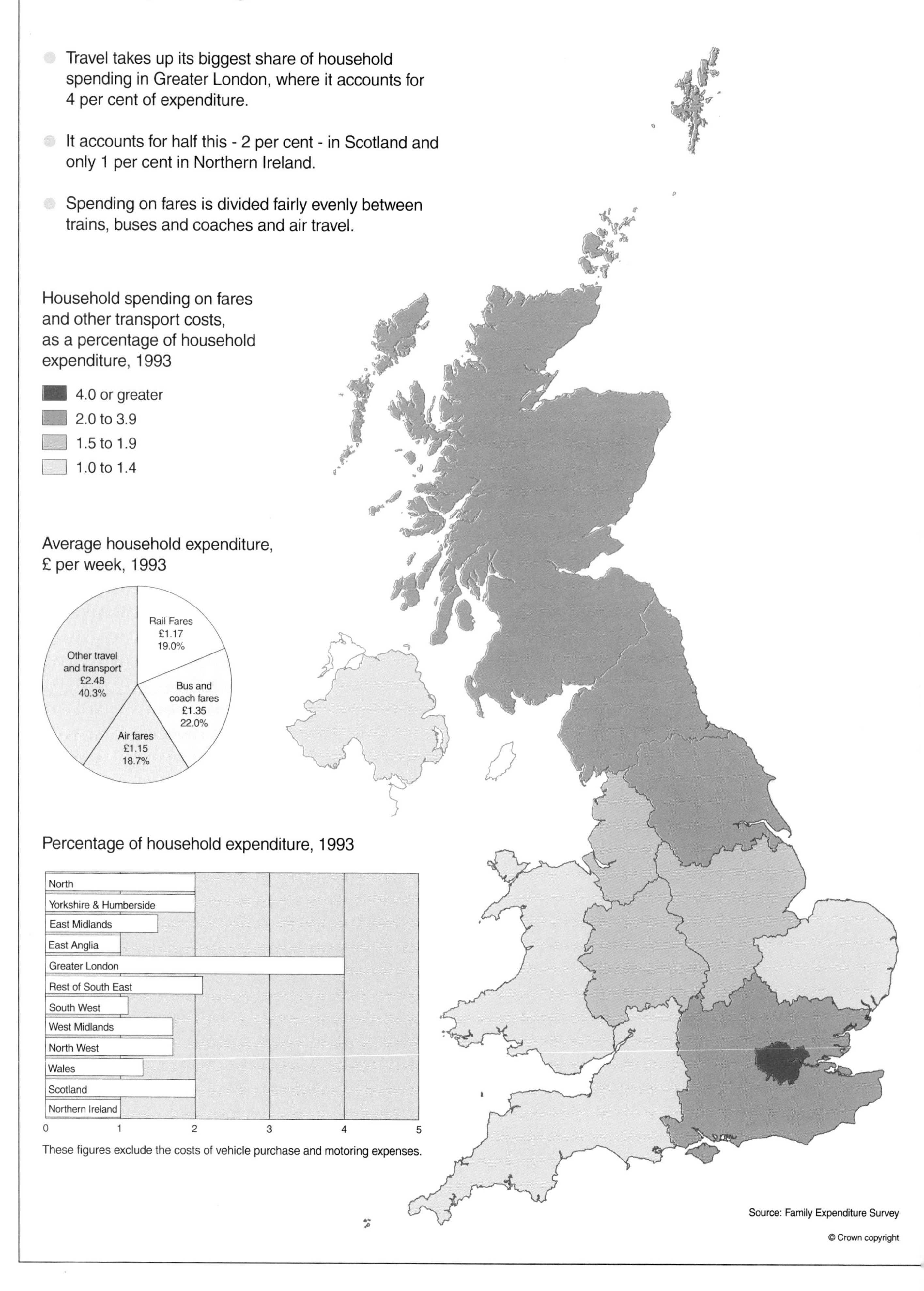

These figures exclude the costs of vehicle purchase and motoring expenses.

Source: Family Expenditure Survey

Major Tourist Attractions

- Many of the United Kingdom's top tourist attractions are in London - these include the British Museum, the National Gallery and Westminster Abbey.
- However, the top attraction of all is the Pleasure Beach at Blackpool.
- 3 Country Parks and 2 Forest Parks each attract over a million visitors a year, rising to 4 million in the case of Strathclyde Country Park.
- As well as Westminster Abbey, other major church buildings to attract visitors include York Minster, Canterbury Cathedral and St Paul's Cathedral.

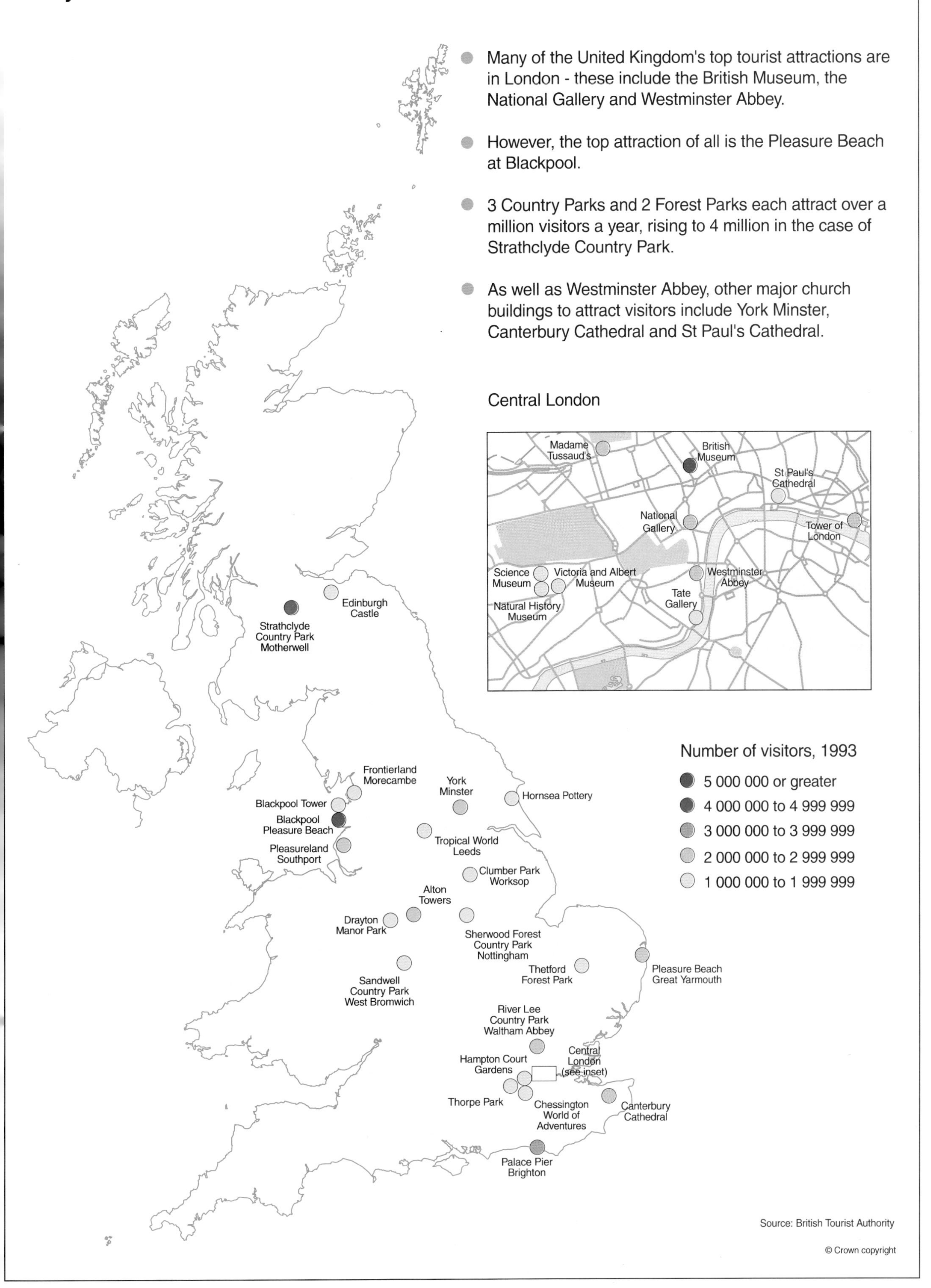

Source: British Tourist Authority

Leisure Goods

- Spending on leisure goods varies between 3.7 and 5.5 per cent of total household expenditure.
- Spending is lowest in Northern Ireland and is also fairly low in the West Midlands.
- It is highest in the South West, with Scotland, East Anglia and Yorkshire and Humberside also having relatively high levels.
- Video recorders have become very widespread, with three-quarters of households in England having one by 1993.
- By contrast, fewer than 2 out of 5 households had a compact disc player.

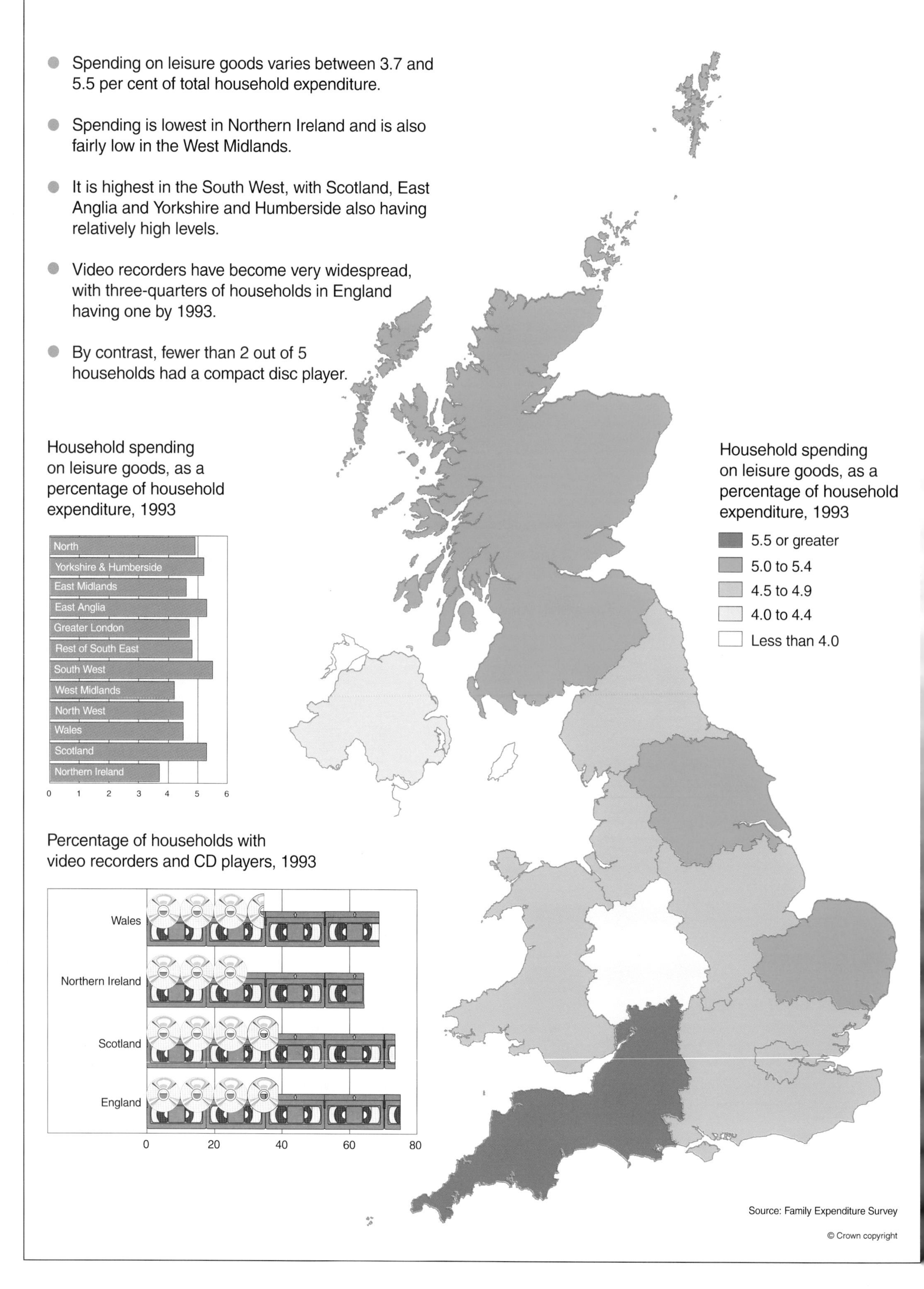

Source: Family Expenditure Survey

Leisure Services

- Leisure services account for a higher proportion of total household spending than do leisure goods.
- A very substantial proportion - over 60 per cent - of spending on leisure services goes on hotel and holiday expenses.
- Spending is highest in Greater London and lowest in the North.

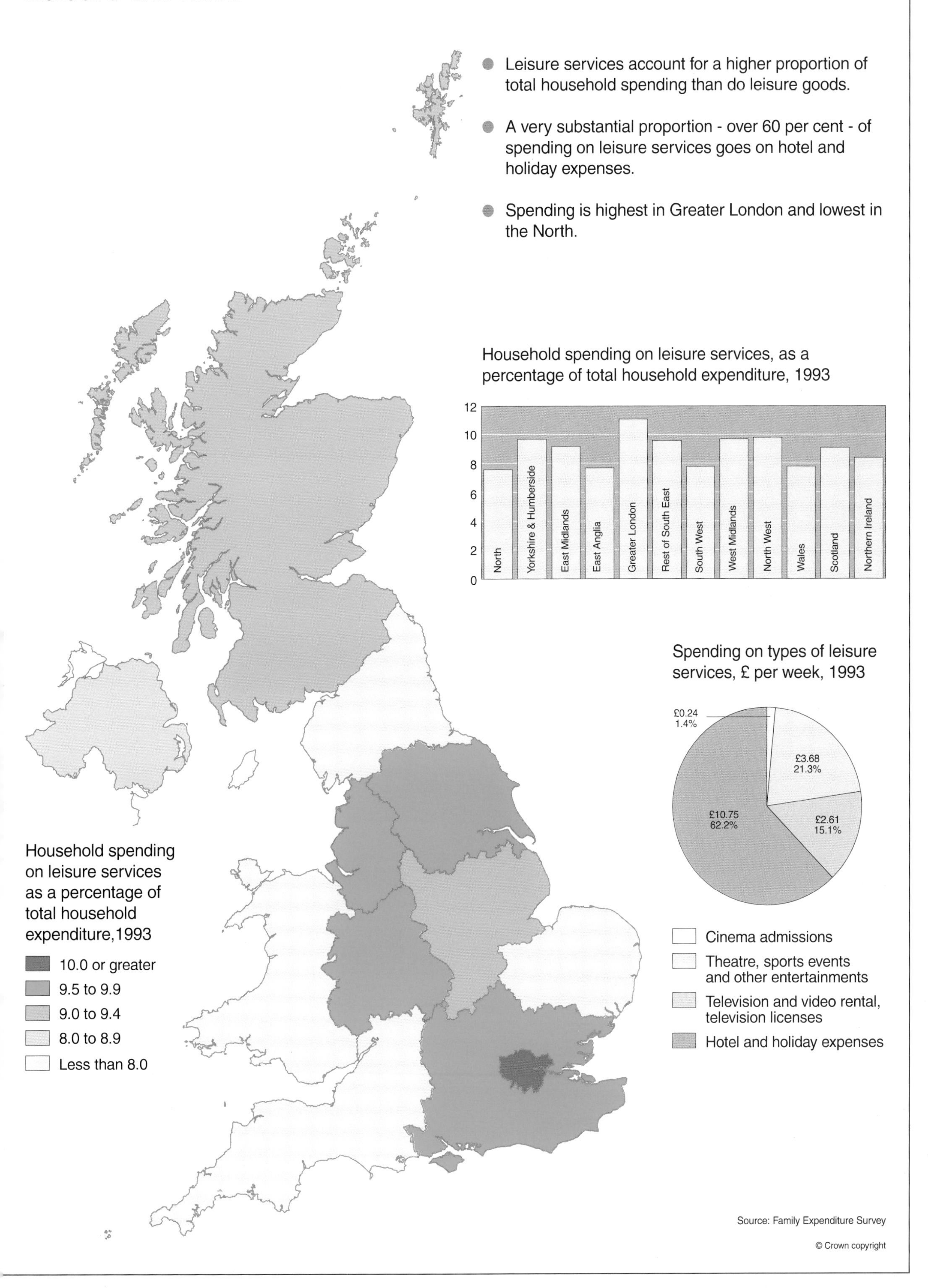

Source: Family Expenditure Survey

Cinema Screens

- The region with the most cinema screens is London, with 420.
- However, the part of the United Kingdom with the highest number of cinema screens relative to population is Northern Ireland.
- The area with the fewest screens relative to population is north Scotland.

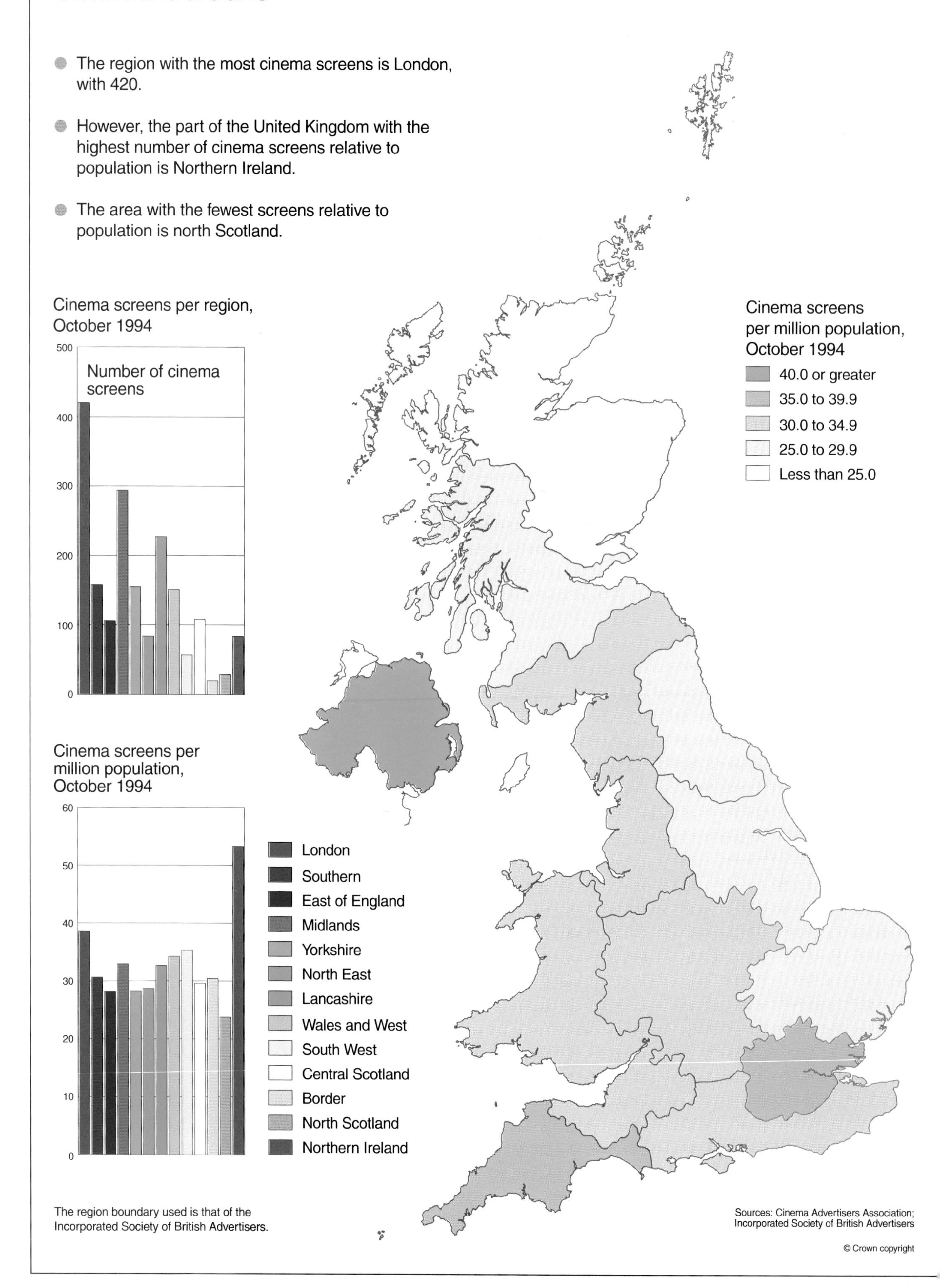

The region boundary used is that of the Incorporated Society of British Advertisers.

Sources: Cinema Advertisers Association; Incorporated Society of British Advertisers

Independent Television Stations

- Licences for the independent Channel 3 stations (formerly knows as 'ITV') are awarded by the Independent Television Commission for a ten-year period following a process of competitive bidding which also involves a quality threshold.
- There are 15 stations holding the licences for the 14 regions (the London licence being split between Carlton and LWT who provide 4 and 3 days output per week respectively); there is also a separate licence for a national breakfast-time service on the Channel 3 network.
- Channel 3 stations are funded largely by selling advertising airtime.

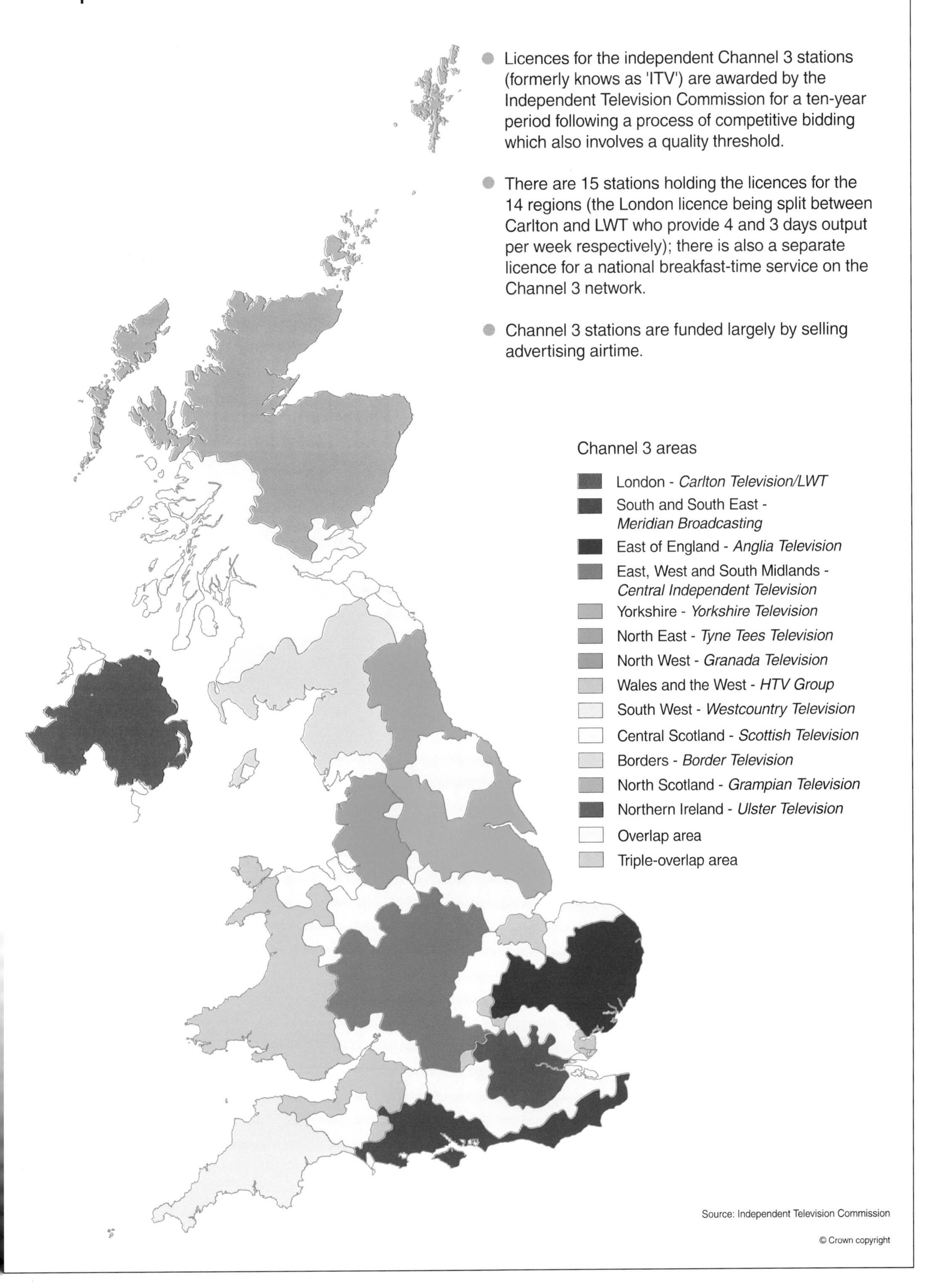

Source: Independent Television Commission

Population Density

- The United Kingdom is the third most densely populated country in the European Union.
- The most densely populated country of the 12 EU states is the Netherlands.
- The North West of England is one of the most densely populated regions in the EU, while Scotland has one of the lowest population densities.
- The Irish Republic is the least densely populated of the 12, with 51 people per square kilometre.
- The populations of the 12 EU member states range from 80 million in Germany to 387 000 in Luxembourg.

Inhabitants per square kilometre, 1990

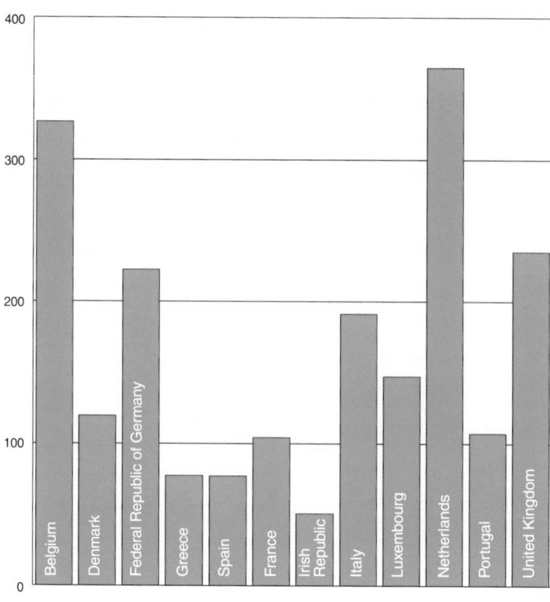

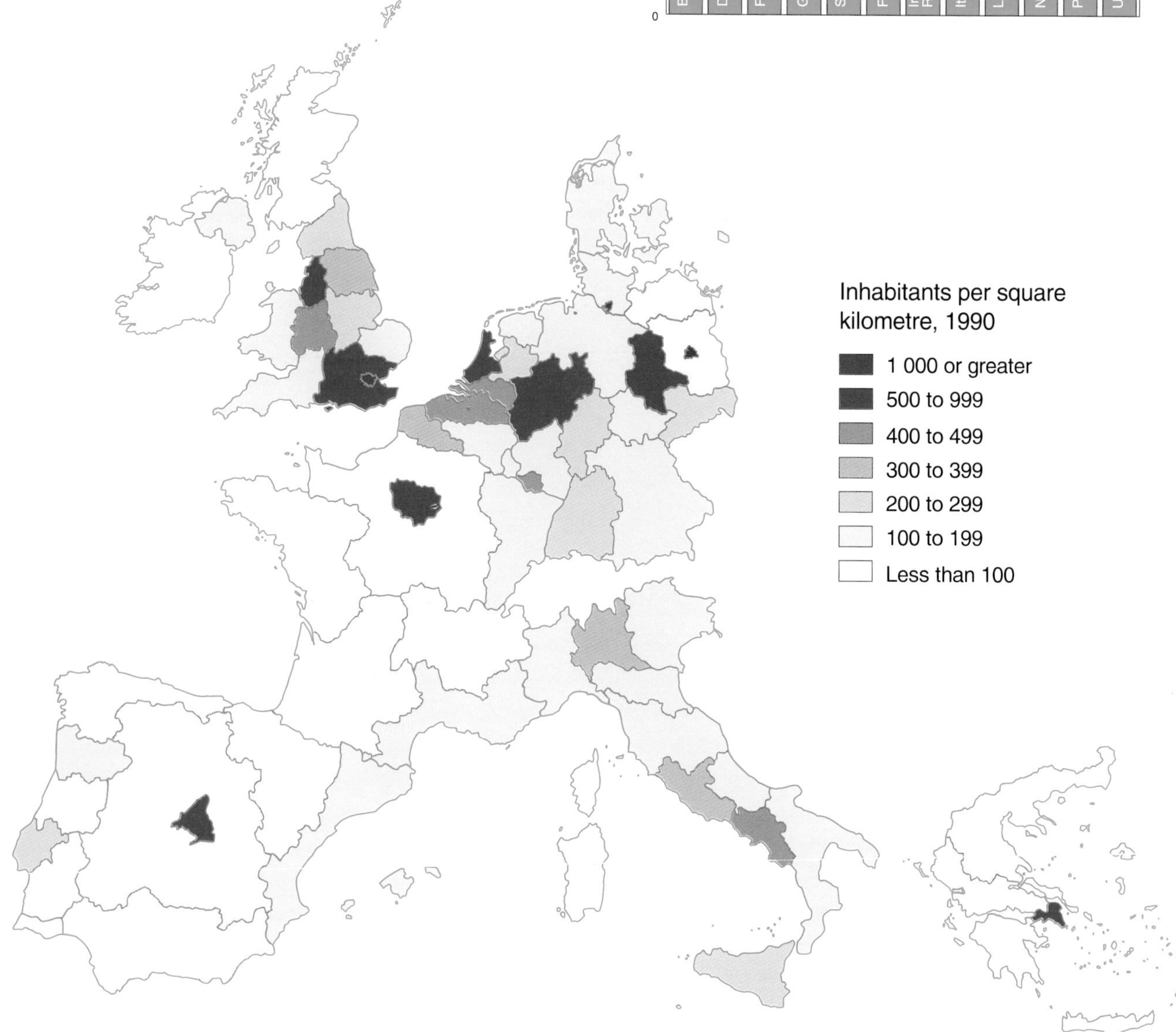

Source: Eurostat

Life Expectancy

- Life expectancy has increased in all countries in the European Union.
- In all countries women have longer life expectancy than men, of around 6 or 7 years.
- Life expectancy in the United Kingdom is around the average for the EU.
- For women, life expectancy is highest in France, and for men it is highest in Greece.
- The lowest levels of life expectancy are in Portugal.

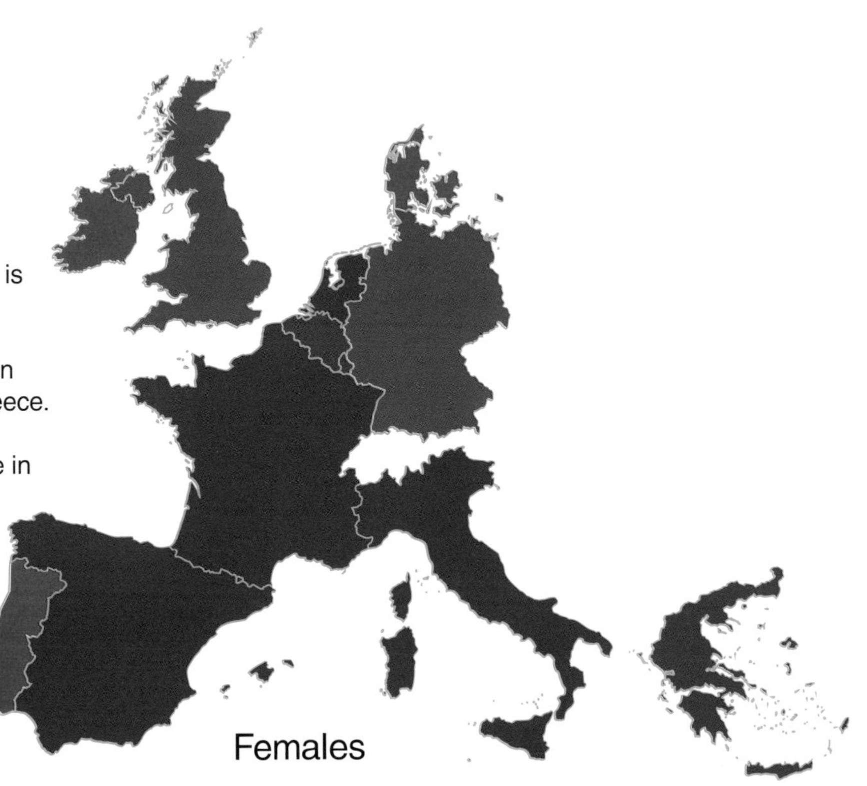

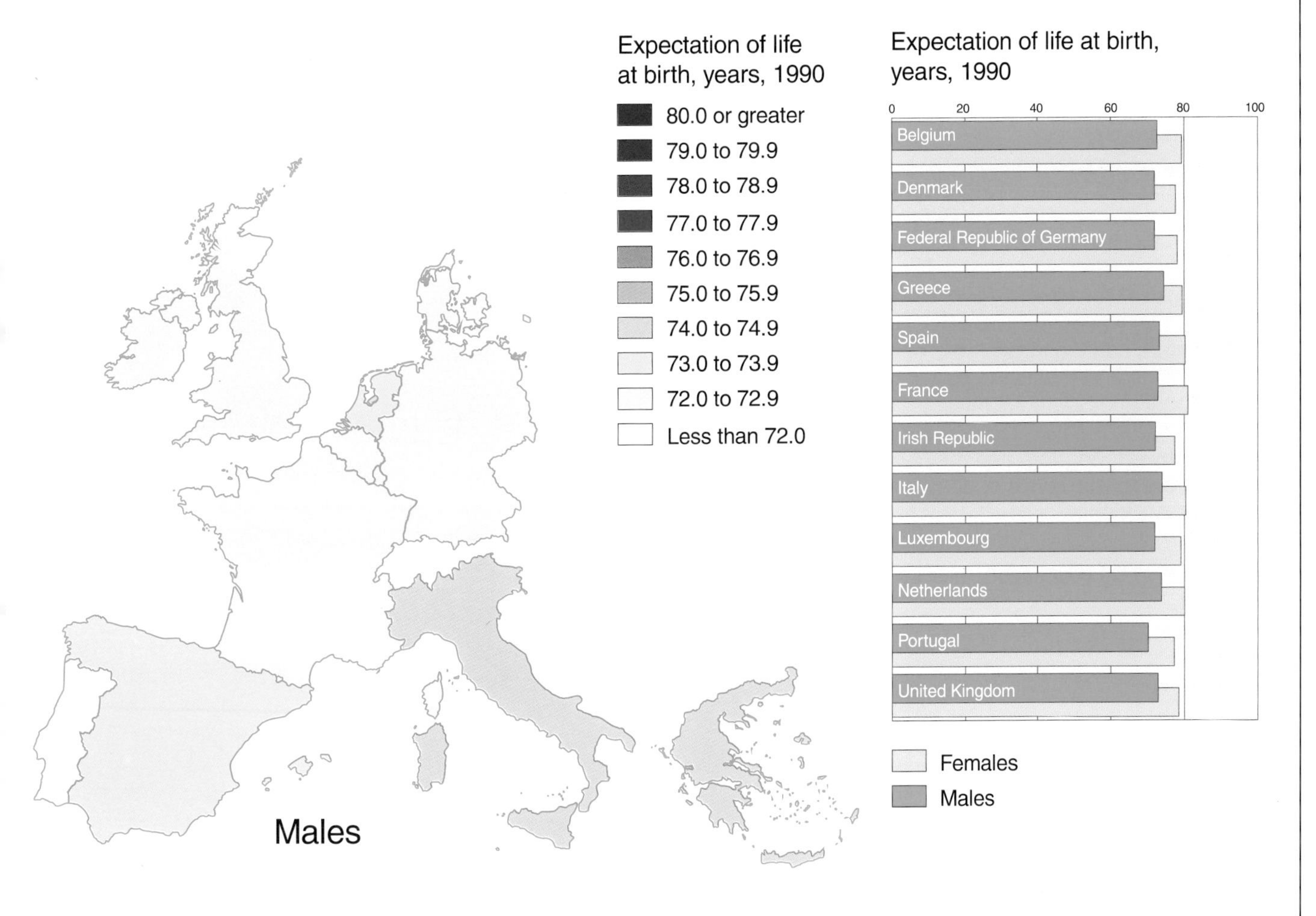

Source: Eurostat

Luxembourg figure is for 1991.

Birth and Death Rates

- Births and fertility rates have generally been falling throughout the EU.
- The United Kingdom has the second highest birth rate among EU countries.
- The highest rate is in the Irish Republic and the lowest in Italy.
- Northern Ireland has the highest birth rate by region in the EU.
- Births outside of marriage have increased considerably in all EU countries and now account for about 20 per cent of births.
- The United Kingdom has the third highest proportion of births outside marriage in the Union, after Denmark and France.
- EU rates for births outside marriage in 1989 ranged from over 46 per cent of births in Denmark to 2 per cent in Greece.
- The United Kingdom has the third highest crude death rate in the European Union, reflecting the above average level of the elderly in its population.
- The United Kingdom has the highest level of deaths in the EU arising from circulatory diseases and the second highest level of deaths from cancer.
- Scotland, the North and the North West of England have some of the highest rates by region for deaths from circulatory diseases, being exceeded only by some regions of Germany.
- Denmark has the largest rate of deaths from cancer in relation to population and Portugal and Spain the lowest.
- The United Kingdom and the Netherlands have the lowest levels of deaths from road traffic accidents.

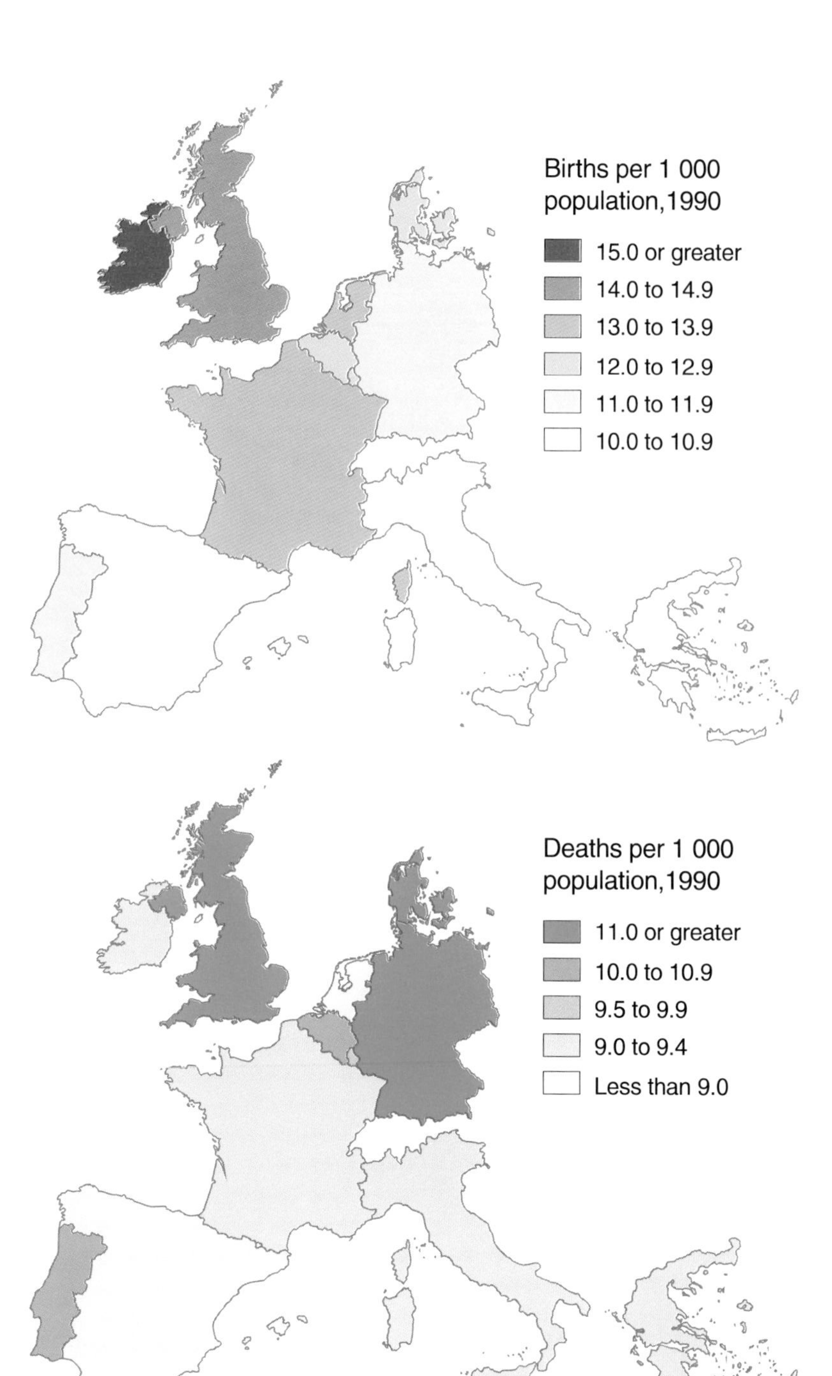

Births per 1 000 population, 1990

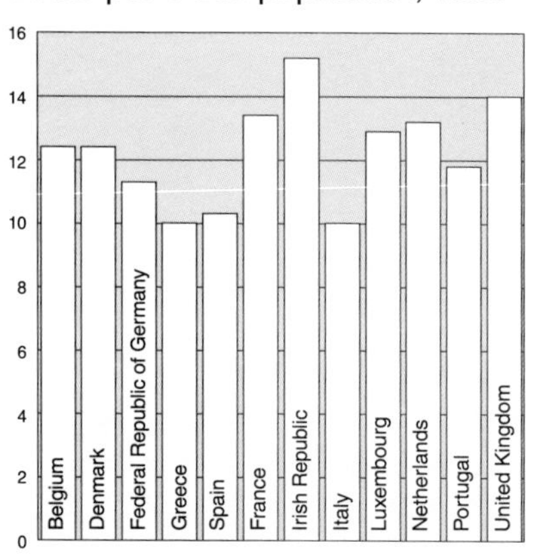

Deaths per 1 000 population, 1990

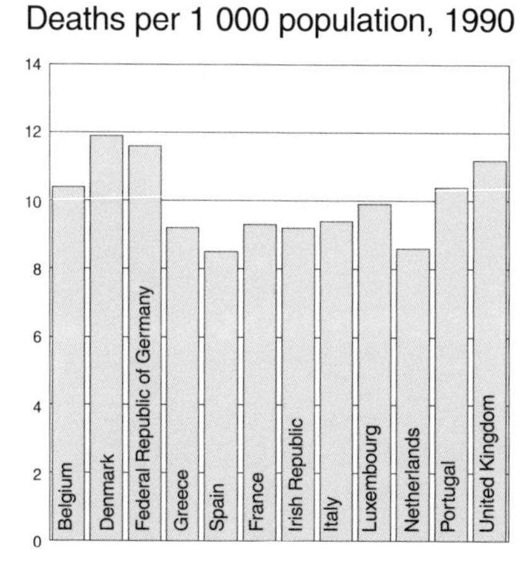

Source: Eurostat

Marriage and Divorce Rates

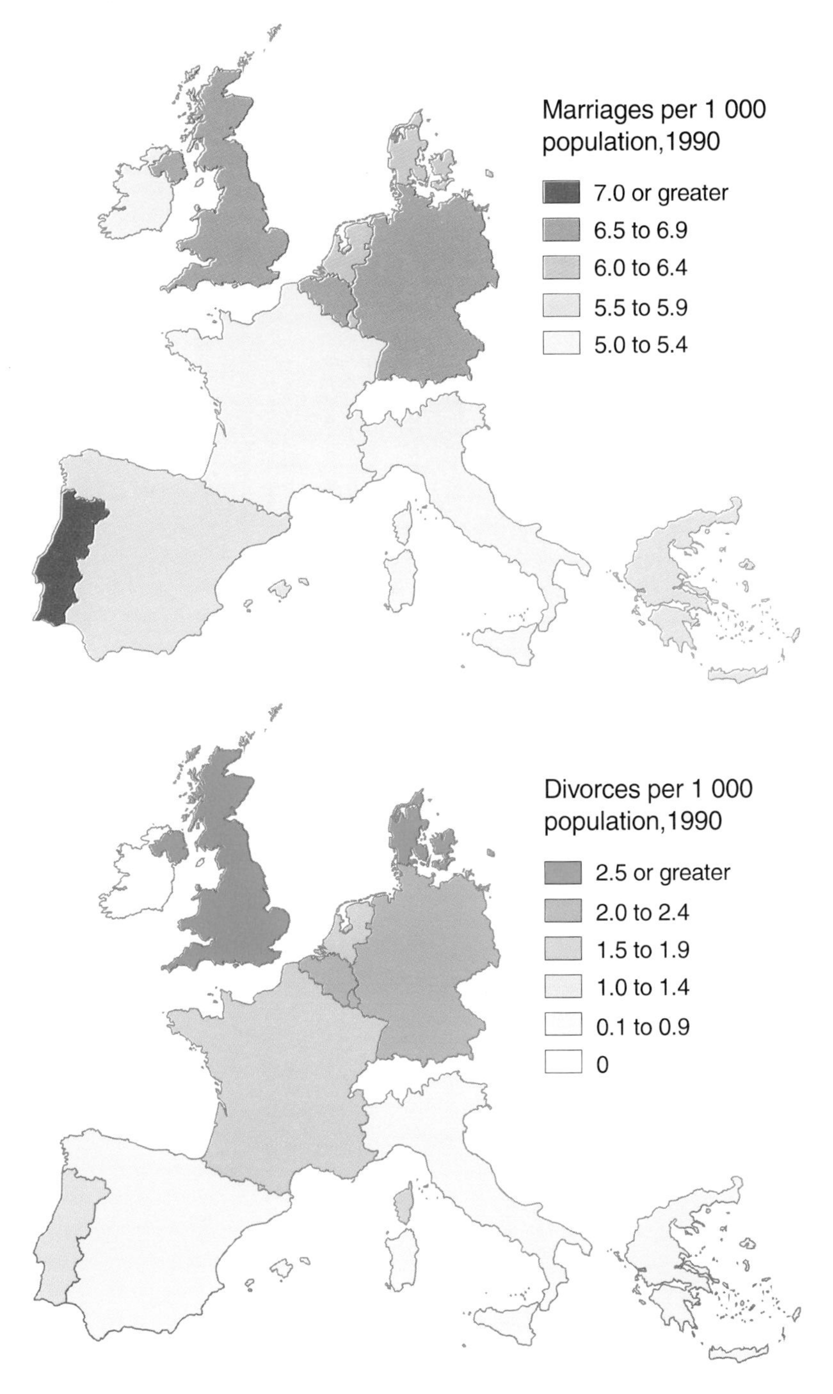

- As in the United Kingdom, the number of marriages in other European Union countries has declined and is at a much lower level than in the 1970s.
- The United Kingdom, however, has the second highest marriage rate in relation to population.
- Portugal has the highest marriage rate in the EU.
- As marriage rates have declined, cohabitation has increased.
- Since the late 1970s the average age of first marriage has risen.
- Although marriages have become less prevalent, the incidence of divorce has grown.
- This has been facilitated by a relaxation in the law governing divorce in most countries.
- Divorce is still not allowed in the Irish Republic.
- The United Kingdom has the second highest divorce rate in the European Union.
- Denmark has the highest divorce rate.
- Apart from the Irish Republic, divorce rates are lowest in Italy, Greece and Spain.

Because of the differences in divorce laws between the EU member states, precise comparisons in divorce rates are difficult. However, these figures do give an indication of general trends.

Marriages per 1 000 population, 1990

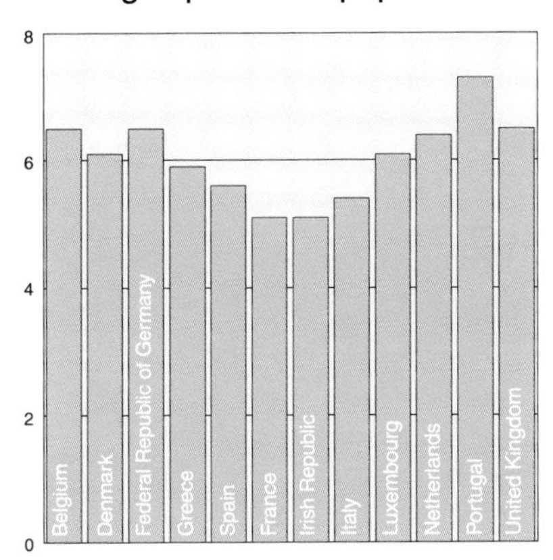

Divorces per 1 000 population, 1990

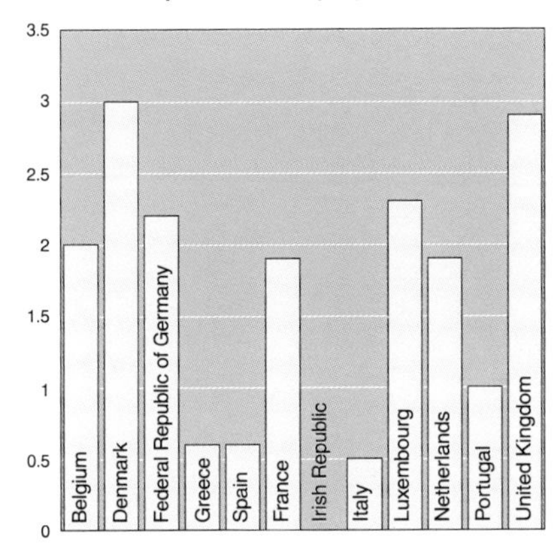

Source: Eurostat

Agriculture

- Employment in agriculture in the European Union has been declining over a long period.
- The United Kingdom has the lowest proportion of people employed in agriculture of any EU state: around 2 per cent of people, compared with the EU average of 6 per cent.
- Less than 2 per cent are employed in the South East, North and North West regions of England.
- By far the highest proportion engaged in agriculture is in Greece - 22 per cent, reaching nearly 40 per cent in the region of Kentriki Ellada.
- The United Kingdom tends to have fewer small agricultural holdings and more large-scale holdings than other countries.

Size of agricultural holdings, percentage less than 20 hectares, 1987

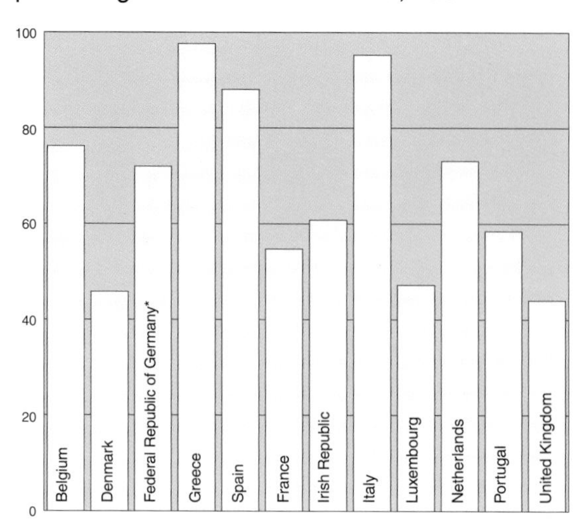

* Former West Germany

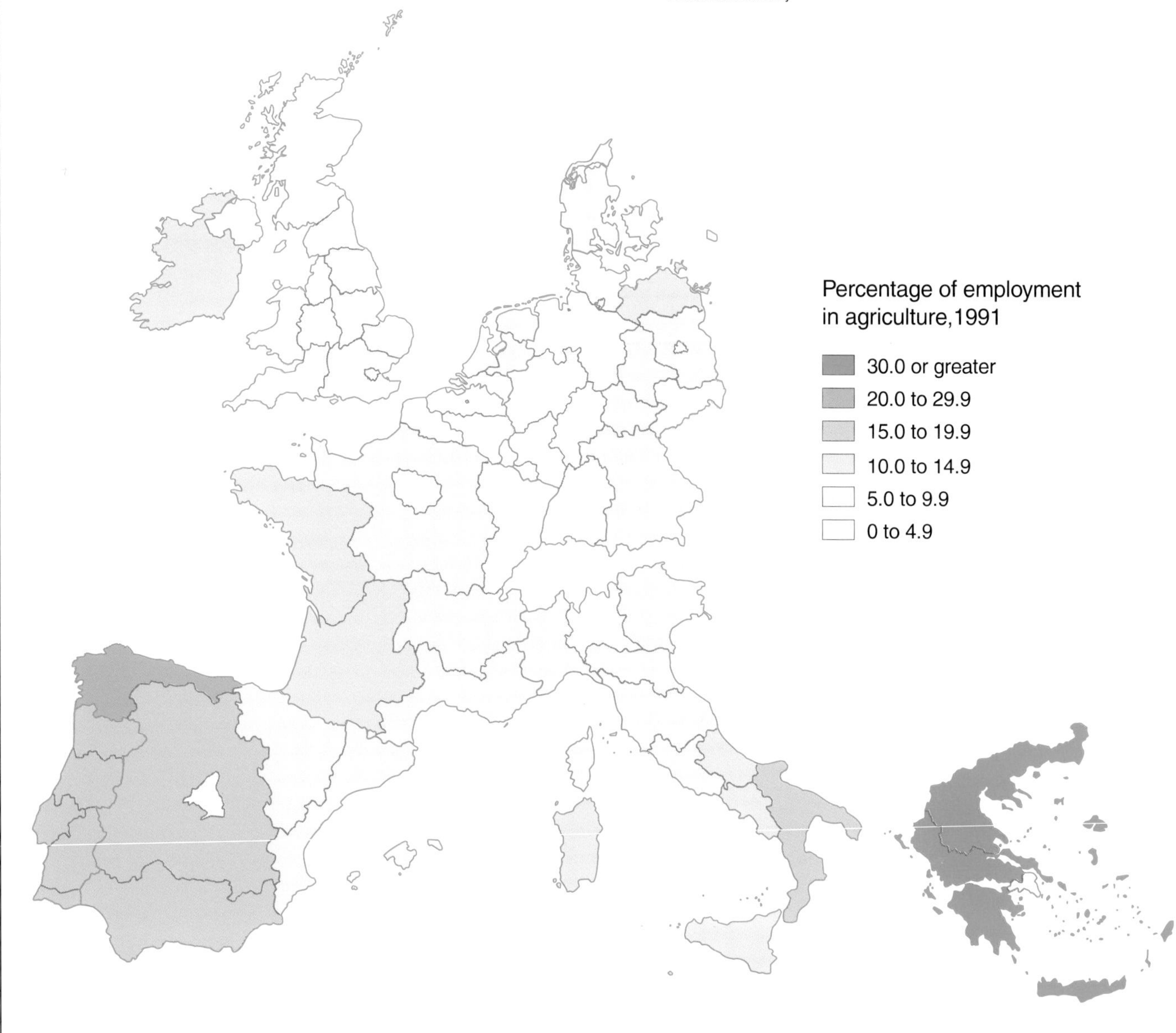

Source: Eurostat

Industry

- About one-third of employees in the European Union are engaged in industry.
- Germany is the country with the biggest proportion of employment in industry: 40 per cent.
- The Netherlands and Greece have the lowest proportions engaged in industry.

Percentage of employment in industry, 1991

- 40.0 or greater
- 35.0 to 39.9
- 30.0 to 34.9
- 25.0 to 29.9
- 20.0 to 24.9
- Less than 20.0

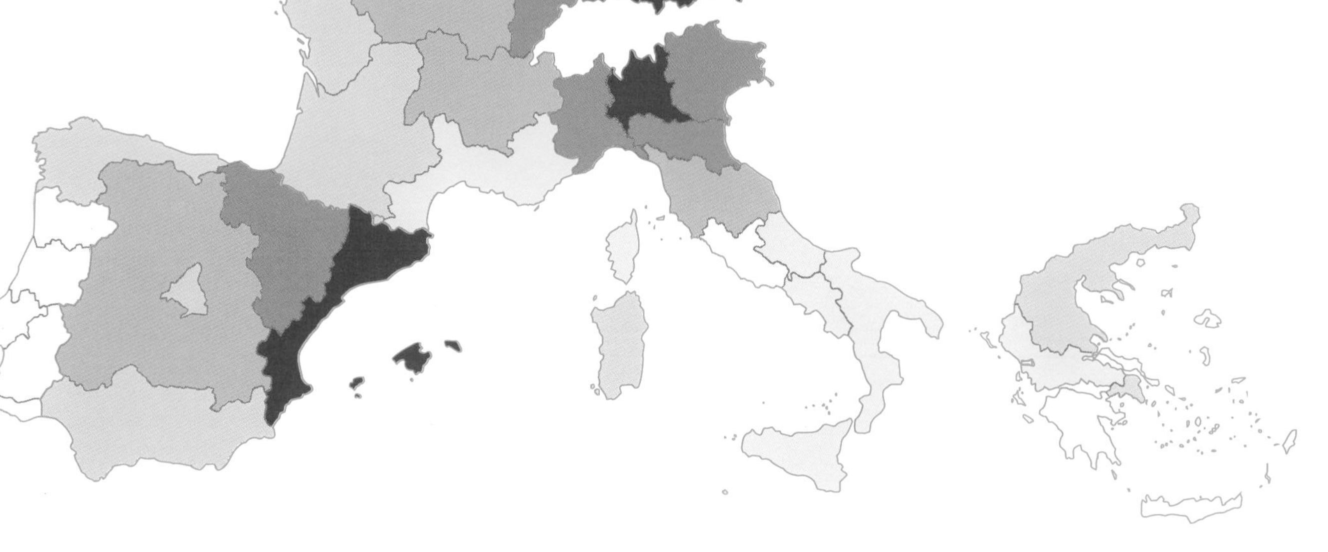

Manufacturing production, percentage change 1985 - 1993

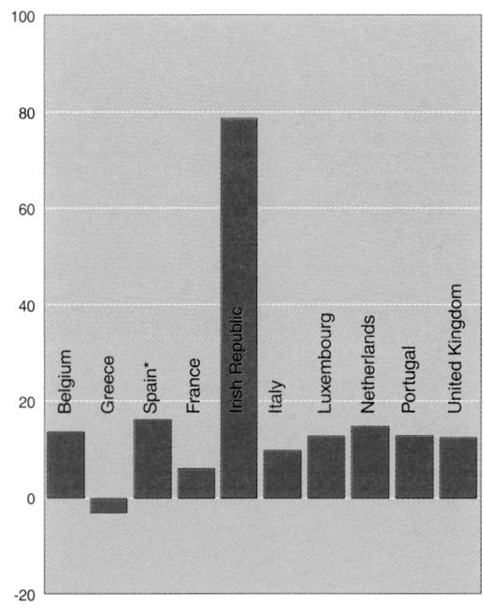

* 1985 - 1991

Data is not available for Denmark and the Federal Republic of Germany.

Source: Eurostat

Trade with the United Kingdom

- Around half of the United Kingdom's exports and imports are with other members of the European Union, as against one-third in 1972.
- European Union member states account for 7 of the United Kingdom's top 10 export markets.
- Germany is the United Kingdom's biggest single export market and import source.

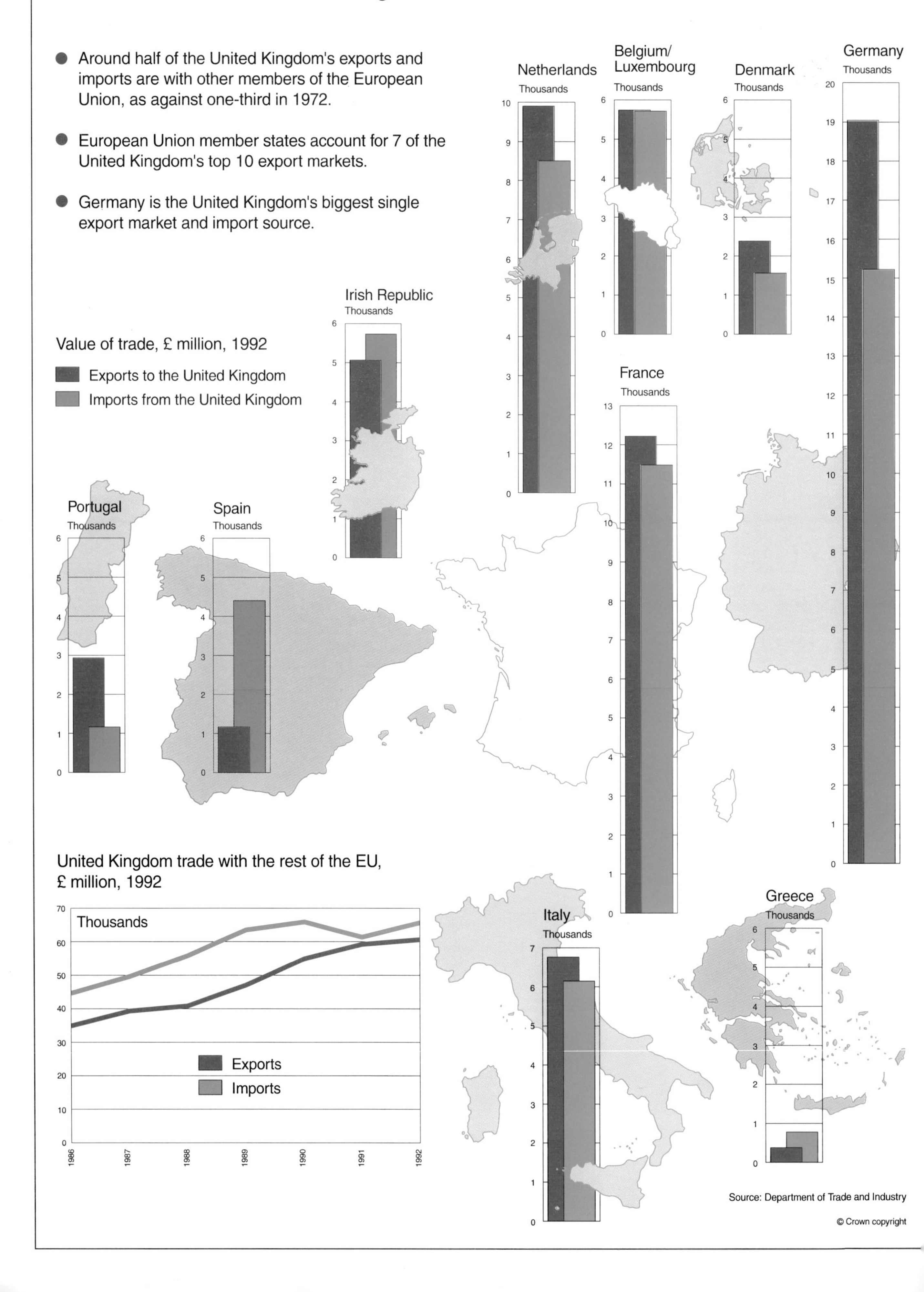

Source: Department of Trade and Industry